QUIET HEROINES

By the same author
'A NURSE'S WAR' . . . Chatto & Windus 1979.
'HANNAH ROBSON' . . . Hodder and Stoughton 1991.

QUIET HEROINES

Nurses of
the Second World War

Brenda McBryde

Published in 1989 by
Cakebreads Publications

Published in 1989 by
Cakebreads Publications
5a The High Street
Saffron Walden
Essex. CB10 1AT

First published in Great Britain by Chatto & Windus 1985.
Copyright Brenda McBryde 1985.

940.53

British Library
Cataloguing in Publication Data
McBryde, Brenda
Quiet heroines: nurses of the Second World War.
1. World War, 1939-1945
2. Nursing
I. Title
940.54'75

ISBN 0-9515308-0-1

Printed in Great Britain by Ipswich Book Co., Ipswich

AUTHOR'S NOTE

In my earlier book, "A Nurse's War", I wrote of my own wartime experiences. This publication produced so many letters from other nurses, both military and civilian, who had served during the second world war, that the need for a second book was made obvious. Aptly titled 'Quiet Heroines', it records the devoted service of some outstanding women whose dedication to duty, often at great personal risk, has never received the recognition it deserves.

Contents

Illustrations

Foreword

I was a wartime nurse. I thought that my experiences, especially in the Normandy Campaign, might be of some interest, and wrote about them in my book *A Nurse's War*, which came out in hardcover in 1979 and in paperback in 1980. To my very great pleasure, my book struck a chord with other wartime nurses, many of whom wrote to me about their experiences in campaigns quite different from my own. From the contacts and correspondence that resulted I realised the need for a much fuller account of nursing in the Second World War than I had been able to give. I also realised what a privilege it would be to record for posterity the stories which had been vouchsafed to me by some remarkable women who are too unassuming to write about themselves.

Thus were the seeds of the present book sown, and I count myself extremely fortunate to have made so many friendships while writing it, and to have been allowed to bring these stories to the public attention which they so well deserve. My only regret is that not all the women I write about have lived to see this book published. I would have liked them to know that they are not forgotten.

I wish to acknowledge the help given to me by my many correspondents, not all of whom are mentioned by name. My questions must have seemed interminable but they wrote and wrote again, giving me facts, sharing their diaries and their memories, not all of which were pleasant.

Future historians will find a wealth of information from other sources about the part played in the Second World War by the Army, the Navy, the Royal Air Force, Air Raid Precautions and the Home Guard. My aim is to make sure that they learn about the nurses, civilian as well as those in the Armed Services, at home and overseas, the students in training, the VADs 'in it for the duration', and the Matrons with a lifetime of experience behind them, in whose capable hands rested the well-being of thousands of casualties.

Among the many letters I received following publication of *A Nurse's War* was one from a trooper whose gratitude to the nurses was touching in its simplicity. 'Dear Nurse,' he wrote, 'I do not know if "nurse" is your correct title, but to me "nurse" is a very honourable

name. As an ex-soldier, I was always aware you were there if the need
arose and your book proves it. Thank you. Respectfully, J. P. Ward,
No./106003437 Trooper.'

Another letter came from Lt General Sir Brian Horrocks, for whom
my book brought back 'so many grateful memories of quiet heroism
behind the lines'. The 'quiet heroism' of the nurses described in this
book will, I believe, be as apparent to readers as it was to me when I
started piecing together their accounts. Being 'there' when the need
arose often meant working under difficult and dangerous conditions.
In situations remote from a higher authority, their personal integrity
was frequently put to the test. Through the violence and tragedy which
stained the war years, the humanity of the doctors and nurses gleams
with a reassuring endurance.

I ask their indulgence if, in attempting to record their work, my
best is not good enough.

Brenda McBryde

I

The Inevitability of War

The 1938 trooping season of the Regular British Army had been about to begin when Hitler sent shock waves throughout Europe by marching into Czechoslovakia. Troopships packed with replacements of men for such overseas stations as India, Malta, Aden, Palestine and the Far East were preparing to sail from Liverpool and the Clyde. Sisters of the Queen Alexandra's Imperial Military Nursing Service (QAIMNS) who would accompany them were already assembled at the Cambridge Military Hospital in Aldershot waiting for orders to embark when the news of the annexation of Czechoslovakia put a stop to all troop movements.

The 'QAs' were instructed to repack their trunks. Out went the garden-party outfits bought for India and the tropical whites for Egypt. Clothing was restricted to their grey and scarlet uniform and, surprisingly, sportswear. Nurses who had never seen a battle casualty waited on two-hour standby while the Prime Minister, Mr Neville Chamberlain, conferred with Herr Hitler in Munich.

When he returned with his treaty of brotherly love between nations and Hitler's assurance that he had no more territorial demands to make, the whole fraught situation collapsed like a pricked bubble. The first reaction by the country in general was one of overwhelming relief. The troopships sailed to their original destinations, and Hitler advanced into Czechoslovakia unopposed. The second and more realistic reaction was to begin construction on air raid shelters with all speed and to repair deficiencies in the Services.

Plans were drawn up for Civil Defence. The Spanish Civil War had shown that modern warfare made no distinction between soldiers and civilians. Air Raid Precautions (ARP) were organised, staffed by eager volunteers, and the Civil Nursing Reserve was formed of trained and assistant nurses who, in time of war, could be augmented by the nursing detachments of the British Red Cross Society and St John Ambulance Brigade. Both these voluntary organisations were composed of young women who had undergone basic training in First Aid and Home Nursing and were known by the initials of their office, Voluntary Aid Detachments (VADs). They could opt for service overseas (Mobile), or service at home (Non-mobile).

As events in Germany continued to cause disquiet, the Ministry of
Defence took stock of London's hospitals and noted that there was
enough room in the cellars beneath St Thomas's to duplicate the
accommodation above ground. With the capital's vulnerability still in
mind, the Ministers earmarked certain country mansions and estates
for possible use as auxiliary hospitals and convalescent depots in an
emergency. Then they turned their attention to an immediate recruiting drive for the nursing services of the Armed Forces.

The figures below show the growth of the three nursing services
between 1939 and 1945.

	1939	*1945* (with reserve)
Queen Alexandra's Imperial Military		
Nursing Service (QAIMNS)	640	12,000
Queen Alexandra's Royal Naval		
Nursing Service (QARNNS)	78	1,341 (inc. VADs)
Princess Mary's Royal Air Force		
Nursing Service (PMRAFNS)	171	1,215

Each of these regular establishments could call upon a small number
of Reservists in time of war, and the Territorial Army Nursing Service
(TANS) would be mobilised to swell the ranks of the QAIMNS.

As a result of the recruiting drive, many student nurses then com-
pleting their four years' training went straight into the Forces. In more
settled times, the majority would have remained in the field of domestic
nursing or joined the Colonial Nursing Service which looked after
British nationals in various parts of the Empire.

Kit Woodman (later Philbrick ARRC, after she received the award
of Associate of the Royal Red Cross) had this latter career in mind
when in 1938 she left her training school at the London Hospital,
Whitechapel Road, but her Matron saw further into the future than
she did herself. In such troubled times, she told Kit, a nurse's duty
lay with the Armed Forces. Kit followed this advice, applied for
entry into the QAIMNS Reserve and was duly introduced to army
nursing.

There were features of service hospitals that were not to everyone's
liking, such as the interminable form-filling, or the slavish attention

that had to be paid to features so unrelated to medicine as the lay-out of a bedside locker. Army regulations stated that the patient's towel must lie thrice folded, and consequently permanently damp, beneath specifically positioned toilet articles such as shaving brush, toothbrush, soap and shaving stick. A photograph was available for those who found the order incomprehensible. The Navy was no better. During 'Captain's Round' of a Naval hospital ward, 'up-patients' were expected to sit at attention by their beds, cap on head, feet properly 'squared off'.

Active service brought more than a touch of common sense. There was no point in taking pains over the appearance of a locker when that piece of furniture was an up-ended rations box wedged in the mud, and when the casualty possessed nothing but his identity disc.

Sister Kit Woodman, in her new grey and scarlet uniform, set off to learn all about army procedures and to give her first timid lectures to a roomful of RAMC orderlies prodded into wakefulness by their relentless Regimental Sergeant-Major.

Barely one year after his annexation of Czechoslovakia, Hitler demonstrated that his promises were as thin as the paper on which he had written them. With the connivance of that other party interested in the Baltic ports, Russia, he began to threaten Poland. Judging Britain and France on past performance, he was convinced that they would not fight – but in this he was mistaken.

These two countries would not back away a second time from their joint pledge, made many years earlier, to go to the aid of any minor nation against an aggressor, so that the balance of power in Europe might be maintained. Czechoslovakia had been sacrificed, but that was where the rot stopped. On 1st September, 1939, when Hitler invaded Poland, the British and French Governments meant every word of the ultimatum they issued, giving Hitler until 9 am on 3rd September to get out of Poland or face war against their two nations.

In an Indian summer of unforgettable tranquillity, Britain prepared for war with sudden energy, as if glad to be finished with cliff-hanger diplomacy. There was a rush to erect observation posts along North Sea and Channel coasts, to close the beaches with barbed wire barricades and to drag doddery experts on trench warfare from their leafy retirement.

Surgeons cancelled operating lists and evacuated their patients from city hospitals to the country. Black-out shades were hastily constructed, and all the light bulbs in hospital wards painted blue. Walls of sand-bags rose outside ground-floor windows.

If war were to be declared, a British Expeditionary Force would be sent to France, and reinforcements sent to Egypt to guard the Suez Canal. Mussolini was then extending his occupation of Abyssinia and might seize upon any preoccupation on the part of the British to attack this vital supply line to India and the Middle East. QAIMNS 'Regulars' who would accompany such troops mustered at various mobilising points under secret orders, together with as many 'Reservists' as could be drummed up in the time available. Their luggage spilled over the pavements outside the Millbank Military Hospital on the Thames Embankment: golf clubs, tennis racquets, favourite Persian rugs, even a sewing-machine and a bird in a cage. In later years, they learned to travel very light indeed.

Senior Sisters at the Millbank Hospital with memories of the First World War were ready with advice. 'Stock up on woolly bloomers,' they urged. 'They'll be in short supply later on.' Many a harassed young QA made a last-minute shopping trip to Harrods before entraining, destination unknown, on the night of Friday, 1st September from dimmed-out Cannon Street Station to the strains of a military band.

When Naval or RAF Sisters undertook a journey, it was usually in comfort and under the kindly eye of an official; this was not so with the QAIMNS. The fact that the latter usually travelled in larger numbers than their colleagues of the smaller Services was not an advantage. A posse of women with the rank of Lieutenant seemed to unnerve even the pluckiest Rail Transport Officer (RTO), whose instinctive reaction was to bury his head in his documents and pray that his visitors would go away.

The party of QAs who left Cannon Street on Friday night at 10 pm did not reach their destination, Glasgow, until 11 pm on Saturday night, having been taken on a troop-collecting tour of England. At least the troops had been provided with a packed meal. The QAs had not had so much as a cup of tea and were in truculent mood when they sighted the RTO in the midst of hundreds of troops on Glasgow Station.

He had no instructions for them, and the problem of finding lodgings for thirty women on a Saturday night in Glasgow, particularly on the night before the probable outbreak of war, was quite beyond him. The Sisters made for the most prominent 'brass hat' on the station, a towering Brigadier, who promptly took them to the comfortable Wallace Hotel and sent the bill to the War Office.

They embarked the next morning on the ships waiting in the Clyde. If war were declared, this would be the first convoy to leave Britain. The SS *Athenia* had already sailed for the United States with repatriating American citizens. When the crucial hour of 9 am came and went, embarkation proceeded. Men in the engine rooms made ready to sail. The Prime Minister's message relayed from the shore by the Tannoy broadcasting circuit commanded instant silence:

'... Germany has not responded to the ultimatum set by ourselves and France and, as a consequence of this, we are now at war.'

As if to underline the gravity of the message, news arrived that the SS *Athenia*, which had sailed twenty-four hours earlier, had been sunk by enemy submarines, with the loss of 112 passengers and crew. The enemy was no doubt aware that the *Athenia* was only one of a large collection of ships preparing to sail from the Clyde, so presumably U-boats would now be monitoring the movements of the convoy.

Amongst all the band-playing and well-wishing, the thought may have occurred to the departing troops that anyone in the cheering crowds lining the riverside could be an enemy agent.

Slowly the ships moved down river to take up convoy positions offshore: the lesson that unescorted vessels were sitting ducks for submarines had been learned in the First World War. One ship hung back. The *Scythia,* dawdled at the mouth of the river. After some delay, a motor launch left the shore and headed swiftly in her direction. As two young army oficers clambered on board, Zena Potter, one of a handful of QAs on the *Scythia* bound for Gibraltar, observed to her companion, 'They must be mighty important to hold back the ship like this.'

They were. One was Lieutenant 'Spider' Deakin, one of only ten men at the time with the knowledge and technical skill to build a radar grid, and he was on his way to do just that on the highest point of the Rock of Gibraltar. The rest of the ships in the convoy now seeking the open sea were bound for Egypt, Palestine and India, with armaments, troops and hospitals. Some of the QAs on board may have felt that the expenditure on so many pairs of woollen knickers had been unnecessary, in view of their destination.

The news that Britain and France were now at war with Germany spread swiftly around the world. Sister Esther Somerville QAIMNS,

RRC (Award of the Royal Red Cross), had just left the theatre of the British Military Hospital at Quetta, India, after an emergency operation – ('My beloved Fusilier Kershaw. Oh God, he had a ghastly appendix!') – and, remembering the tense political situation, made for the wireless set in the Warrant Officers' side ward. One of a group of silent men held up a warning finger as the voice of Britain's Prime Minister, heavy with foreboding, filled the room.

QAs serving in Cairo heard the news in their Mess, the former residence of a Caliph's harem, and reflected that their hospital, housed in the ancient Citadel, was now in an uncomfortably vulnerable position.

In Australia, the British Prime Minister's announcement was followed almost immediately by the Australian Prime Minister pledging support for the Mother Country. His government turned over a newly-built interstate cruising vessel, the SS *Manunda*, for use as a hospital ship, and men and women wasted no time in enlisting. The Australian Army Nursing Service set up an enrolment centre in Sydney showground, and recruits poured in.

Ann Ramsden RRC (later QARNNS Cooper), one of two trained nurses employed by the P & O Line to look after passengers on the *Strathnaver*, ruefully reflected, on hearing the news, that she would now be out of a job. All merchant shipping passed to the control of the Royal Navy at the outbreak of war. Even as the ship berthed in Sydney harbour, her crew, armed with ropes and buckets of paint, were transforming her sparkling white superstructure into drab battleship grey. The anti-aircraft gun taken on board at Liverpool as a precaution and stowed away until now in the hold, was winched up and mounted on the afterdeck. With the sinking of the *Athenia*, the submarine war had already begun, and the homeward voyage, unescorted by protecting convoy, would not be without danger. Duties for the staff on the homeward voyage changed overnight.

'The senior Ship's Surgeon, Major A. Saunders RAMC (Retired), became officer-in-charge of blackout,' wrote Miss Ramsden. ' "Darken Ship" was announced on the radio every night before sunset. Portholes and doors were closed. All electric light bulbs had been removed from the decks, and exit doors were screened to prevent passage of light from within. Double layers of tarpaulin were hung about a yard apart so that one fell into place before the second one was lifted. Smoking on deck was forbidden; not even a match was to be struck. Extra watchkeepers were recruited from the passengers to keep a day and night look-out for periscopes.'

The *Strathnaver* made for home with all speed. From now on she would be on trooping duties.

2

Mobilisation

For Britain, the way ahead was now clear. The true facts of the European crisis to which she was now deeply committed were plain to see, without further humbug or procrastination. Germany was an aggressor bent on acquiring territory for herself at the sacrifice of weaker nations, and she must be stopped. Russia was in the same camp, aiming to get her slice of Poland and possibly Finland as well.

Britain and France mobilised at once. Since there was no possibility of sending troops to Poland itself, isolated between her attackers and fronted by neutral neighbours, they fell back on the First World War concept of a Western Front along the northern borders of France. They took up positions behind the French Maginot Line of fortifications, facing the German Siegfried Line of similar construction. The fact that the Maginot Line did not extend across the borders of Belgium seemed of no significance, since that small country was determined to stay neutral in this European conflict and so would present a natural buffer for the Allies.

The fallacy of this line of reasoning had been proved at considerable cost twenty-five years earlier, and was now to be repeated. The First British Expeditionary Force proceeded to dig themselves in to the same positions that an earlier generation had learned to loathe. There was a great deal of enthusiastic drilling and soldiering, and a confident feeling that it would all be over by Christmas. Hitler would be given a bloody nose, and the Reservists would go back to their desks in Civvy Street once more. Meanwhile, the plunder of Poland went on.

At home in Britain, preparations went ahead to meet the air attacks which were expected hourly. Barrages of balloons tethered to steel cables rose like huge silver fishes over London and over the mouths of important rivers. The carefully planned Air Raid Precautions fell into place, with volunteer wardens for each district, First Aid Posts and fire-fighting teams. Over the country, in traditional hospitals and buildings requisitioned by the Emergency Medical Service (EMS), a total of 250,000 beds were made ready for victims of air raids.

There was an 'Alert' immediately following the declaration of war. It came as student nurses from the London Hospital were being evacuated to a place of greater safety in Billericay, Essex. As the unfamiliar wail of sirens filled the air, they flung themselves face down in the road, to the consternation of their Matron.

'Spread out!' ordered that practical woman. 'I don't want all my nurses killed at once!'

The Alert proved to be a false alarm.

The evacuation of student nurses was in accordance with an agreement between the Royal College of Nursing and the Government. With no knowledge of what the future might hold, the RCN was understandably anxious about the continued supply of adequately trained nurses. The large London hospitals were obviously at greater risk from air raids than hospitals in other parts of the country, and it was decided that student nurses from these high-risk institutions would move to the country for long periods of work and study. These 'safe' centres would be shared by students from various hospitals.

Park Prewitt, a one-time mental institution near Basingstoke, was one such complex, and was shared by students and their tutors from St Mary's Paddington, St Thomas's and the Westminster. Botley's Park near Chertsey, Ashridge College Hertfordshire and Hydestile near Godalming were similar shared centres. St George's, Hyde Park, sent some of its student nurses to Romford, the London Hospital to Billericay, while as much as possible was done to improve the safety of the parent hospitals in the capital.

The historic cellars beneath St Thomas's were cleaned, whitewashed and made ready for patients. As anticipated, there was enough room below ground for wards, operating theatre and all ancillary departments. The basement ward at University College Hospital was set aside for mothers and babies, since women will give birth during air raids just as at any other time. Walls were buttressed with sandbags, windows strapped across with adhesive tape. All nurses were issued with a special identity card which allowed them priority transport to their hospital should they be off duty during an air raid.

There was movement all over Britain – of troops, of civilians leaving sensitive coastal areas and of children weaving in crocodiles down to the stations, each child with a small case of precious belongings in his hand and a gas mask slung around his neck on a string, on their way to farms and country places. Left behind, their red-eyed Mums would agonise for ever over their decision.

Groups of VADs could be seen on railway platforms, clad in their navy blue serge coats shaped like drainpipes and their unbecoming pork-pie hats, a uniform which had not changed since the First World War. The hats were later replaced by more attractive headgear and the skirts crept up, but never became so short as to display the chaste popliteal space behind the knee when bending.

VADs classified as 'Mobile' were on their way to join the Navy at Haslar Hospital near Portsmouth, the RAF at Halton Hospital in Buckinghamshire or the Army at any one of the many military hospitals dotted about the country. Some had already sailed with Regular QAs to Egypt.

The 'Non-Mobile' VADs reported as auxiliaries to the Civil Nursing Reserve, as staff for the EMS Hospitals. These could be in buildings as grand as Leeds Castle or as homely as a northern Working Men's Club, which now frequently functioned as Camp Reception units for medical examinations.

When VAD Phyllis Harris arrived at Shenley Mental Hospital in Hertfordshire, now a military hospital, she was understandably dismayed to find that her chief responsibility was to be the cleaning and maintenance of a cumbersome old cooking stove in the vast Victorian kitchen. She had diligently practised her First Aid and Home Nursing, as laid down in the St John Ambulance Brigade Manual, and had worked on the wards of her local hospital every weekend for the last twelve months. To be given a stove to look after was distinctly disheartening.

'Never seen one like it for grease,' she marvels.

Her fellow VADs were a mixed crowd. Some came from very privileged backgrounds and, to their credit, undertook whatever tasks were asked of them, from polishing floors to surgical dressings. VAD Rosemary Bowes-Lyon, caught one cold night with her feet in the ward oven, came in for a sharp rebuke from the Night Superintendent, despite her friends at the Palace. Inexperienced at the beginning, the VADs quickly made themselves indispensable assistants to the trained staff and were able to release male orderlies for more onerous duties. They were a godsend to hard-pressed junior probationers, who were delighted to share their heavy routine, and who enjoyed the company of newcomers not yet terrified out of their wits by disciplinarians of the old school of ward Sisters.

August Matrons of the Army, Naval and Air Force Nursing Services interviewed applicants for their respective establishments with a critical eye.

'You look very young,' they objected when Marjorie Lloyd appeared before them. Straight out of training school, she had just spent a month's salary on a new hat and gloves in order to impress them with her maturity.

'Oh no, I'm not,' she corrected them. 'I'm in my twenties.'

Many trained nurses on holiday from the Dominions, finding themselves on the wrong side of the world when war broke out, chose to join the British Services rather than wait an indefinite period for repatriation. Teddy Head and Lynette Walsh from Australia applied to join the QAIMNS Reserve '... but only if we can stay together,' they told the selection committee.

'We will pin your papers together,' the Matrons said gravely, and they stayed that way until Lynette met and married Wing Commander Larking in Heliopolis in 1942.

Regimental tailors were inundated with rush orders as newly enlisted nursing Sisters took up their appointments. Naval Sisters served in Haslar Hospital or took charge of sick bays for casualties from minesweepers and coastal patrol boats. A staff of one Naval Sister and one Naval VAD, affectionately known as 'Siss' and 'Nuss', was attached to each Women's Royal Naval Service (WRNS) station, to look after their welfare. Only a few were given the chance to serve on hospital ships, as most of these vessels were administered by the Army and staffed with RAMC and QAIMNS personnel.

Sisters of Princess Mary's Royal Air Force Nursing Service staffed the main hospital at Halton and the sick bays attached to the many Training Wings which proliferated like mushrooms in this first truly air-conscious war. In addition, they turned now-deserted seaside hotels into convalescent centres.

Army Sisters reported to the military hospitals then mustering for France. Number 6 and Number 2 British General Hospitals (BGH) were mustering at Cookham bound for Le Treport and Offranville near Dieppe. Number 5 BGH, also bound for Le Treport, was at Shorncliffe, Number 3 BGH was at Millbank, destined for Offranville, Number 4 BGH at Netley for La Baule, and Number 9 BGH, at Preston, was preparing to move to Le Mans.

One week after the declaration of war, the first six Sisters of the QAIMNS landed in Cherbourg with the advance party of the First

British Expeditionary Force. They were followed by 1,300 more within the next three weeks, made up of the Regulars, who knew the whole game backwards and the correct Army procedure for every eventuality; the Reserves, who were not entitled to wear the jealously prized scarlet shoulder cape of the Regulars, and many of whom were straight from hospital training school with a lot to learn about life; and the TANS, the Territorials, a different establishment with their own high reputation who merge with the QAIMNS in time of war.

'It never occurred to me to resign from the TANS at the end of the First World War.' Miss Jean Mitchell from Broughty Ferry near Dundee had been nursing Serbs in Macedonia in 1916; she was forty-eight years old when she was called up in 1939 and put in charge of number 10 Casualty Clearing Station bound for France. Skirts were shorter and the pay was better, but, in other respects, this war looked very much like the last one.

The 1st BEF dug itself in alongside the French Army and absolutely nothing happened but Poland was overrun and by the end of September, the Polish National Anthem was no longer heard on Warsaw Radio.

The Casualty Clearing Station (CCS) was, at this time, the most forward position in which Sisters were permitted to serve. Later in the war, circumstances frequently caused the structured plan of medical care to be more flexible, and Sisters worked wherever they were needed. The CCS acted as a short-term holding unit, receiving casualties from such forward outfits as Field Dressing Stations and Advanced Surgical Units, whose function was to resuscitate, operate and evacuate. Only urgent surgery was dealt with in the field, where there was no provision for post-operative care. Less immediate surgery waited until the casualty reached the CCS, where a staff of eight or ten Sisters nursed the wounded until they were fit to be transferred, usually by ambulance, to the base hospitals. But the tide of battle does not always proceed according to plan. Field Dressing Stations (FDS) have been forced to hold patients and base hospitals have been known to act as Casualty Clearing Stations.

The system was working with copybook precision, however, that first winter of the war in France. Casualty Clearing Stations were sited in requisitioned buildings within easy access of forward dressing stations. Ambulance trains transferred patients to base hospitals ranged around the Channel ports where hospital carriers, smaller vessels than hospital ships and therefore more suited to duties in the Channel, waited to carry them to England. The only unusual feature in all this organisation was that, up till Christmas, a total of three British soldiers had been killed. There were no battle injuries in the hospitals. The services of specialist surgeons and physicians and trained nurses were at the disposal of men who, so far, suffered from nothing worse than stomach trouble and Athlete's Foot.

Many Reservists had been sent to France in the first batch of men without adequate training or careful selection.

'They were a lot of old crocks.' Kit Woodman, who had wanted to join the Colonial Service in order to travel, was having her wish granted in the QAIMNS/R. She was stationed at Offranville with the 2nd BGH and had a ward of unfit men. 'One complained that he could not sleep. "It's the pains in me legs, Sister," he said. I asked him how long he'd had pains in his legs. "All me life," he said. That's the kind of patient we were nursing. There were many like him.'

With the advent of colder weather, the troops succumbed to bronchitis and pneumonia. These were the days before penicillin and antibiotics. Reliance was placed on the new sulphonilamide drugs, of which M&B 693 was especially helpful in the treatment of chest infections. Apart from that, nursing was still dependent on linseed and antiphlogistine poultices to the chest and steam inhalations, not easy to carry out in tented wards during a winter which turned out to be very severe.

At first there was mud. No concessions to local conditions were made with regard to the Sisters' uniform, and they still struggled to keep their white coats clean with only the sketchiest of laundry facilities. After the mud came the snow. At times it lay four inches thick on the canvas of the tents and the few coal-burning stoves did little to heat the draughty wards.

Miss Bremner, QAIMNS, Assistant Matron of 2nd BGH, set off on a round of the wards accompanied by an orderly carrying a hurricane lamp one particularly foul night. She was seen, on her return, to be supporting the orderly with one arm while the other arm held aloft her umbrella, frozen in the extended position. Conditions were miserable for staff and patients alike.

With the approach of Christmas 1939, the British Broadcasting Corporation planned a programme of greetings from 'Our Boys at the Front' to the people at home who were still wondering when the war was going to start. Patients had long since drifted back to the civilian hospitals, leaving only a small proportion of beds for air raid victims, if and when they ever materialised. Domestic commodities were growing more scarce, for an alarming number of merchant ships were being sunk by submarines, but in all other respects this period was earning the title of 'the phony war'. Some messages from the boys in hospital would liven up Christmas for many families and, with this in mind, two representatives of the BBC paid a visit to Colonel Kenneth Thomeroy, Commanding Officer of 3rd CCS, and its Matron, Miss Monica Johnson (later Golding, DBE, RRC, Matron-in-Chief QARANC).

Number 3 CCS occupied the grounds of an old château at Mondicourt near Le Mans and, after a good deal of hard work initially in unprepossessing surroundings, had achieved an efficiently working unit. Outbuildings grouped around the central courtyard provided a surgical ward and duty-officer's room. The stable became a dispensary, and a large tent was erected as a medical ward. The château kitchen, such as it was, with neither light nor running water, was put at the disposal of the unit and a tented extension from here formed the operating theatre.

The Engineers transformed the situation with their magic. They laid a pipe to the village pump, and there was water. They set up a dynamo, and there was light. They fashioned first class shadowless operating lamps from petrol tins, which were tried for the first time on a soldier with a ruptured gastric ulcer. He was successfully operated upon and made a swift, uncomplicated recovery, which was not surprising since the surgeon was Mr Bill Underwood, until recently an eminent figure in Harley Street.

RAMC men were quartered in the barn and the QAs had tents in a nearby field. The CO and Matron were each given a tiny room in the château for use as an office, and it was here that Miss Johnson entertained Richard Dimbleby from the BBC to a cup of hot Bovril.

Arrangements were made for the patients to send their messages home, and in return for Miss Johnson's co-operation, Mr Dimbleby and his partner, David Haworth, went to Paris on a shopping spree for the CCS which until then had nothing but a pudding in the way of Christmas preparation. They brought back eleven turkeys, ten for the men and one for the Sisters' Mess, a present for each patient and a car-load of apples, nuts and crackers.

'That is what the BBC did for me.' Dame Monica Golding, as she is today, remembers with undimmed gratitude the last good Christmas for many years to come.

A line or two in the British Press reported that Herr Hitler was spending Christmas inspecting the defences of the Western Front, which was entirely reasonable considering what he had in mind.

3
Dunkirk

The spring of 1940 came to Offranville, touching the grubby, over-wintered tents of the hospitals there with pale sunshine. End-flaps could now be fastened back to let the patients glimpse a gleam of daffodils planted by the Sisters during the previous autumn. Their brightness brought cheer to drab wards and the message that the long, cold, uncomfortable winter was over.

So, it seemed, was the period of waiting upon events. Germany was showing interest in certain Norwegian ports, and when, in early April, a party of German troops landed in Narvik under the guise of trading, Norway appealed to Britain for assistance. A small force of British troops was hastily dispatched, and at the same time a similar party was sent to Iceland to forestall any German initiative there. Each group was to be accompanied by a military hospital, but in the case of Norway, the order was overtaken by the speed of events. The advance party of the hospital, composed of medical officers and orderlies, had scarcely landed before Norway was overrun and they escaped by the skin of their teeth.

A chain of disasters followed. German troops, with the element of surprise in their favour, went on to overwhelm Denmark, and before Holland had time to appreciate her suddenly vulnerable position, she, too, was invaded. Belgium, with the enemy breaking over her borders, realised that further protests of neutrality were useless, and she threw in her lot with the Allies.

The BEF had a fight on its hands at last. The weaker elements had been weeded out long ago, and it was a supremely fit and confident army which now moved cheerfully up to the Western Front. Ambulance trains began to evacuate patients from forward CCSs to base hospitals in order to free beds for the anticipated engagements.

There were thirteen such trains in France, converted from conventional rolling stock in Britain and ferried across the Channel. Fitted with a kitchen-car, a dispensary and accommodation for both sitting and stretcher cases, they could transport more than 300 patients in comfort on each journey. Until now, their staff of three medical officers, three QAIMNS Sisters and forty RAMC orderlies had not been overworked in the routine shuffling back and forth from one hospital to another, but that situation was soon to be drastically changed.

The CCSs put their units in a state of absolute readiness. Drums were filled with sterilised dressings, gloves, gowns and towels. Transfusion units, 'Vampire Vans' in the vernacular of the troops trucking by, checked their supplies of blood, plasma and glucose. Preparation was orderly and cool. There was no alarm, for this was the action everyone had been waiting for. The French and British armies went forward to meet the invaders in good heart.

The highly mechanised German Army, however, had gained a formidable momentum by this time, and could not be stayed by the hastily formed line of Dutch and Belgian soldiers nor by the breached dykes of Holland. Their advance was measured by the sudden urgent issue of civilian refugees from Belgium who poured into France; old people, women and children, pushing prams and handcarts heaped with household goods, over-burdened motor vehicles honking their way through the congestion for as long as the petrol lasted; all streaming fecklessly by without knowing where they were bound, clogging up the routes and hindering the movement north of troops and supplies. They presented an easy target for dive-bombing German planes and were the first patients to be brought to Number 10 CCS near Lille, not far from the border of France and Belgium.

'We began operating at 1000 hours', Miss Mitchell, Matron of the CCS records, 'and continued without pause until 0100 hours the next morning. I remember a wee girlie brought in with her grannie, picked out of a ditch where they had been sheltering with the child's mother. The child and her granny were both wounded and the mother was killed.'

The plight of the refugees hurrying by was heartbreaking to see. 'I mind one old man in a wheelchair accompanied by two old ladies.' This memory, more than any other, casts a shadow across Miss Mitchell's long and eventful life. 'One of the ladies pushed the chair while the other tried to carry two suitcases. As I watched them go by, I wondered how far they would get.'

Amongst the first British casualties to arrive was a lucky Duke of Gloucester with shrapnel wounds and a large dent in his tin hat. He was soon followed by an increasing flow of wounded but there was, as yet, no cause for alarm at the Front; Belgian troops were now reinforced by strong British and French forces on a line stretching from the coast at Antwerp to the start of the Maginot Line. On 15th May, however, German armies broke through a section of the French line at Sedan, where an attack had been least expected, over terrain mistakenly judged to be impossible for tank warfare. The whole Allied line was compelled to fall back hurriedly as a phalanx of German armour swept through the gap.

The German thrust could not be stopped. Experienced by this time in the art of the 'Blitzkrieg', Hitler's Panzer divisions drove south from Sedan and then swung westwards towards the Channel. Confused reports of the enemy's headlong advance came from all sides, and wounded men admitted to the hospitals were bewildered by the rapid deterioration of the situation. The possibility of the whole of the BEF and a great many French and Belgian troops being cut off and encircled was glaringly obvious. Air attacks over Allied lines increased and medical units began to pull back out of the net, edging towards the Channel ports.

Number 3 CCS had moved from Le Mans some weeks previously and was now working at St Pôl near Béthune in northern France. Matron Miss Johnson's first intimation that the military situation was getting out of hand came with an instruction to evacuate all patients on the second day after operation, instead of on the third as was customary. There was scarcely time to put this ruling into effect when the order was changed: for 'Second Day' read 'Day Following Operation'. Not long after this, patients were not permitted to rest even for one night following operation. 'Treat and Pass on' was the instruction and, finally, the saddest message of all, 'Do Not Treat. Pass to the Rear Unit and prepare to evacuate the CCS'.

'We didn't know what was happening, but we knew something was going wrong, so I went to my Red Cross store. I had been supplied with the most wonderful gifts, men's socks, scarves and theatre stockings, all made by women in the north-east of England, and I was determined that the Germans should not get them. We had evacuated all but ten patients and they were preparing to go. I went round them all, and then around the RAMC personnel.

'"What size socks? Would you like a scarf?" I went down to the Quartermaster's Store. "Little Tich" was there. I can't remember his real name. He was a wonderful Quartermaster.

'"Well, Matron," he said. "Are you ready to go?"

'I said we were and gave him some socks, then in came the Company Officer, very important, Territorial. Gaitered. Came smartly to the salute.

'"Matron. Your orders have come. Immediate movement."

'"Thank you," I said, and Little Tich said, "See you later, Matron" and off I went to round up my Sisters. There was no time to pack, We went as we were, We climbed aboard two ambulances, not knowing where we were going.'

Number 12 CCS was in an old Sports Pavilion at Béthune. Casualties streamed in, convoy after convoy, and surgical teams were operating round the clock. When Kathleen Smith, TANS, went on duty on the night of 19th May she discovered that she had 200 post-operative cases in her care, and more undergoing surgery in the theatre. Working in tin hats as one air raid followed another with barely a pause, Sister Smith and her orderlies were scarcely aware that the sound of gunfire was creeping nearer, until the day staff appeared in the ward, fully dressed. The CCS was to be evacuated immediately, and two ambulances were waiting for the Sisters.

Commanding Officers of medical units had been given orders to ensure that Sisters on their staff were never in a position to be taken prisoner. These instructions were most gallantly carried out, although the Sisters themselves were utterly dismayed to leave their colleagues in the RAMC and their patients at a time when their assistance was most needed.

At the order to evacuate, Kathleen Smith, well-schooled in military procedure, hastily began an inventory before handing over her wards to the medical officers but a Movements Control Officer interrupted. 'No time for that,' he said, and hustled her off to collect her ready-packed case. It was then that she realised the true gravity of the situation. To move without a signed inventory was unthinkable in the Army.

She need not have troubled about the suitcase. At some point during the uneasy, moonlit night that followed, the ambulance carrying the Sisters' luggage became separated from the slow procession of refugees and wounded jerking its way along the congested road towards Dieppe. The driver, approaching a group of army vehicles to ask directions, noticed too late the black Maltese Cross markings and spent the rest of his war in a POW camp.

While still some distance from Dieppe, the rest of the cavalcade was halted by a Military Policeman and turned about. Ahead of them, Amiens was being shelled by German troops advancing towards the east, and the way to Dieppe was barred. They must now make for Boulogne, before that, too, fell to the Germans.

Ambulance trains were working under increasingly difficult conditions, their progress delayed by blown-up track and by abandoned French rolling stock. Casualties awaited the trains at every station and, throughout all the shunting and manoeuvring and sporadic shelling, surgeons operated, Sisters and orderlies renewed dressings, fed and washed the weary troops and refugees.

Number 4 Ambulance Train reached Dieppe harbour safely, but was attacked by German planes as patients were being transferred to the two waiting hospital carriers, the *Maid of Kent* and the *Brighton*. Men with limbs in plaster and splints scuttled for cover as machine guns strafed the wharves. A tanker tied up alongside the carriers was set on fire, and soon all three ships were blazing out of control. Flames spread to the wharf buildings and to the rear carriages of the train. With great presence of mind, the Commanding Officer of the train detached the burning coaches and drove the rest of the train away from the danger area, leaving an MO and orderlies to look after the wounded on the wharf. All three ships in the harbour were sunk, but Number 4 Ambulance Train eventually turned up at Cherbourg with its remaining patients and shipped them safely to England.

Altogether, nine ambulance trains were lost in France, destroyed or captured, but before they were brought to a standstill they made forty-seven journeys, transporting 31,000 Service casualties who were eventually received in England.

Number 6 Ambulance Train, filled with casualties, was finally stranded in the station at Albert, with the track blown up on either side. The Germans were not far away. The looted, deserted town was in flames, and the local population had fled. RAMC personnel and the three QAs on the train went about their work, intent on doing as much as possible to help their patients before the Germans arrived. The Commanding Officer had no transport to offer the Sisters, but as the sound of the guns drew nearer, he urged them, in desperation, to join a party of French railway workers who were setting off to walk to the next town. There was a chance that they might pick up a lift to the coast. Twenty-four hours after they left, all on board the train were taken prisoner. Their own position was full of danger, for there was no room for three able-bodied women on trucks packed with troops and wounded. They had to fend for themselves with whatever help they could find. By bicycle, on farmcarts and in a Salvation Army canteen van, they arrived in Cherbourg seven days later, hungry and bedraggled and overjoyed to see a British ship waiting there.

They were luckier than the frantic civilians who crowded the quay, hoping for a passage to England. There was no room on the ships for most of these unfortunate people, and soldiers with fixed bayonets were needed to clear a passage for the Sisters. There were similar scenes at Boulogne where QA Kit Woodman was being evacuated with the 2nd BGH. She did not find it easy to walk past all those imploring eyes.

'I felt ashamed that so much was being done for us and so little for the refugees.'

By 22nd May, Number 10 CCS had to get out of Lille and seek a safer site. To move south was now out of the question, as the neck of the bag which held the greater part of the BEF was being drawn tighter. Instead, they went into Belgium, to the village of Krouhelse, where they took over the church as a hospital and the schoolhouse as an operating theatre. Casualties appeared almost before the unit had time to unpack, and no matter how swiftly the surgeons worked, the long lines of stretchers carrying men in need of urgent surgery continued to grow. When medical supplies began to reach the CCS in unstinted quantities, the staff knew that the base hospitals had left the country. Casualty Clearing Stations, Field Dressing Stations and Advanced Surgical Units were now handling Belgian, French, British and sometimes German casualties on an unprecedented scale.

At midnight on 27th May, the King of the Belgians capitulated. The staff of 10 CCS worked on, in tin hats, expecting capture at any moment. The evacuation of patients was now impossible, yet fresh convoys continued to arrive.

'We now held about 800 casualties,' says Miss Mitchell. 'Every inch of the church floor was taken up with stretchers, and we had to do a terrible thing,' She is a devout woman with a proper respect for sacred places. 'When a man was dying, sometimes in great distress, the only place where we could put him so that he would be out of sight of the rest of the men was behind the altar.'

The whole countryside around the CCS seemed to be going up in flames. Bridges, houses and trucks burned as shells smashed down, drowning the cries of wounded men with their noise. When groups of soldiers, sometimes in two and threes, sometimes in whole companies, stopped to ask the way to the coast, the message was desperately clear. A major disaster was about to overtake the Allies.

Almost at the eleventh hour, on 29th May, a nearby FDS put one of its ambulances at the disposal of the Sisters at 10 CCS. There was still a chance that they might escape. Unwilling as they were to leave their colleagues in the RAMC to carry the burden, they had no choice.

'We had to say goodbye to our doctors, orderlies and patients. They were all taken prisoner. The doctors and orderlies had to walk all the way to Germany.'

With the collapse of the Belgian Front, the perimeters of that area of northern France not yet occupied by the Germans had narrowed to a funnel leading to the only ports still open for evacuation, Dunkirk and La Panne. Both were under constant attack from enemy artillery and dive-bombing planes. Dunkirk was burning fiercely when the Sisters' ambulance drew near and their driver, finding his way blocked with blazing rubble, made for nearby La Panne. There on the sand dunes he brought his vehicle to a halt. Waiting off-shore amongst the pluming waterspouts of falling shells were vessels of every description from pleasure boats to Royal Naval destroyers and, trying to reach them, were long black lines of men wading out from the beaches. The driver was at a loss as to what to do next. Could his ladies wade out with the men? There were no instructions for this situation.

Two Tommies sat on a nearby fence as unconcerned as if they were waiting for the next bus to Brighton.

'Where do we go from here?' Miss Mitchell called out. They jerked a thumb in the direction of a house, half-hidden in the dunes. 'That's HQ,' they said. 'You have to report.'

A short stocky officer of very senior rank was in earnest conversation with a subordinate when Miss Mitchell appeared at the open door. His voice tailed away at the sight of her. 'Good God,' he said. 'Who are you?'

In her unhurried Dundee way, she told him that she was Matron of Number 10 CCS.

His voice rose with a touch of hysteria. 'You can't be! We've got all the nurses away.'

Gently she corrected him. Thirteen more were waiting outside on the dunes.

He turned to the junior officer. 'Get these ladies on a ship at once.'

'I will never get the picture of La Panne out of my mind.' Miss Mitchell, today a very old lady, recalls the scene as if it were yesterday. 'All those men in the water, swimming, wading out to the ships, all under constant fire. One ship was hit and sunk as we went on board the *Oriel*, a minesweeper which had gone aground and was now re-floated.'

Standing next to her at the rails, taking a last long look at his ruined country, was a high-ranking Belgian officer.

'It's a pity King Leopold ratted on us,' Miss Mitchell said boldly.

'Sister,' he said. 'We had nothing to fight with.'

Two days later, the Chief of the Imperial General Staff, Lord Gort, a short, stocky man, left his HQ in the dunes at La Panne and sailed for England, carrying with him the bitter defeat of the First British Expeditionary Force in France.

4
Britain Alone

Sister Kathleen Smith sat in the corner of a first-class compartment of the 5.25 from King's Cross on the evening of 20th May. She studied her fellow travellers with some curiosity. The gravity of the situation in France had not yet penetrated to the civilians in Britain, and businessmen from the City joggled comfortably homewards behind evening papers which as yet showed no pictures of troops on the run and no casualty figures.

In the luggage racks above them lay their bowler hats and briefcases. No-one spoke. No-one dived for cover or scanned the sky for raiders. In the peaceful fields spinning past the windows, farmers gathered in the hay with no sense of urgency on this serene summer evening. Kathleen closed her eyes and more recent images crowded into her tired mind – images of grey-faced men awaiting blood transfusion, of refugees lying wounded and untended by the roadside.

She had spent the previous night seated next to the driver in the ambulance as it crawled towards Boulogne, stopping and starting, taking bumpy short-cuts across the fields to beat the traffic blocks. It had been a night of white moonlight and blackness flashed with the orange of shellfire. Her head under its heavy tin hat had bumped like a turnip every time she dozed off.

After the weeping and the chaos of Boulogne, everything was so sane at Dover: 'Name, Rank and Number' and a wonderful cup of tea, a railway warrant home and seven days leave.

'Would Madam like to order tea?' She opened her eyes. A steward hovered, band-box clean and stiffly starched. She shook her head. Madam's purse and luggage were somewhere in France. All she possessed was a comb and a travel warrant.

'Excuse me,' said the man in the next seat, who had been hoping she would open her eyes. 'Would you mind telling me what uniform you are wearing?'

There were many different uniforms about the streets of Britain, relating to all the dispossessed nationals of Europe, and the grey suit with scarlet facings of the Army Nursing Service was not well known to the general public. Kathleen's skirt was crumpled, her shirt no longer clean, and her stockings spattered with somebody's haemorrhage.

'I am in the Territorial Army Nursing Service,' she said, 'and I apologise for the state I am in, but I have just escaped from France.'

The evening papers were lowered. Miss Smith was the hottest news on the train that night. From Calais to Dover is but a short trip in a fast boat, and that little stretch of water was all that stood between Britain and Germany's as yet unbeaten armies. Thoughtfully the commuters peeled off at their various stations and hurried to their quiet houses in the country. The steward returned with a tray of tea and biscuits.

'Oh no,' she protested, angered to have to turn away for the second time that lifesaving cup of tea.

'With the compliments of the gentlemen who have just left the train,' the steward said politely.

If any doubts lingered about the extent of the collapse in France they were soon dispelled by the shiploads of troops who began to arrive at southern ports. No sooner were they disembarked than the ferrying vessels turned about for the return trip. The first casualties were taken straight to the EMS Hospital at Dover, which was neither designed nor groomed for the heroic part it had now to play.

Little had been done to modernise the building since the reign of Queen Victoria, when it had been a Poor Law institution. There were no lifts, and an awkward bend in the main staircase posed a difficult manoeuvre for stretcher-bearers. One room had been converted into an operating theatre and was equipped with two antiquated operating tables. Yet, in spite of the building's obvious drawbacks, magnificent work was done there from the time of Dunkirk to the end of the war.

When the first casualties arrived from Dunkirk, no-one at the hospital had any experience of battle wounds, or of dealing with such overwhelming numbers. As the ships came in to dock, civilians from the town hastened to help. Bank clerks, railway porters, clergymen, even hospital visitors grabbed a stretcher and carried the wounded men ashore.

The question of who should have priority treatment was a difficult one for the Civil Nursing Reserve staff of four trained nurses, one assistant nurse and one VAD. Betty Le Grys was preparing to treat a desperately wounded man when the Medical Superintendent took her aside. She must give her time to those who, unlike the man she was treating, could still be saved. This was a hard lesson for a young woman just out of training school. A light caress to his clammy brow was the only sign of caring she could give to the dying man before passing to the next stretcher.

Auxiliary hospitals in other parts of the country were prepared for casualties, but the scale of this evacuation from France and the exhausted state of the men on arrival confounded everyone's expectations.

Ashridge College Hertfordshire, once the scene of Queen Mary's 'coming-out' ball, was now home to student nurses evacuated from University College Hospital, London. Neat white beds filled the large rooms, and Nissen huts equipped as wards disfigured the neatly tailored grounds. One fine day towards the end of May, the students sat in the sunshine, knitting long theatre stockings, as they waited for the first ambulances to arrive. Everything was in readiness. Every bedside locker was equipped with temperature chart and case-notes holder, sputum mug, ashtray, denture bowl, soap and towel.

The casualties, who had been expected in tens, came in hundreds. In the space of a few hours, the tidy wards were cluttered with dirty boots, soiled uniforms, packs, respirators and rifles, all pushed under the beds until someone had time to clear them away.

The men fell asleep as soon as they were laid on a bed. For some, an anaesthetic before operation scarcely seemed necessary. The walking wounded fell asleep in the grounds where they were halted, under the trees, even on the asphalt paths.

'Sorry, nurse,' they apologised to the young girls who undressed them, 'I haven't had my boots off for ten days.'

Marison Orfeur was a first-year student nurse. 'Like most of my friends, I grew up that night. The suffering of the wounded was a nightmare. A theatre team lent to us by Charing Cross Hospital operated day and night continuously for a week, while we inexperienced and humble student nurses did what we were told and wished that we were qualified so that we could do more.'

On night duty, a little while later, she writes home during a quiet half-hour before dawn.

'Three hundred soldiers have arrived, and two hundred and fifty more are expected. Sometimes I accompany a patient to the theatre and sometimes I cook the porridge. Convalescent men help me to serve the breakfast. It is two o'clock now and I must go and cut mountains of bread and butter.'

In the confusion of retreat, a number of injuries had been left untreated for too long and were infected and gangrenous by the time the wounded men reached hospital, leaving no alternative for the surgeon but amputation. Those injuries which had been enveloped in plaster of paris for ease of transport were in much better condition, despite the fact that when the plaster was removed, sometimes after an interval of three weeks or more, a stinking wound crawling with maggots was revealed. Miraculously, the loathsome creatures disposed of all the septic matter and left the wound clean and granulating. This trick of nature had been discovered in the Spanish Civil War, and was first used by Professor Trueta, who later became the Professor of Orthopaedics in the University of Oxford. The enclosing of open wounds in plaster was to become standard practice in the Second World War.

Time was running out for those troops still waiting on the beaches of Dunkirk and La Panne. Medical officers and orderlies sought what shelter there was in the dunes for the wounded in their care, and got them on board a rescue ship whenever the opportunity presented itself.

The hospital carrier *Isle of Guernsey*, with six QAs on board, made her sixth and final splendid rescue bid on 9th June, by which time all but one of the piers at Dunkirk were destroyed and the harbour was a mass of wrecks. Before she could begin to embark casualties, this last remaining pier was struck by a shell and began to disintegrate. Ship's officers and crew as well as orderlies ran with loaded stretchers from the beach. Willing hands at the ship's side hustled the wounded on board. Stretcher cases somehow managed to pull themselves over the ship's rail while the stretcher-bearers ran back to the beach for more, even as the whole structure of the pier was beginning to crumble into the sea. 600 wounded men were lifted from the beach before this last lifeline collapsed.

Nothing more could be done for the remaining casualties. Their dedicated doctors and orderlies stayed with them, and were taken prisoner with them. The *Isle of Guernsey* was attacked several times on her way home but was not incapacitated. Her sister ship, the *Paris*, was not so lucky, and became the third hospital carrier to be sunk during the Dunkirk evacuation, despite their regulation markings of Red Crosses.

When the rescue operation could be properly assessed, it was seen as a remarkable achievement. The greater part of the BEF and thousands of French and Belgian soldiers had been taken from a trap which seemed likely to engulf the entire Allied forces. So great was the relief felt in Britain that the whole exodus began to take on the appearance of a victory – but it was, in truth, a terrible defeat. And, although the majority of the fighting men had been saved, all their armaments, tanks and guns had been left behind.

Nevertheless, a Second British Expeditionary Force was hastily formed, with the object of returning to France, but even as it prepared to leave, France capitulated, on 17th June.

The war, from Britain's point of view, suddenly changed from a liberating crusade to a fight for her own survival. She now stood alone. Europe belonged to Hitler. Without warning, explosions began to rock the town of Dover, and mystified inhabitants looked in vain for culprit bombers in the sky. A powerful German gun had been mounted at Calais and the crew had just found the measure of the south-east corner of England. For the first time in nearly a thousand years, Britain faced invasion. Would she, too, kiss goodbye to freedom after the manner of Czechoslovakia, Poland, Norway, Denmark, Holland, Belgium, and now France?

Premonition of disaster can always be relied upon to light a fuse under the otherwise phlegmatic inhabitants of Great Britain, and the notion that the Germans might dare to set foot on the 'sceptred isle' was enough to set the nation afire. Guns, tanks and planes were rushed off assembly lines to replace those lost at sea. Look-outs manned the cliff tops. Place names on Post Offices and shops were painted out to confuse enemy parachutists. The ringing of church bells would be the signal that the enemy had landed, and they would not be rung otherwise.

In addition to the Home Guard, formed of men too old to fight and those in reserved occupations, another and more secret band held themselves in readiness for what would certainly be a terminal service. Made up of countrymen, gamekeepers and farmers, they knew the ways of the land from childhood. At the first sign of invasion, they would go to ground, to prepared hideouts pre-stocked with food and ammunition. There they would hide until the first wave of invaders passed over, then they would emerge behind the enemy's lines, to blow up petrol supplies and ammunition dumps and to disrupt his communications. They did not expect to survive for long, but the quality of their going would be memorable.

Joe Lowes was one of these men. He had been a Sergeant in the First World War, and was as mad as a gnat to be over age for this one. A gamekeeper by day and a platoon commander by night, he trained his men in a cell scooped-out under the roots of a great elm tree near an Essex estuary. His wife was as mystified as all the other women at their husbands' nocturnal absences, but knew better than to question muddy boots and blankets.

The decisive Battle of Britain, however, was to be fought in the skies, since Hitler was not prepared to send in his assault troops until the RAF had been wiped out. With his Luftwaffe now so conveniently placed in Northern France, he gave orders for the air attack to begin in the summer of 1940. Day after day, his bombing planes came over the Channel in dense formation, their aim being to destroy the airfields and wipe out the RAF in the air and on the ground.

Outmatched in numbers but not in performance, the RAF proceeded to deal out harsh punishment to Goering's hitherto unbeaten air force. With every day that passed during that fraught August, planes fell burning out of the skies over Kent, Essex, Surrey, Sussex and Hampshire, and hospitals became acquainted for the first time with 'airman's burn'. An aircraft on fire, travelling at high speed, was as lethal as a blow lamp, producing deep destruction of tissues.

The medical profession was tireless in its search for more efficient, less painful methods of treating these cases, for no matter what ointment or lotion was applied, dressings could not be changed without causing the patient intense pain. Two young RAF doctors were discovered one day in a side ward at Halton RAF Hospital, drenched to the skin, experimenting with ways of providing continuous antiseptic irrigation of burned limbs encased in waterproof sleeves. What emerged was the Bunyan-Stannard Irrigation Envelope, named after its two wet innovators, which found its way onto most of the hospital wards in Britain and achieved considerable success in certain cases. As the war progressed, there was much intensive research into this most painful injury. Tanks, ships and planes all caught fire and provided a large proportion of the wounded.

At his newly-established plastic surgery centre at Park Prewitt near Basingstoke, Sir Harold Gillies, with infinite patience, began to repair scarred and burned victims, giving back function to distorted limbs and making noses, jaws and eyelids for men with little left of their original faces.

That summer had a strangely unreal quality for those going about their daily business on the ground. For Dorothy Harper (later Dye), Sir Harold's ward Sister, this was an unreal period of conflicting sensations.

'The beautiful weather was at odds with the desperate plight of the nation. The call of the cuckoo and the song of the nightingale were drowned by the noise of dog-fights overhead. The smell of lilac and of pinks was overpowered by the stink of rotting plasters. In the darkness of the night on the wards, men with phosphorus burns glowed eerily in their beds.'

History was being written in the skies by young pilots whose lives, in many cases, ended shortly after they had left school. VAD Dorothy Jacob (later Lewes), was 'special' nurse to two such young men, both pilots, both nineteen years old. One was English, the other German, and they lay side by side, critically wounded, in a small room at Haslar Naval Hospital, Portsmouth. They died within minutes of each other. Their young and inexperienced nurse saw tears in the eyes of the ward Sister as she turned away from the two dead youths.

'Lay them out, please, Nurse.'

'I dared not confess that I had not performed this service before,' writes Dorothy Jacob, 'and I hoped that the Sick Berth Attendant sent to help me would be more experienced than I, but he was a peacetime ballet dancer without any knowledge of Last Offices. Fortunately, I was able to remember the last chapter in our Red Cross manual, and completed our sad task.'

As the weeks went by, the truth began to dawn on Hitler: his Luftwaffe was not winning the war against the RAF. At the end of August, student nurse Marison Orfeur was able to write to her parents:

'The Nazis are losing so many planes that I'm sure we must come out on top soon. Tomorrow there is to be a Jumble Sale in aid of the Spitfire Fund. We will be wearing each other's clothes, but at least they won't cost coupons. Are you still sleeping in the cellar?'

By mid-September, the battle for supremacy in the air had been won by the RAF, and the invasion of Britain was called off. As a parting shot, the RAF blew up all the invasion barges waiting to sail from the estuaries of the Meuse and the Scheldt. In fury, the Luftwaffe turned its attention to Britain's cities and centres of industry. Civilians were soon to find war in their own streets in what was known forever afterwards as 'the blitz'.

5

The Suez Canal under Threat

Having judiciously waited until Hitler's victory in France was assured before committing himself to the conflict, Mussolini declared war on the Allies on 10th June, 1940, and in so doing dropped one more huge burden of responsibility into Britain's lap.

Egypt and the Suez Canal were now ringed with enemies. After the collapse of France, the French-administered territory of Syria was taken over by Nazi sympathisers in the Vichy French Government, thus constituting a threat to the Canal from the north. Mussolini could attack from Abyssinia through the Sudan at any time and his maritime provinces bordering the Mediterranean carried a fine road, equipped with depots and forts, right to the borders of Egypt.

Reinforcement troops for these danger areas were sent from Britain without delay, even though her own continued existence as a free nation was in doubt that summer of 1940. Convoys of ships carrying men and military supplies left the ports of Glasgow, Liverpool and Southampton for the Middle East. With an enemy now straddling the Mediterranean, the longer route via the Cape was chosen, although escalating submarine warfare was soon to make this voyage equally perilous.

Great ships sailed with lesser ships and were not always pleased to match their speed to that of the slowest. The *Queen Mary* was out of her class when she set out for Australia to pick up troops. 'Nineteen knots!' roared her Captain. 'I'll have to go astern on one engine to maintain that speed.' History does not record the comments of less patrician Masters.

Servicewomen accompanied the troops, women of the Auxiliary Territorial Service (ATS), the Women's Royal Naval Service (WRNS), the Women's Auxiliary Air Force (WAAF), the First Aid Nursing Yeomanry (FANY) and all three nursing services with their VADs.

Preparations for the departure of convoys from Britain were carried out under tight security. The date of sailing was not disclosed until the last possible moment, after which time telephones were out of bounds to all personnel. Movements from billets frequently took place under cover of darkness and many a ghostly procession of QAIMNS

Sisters, laden with baggage, was silently escorted down the hill from Hatfield House in Hertfordshire, now a military hospital, to the railway station, past houses where occupants were blissfully sleeping – until some over-burdened young lady would drop her tin hat and blow the whole exercise.

The next stage of the journey was rarely straightforward. Sailing dates were frequently postponed and women waiting to embark were allotted whatever accommodation was available. QAs Judy Price (later Martin) and Joyce Pool slept head to toe in a double bed in the 'Taverners' Arms' in Plymouth, a run-down, jolly establishment with sing-songs around the piano and a staff of one very pregnant maid. Two VADs spent a restless night in Liverpool holding a chairback against the bedroom door of their strongly suspect 'hotel' and shouting discouragement through the keyhole to a long line of hopeful clients.

Amongst the QAs now setting out for the Middle East were many who had recently escaped from France. Ever since the dramatic rescue by minesweeper of Number 10 CCS from La Panne, Miss Mitchell had waited impatiently at her home in Scotland for recall from leave.

'I was just thinking, here I am, stuck in Broughty Ferry for ever-more, when embarkation orders arrived.' She boarded the Cunard Line SS *Franconia*, bound for Egypt. Sister Kathleen Smith, still with Number 12 CCS, was on the *Mauretania* (Cunard Line) and Miss Monica Johnson, promoted from Number 3 CCS, was now Assistant-Matron of Number 9 BGH on board the *Andes* (Royal Mail Line).

A state of alert was maintained throughout the voyage, and women were advised to sleep in 'slacks' in case of shipwreck. On all other occasions, QAs were forbidden to wear trousers at the express wish of their patron, Queen Mary. The vicissitudes of war, however, were to bring about a certain bending of the rules, despite royal disapproval.

There was a welcome port of call at the Cape for all convoys. Passengers were given shore leave in Cape Town or Durban while oil and water were taken on board. The hospitality of the people of South Africa, which was to become legendary, was showered on the troops as soon as they set foot ashore. Homes were opened to them; parties, picnics and dances arranged for their entertainment. Local wives ran a canteen for the troops where, for a shilling, a soldier could buy a meal of sausages, bacon, eggs and tomatoes followed by fruit salad and a cup of tea. When the time came to leave, a female singer dressed in white took up her position at the furthest end of the Durban pier and sang a song of farewell to each departing convoy. Servicemen and women who called there will remember forever the kindness they met in South Africa and their last sight of Durban, 'the woman in white'.

On arrival at the port of Suez at the southern end of the Canal, the Women's Services went their separate ways. The Military Hospitals with their staffs of doctors, Sisters and VADs took up their appointed sites. Some continued to the Sudan and Palestine, but most proceeded to a spot in the desert marked with a cross and having no distinguishing features but unrelieved sand. The 13th BGH put up its tents near the town of Suez to function as a point of departure for evacuating patients, and was known thereafter as the 'bed-and-breakfast' hospital.

Egypt was accustomed to visitations of British Army Sisters over the years. The first contingent served there in 1879, when British troops were sent to guard the Canal on behalf of a bankrupt Egypt. Again, in the First World War, QAs and VADs nursed here the wounded from Gallipoli. Perhaps the ghosts of the 24th Stationary Hospital gathered to watch Number 1 BGH put up its tents, twenty-two years later, on the same site, at Kantara on the Egyptian side of the Canal, some twenty miles from Port Said.

The men from Gallipoli were fed and rested here, their wounds dressed before being passed along to the Cairo hospital. VAD Sadie Apperley, a vicar's daughter from Durham, in a uniform more suitable for the vicarage than the desert, was on night duty in 1917 in a ward of very ill men when she wrote in her diary, 'The wind is rude and rough with me tonight. I tramp around the camp with both hands full of medicine glasses and a lamp, and it swishes my hat over my eyes and throws my skirt over my head and I trip over a tent peg.'

These were the days before even the sulphonamides had been invented, and the demands made on the nurse were strenuous.

'Convoys are coming in every day and the wards are overflowing. Case after case of malignant malaria with patients running temperatures of 104 and 105 degrees. We have four delirious pneumonias on the ward, all trying to get out of bed at the same time and so strong that the orderly and I can hardly hold them down. I hope they will be given morphia tonight before I go on duty.'

Sadie's friend, VAD Pepper, died here of a septic finger, and is buried in the English cemetery under the Roman aqueduct in Old Cairo.

The nurses of Number 1 BGH were a different generation, with short skirts and cropped hair, but Egypt had not changed. Medical treatments had advanced since Sadie Apperley's day, but living conditions for the hospital staff were no less primitive in 1940. The Sisters slept four to a tent on camp beds, and pressed their uniforms on the top of a tin trunk with a flat-iron heated on a 'Beatrice' oil stove. The sand blew from sun-up to sun-down and, for all their needs, they had an allowance of one bucket of water per day. They had to learn to live with bugs, mosquitoes, flies, scorpions and rats.

Everyone going to the latrines carried a stick to beat off the rats. The desert was full of them. They built their nests in the short concrete walls constructed at the base of the tent sides and would scurry up the mosquito netting over the patients' beds. They developed a taste for plaster of paris, and nibbled away at any exposed piece they could find. Immobilised patients beat them off their plastered limbs with long poles. A Sister was attacked by a horde of the creatures as she went about the ward one night by the light of a torch. In terror, she leapt into the nearest bed, to be received with delighted surprise by its New Zealand occupant.

Bugs were no less of a problem. They found their way inside the patients' plasters and caused such irritation that the plasters had to be removed and fresh ones applied. The legs of the patients' beds were placed in tins of paraffin to prevent the creatures from climbing up into the mattress, and the bed frames of 'up-patients' were seared with a blow torch, but still the bugs increased. A ward tent could be emptied, disinfested, refilled with clean equipment and, as soon as the exercise was completed, the bugs would return. Every effort to exterminate them met with failure.

'The nights were so beautiful,' wrote one Sister on night duty. 'Tall palm trees silhouetted against the night sky swayed with the breeze, their leaves making a gentle swish-swish. The Bedouin guards on duty in the camp would call to each other at intervals, a strange, weird cry that echoed across the desert. On one such night, I sat outside the ward tent to enjoy the evening instead of going for a meal but, within minutes, I felt something crawling across my face. When I went to the ablutions, there were five bugs on my cap and I had to strip to the skin and change all my clothing.'

Those hospitals not sited in the desert enjoyed more comfortable conditions. Number 9 BGH took over the magnificent Heliopolis Hotel near Cairo. The 25th BGH moved into a Boys' College near Alexandria, operating jointly with a Naval medical unit to form the 64th BGH, staffed by both Services.

There were nice differences in the *modus vivendi*. Teddy Head and Lynette Walsh, the two Australian nurses who had joined the QAIMNS in London, were astonished to find silver finger bowls in the Mess. Conversely, the tin plates of the 'Pongos' were not appreciated by Naval Sisters accustomed to crested china. The two Services worked well together, however, in this strategically important position which served the Eastern Mediterranean Fleet at Alexandria and also acted as first base to troops in the desert.

The Regular Military Hospital in Cairo moved from the Citadel to less conspicuous premises with few regrets, since the very grand palace of a twelfth-century Caliph had left a great deal to be desired as a hospital. Birds nesting inside the high, domed roof were a perpetual nuisance, spattering the mosaic floor with their droppings and swooping low over defenceless patients at meal-times to snatch the food from their plates. The barracks at Helmieh, recently vacated by the Hussars who had moved up to guard the railhead at Mersa Matruh, were in every way more suitable. The hospital, which became known as the 63rd BGH, was to expand into one of the most important medical centres in Egypt.

Mussolini's long expected invasion from Libya came about on 17th September, 1940, and succeeded in penetrating into Egypt as far as Sidi Barrani, a distance of sixty miles. Here the attacking force paused to pull up their extended supply lines and, fortunately for Britain, did not appear to be in any hurry to renew the attack. This allowed time for the shiploads of men arriving from Britain with every convoy to be built up into a strong fighting force.

As well as troops from Britain, volunteers from Australia, New Zealand, South Africa and India were assembling in the Middle East, and none were more anxious to get to grips with the 'Eyeties' than the Australians. Bored with the inactivity of the voyage, they were spoiling for a fight as the *Queen Mary* nosed in to dock at Suez, but there was no Front Line station for them. Instead, a message calculated to strike fear into the heart of any British ward Sister was dispatched to the 13th BGH:- 'Prepare to receive boatload of Australians.' Coming from their isolated continent, they had no immunity to Western diseases and the voyage from Australia had provided perfect incubating conditions for every quiescent germ on the ship. As soon as they came ashore, they were led to hospital, protesting wildly, and put to bed with their measles, chicken pox and mumps. The midnight round, however, frequently revealed empty beds stuffed with pillows, for the Diggers saw no reason to miss out on the night life of Suez because of a few spots and lumps.

There were few battle casualties at this stage, apart from the results of sporadic sniping at the frontiers, but the endemic diseases of the Middle East soon made a serious impact on the strength of the regiments. Dysentery was a terrible scourge, keeping the laboratories as well as the wards busy. The new drug sulphaguanidine was so precious that it could be prescribed only for the very sick. Surgeon Commander Wilson of the 64th BGH would not let his small supply out of his sight and carried it wrapped in small packets in his uniform pocket. For most patients, nothing but the old-fashioned 'salts and castor oil' treatment could be offered, with its limited promise of a slow recovery at best. Sand-fly fever, scrub typhus, malaria and typhoid fever claimed many victims and, in those regions like the Sudan, where high humidity equalled high temperatures, heat stroke was a killer.

A man would collapse suddenly in a dehydrated condition. Sweating stopped, and the whole of the body's heat-regulating mechanism was thrown out of gear. Left untreated, his temperature would continue to rise to 108 and sometimes 110 degrees, taking him through convulsions and coma to death.

To bring his temperature down when no air conditioning was available was no easy task. Treatment was immediate and intensive. Naked except for a covering sheet, he was placed on a bed beneath an electric fan. Ice was packed around his groins, armpits and spine, and he was doused from time to time with cold water. To reduce internal heat, he was given cold enemata and intravenous transfusions of saline and glucose. When he began to respond, his chilled body had to be gently rewarmed with most assiduous monitoring.

From time to time there were outbreaks of poliomyelitis, not then covered by a prophylactic serum, and of diphtheria, both needing the utmost care in nursing at great personal risk on the part of the nurses.

Miss Monica Johnson, after a short time as Assistant Matron of Number 9 GBH, was posted to the 63rd BGH at Helmieh as Matron. Each day began with a discussion concerning those men who were on the Dangerously Ill List (DIL), or the Seriously Ill List (SIL), between herself and the Regimental Sergeant-Major who occupied the position of Wardmaster.

'We were becoming increasingly concerned about a soldier suffering from diphtheria,' writes Miss Johnson. 'The Wardmaster had just seen the man and didn't think he was going to "make it". He was experiencing great difficulty in breathing.

' "But he's got a tracheotomy," I said.

' "He's no better off, ma'am," he said.

'So I hurried to the soldier's bedside, for it was obvious that a plug of mucus must be blocking the airway. I found Sister Anne Roberts, who was specialling the patient, behind the screens, quite cool and calm.

' "He's all right now, Matron," she said.

'The man was indeed all right and breathing easily through his tracheotomy tube. On his locker was a bowl and a catheter. Sister Roberts had saved his life, and put her own in extreme danger, by sucking out the plug of mucus from his throat through the catheter. God must have been watching over that brave woman, for she did not catch the disease.'

A case of bubonic plague was identified at the 64th BGH and a course of M&B was started immediately. The man recovered and none of those who nursed him were infected. However, two Basutos, who were admitted to Number 1 BGH well advanced with the disease, died from it, and in spite of inoculation the doctor and the Sister who had attended them both caught the disease and were gravely ill for several weeks before they recovered.

The appearance of a case of smallpox from time to time triggered off stringent isolation precautions. In spite of these, in one instance at Number 1 BGH, the infection unaccountably continued to spread.

The original sufferer was being nursed under strict barrier conditions by an RAMC Sergeant SRN (State Registered Nurse) in a tent pitched one mile away from the rest of the hospital, yet three more patients in a ward on the perimeter contracted the disease. Thorough investigation failed to reveal the cause of the spread of infection, and the Commanding Officer himself paid a visit to the Isolation Tent, in search of possible clues.

His eye fell on a thin trail of ants crossing the tent floor. This was not an unusual sight in the desert, but these ants carried the dried crusts which had dropped from the skin of the sick man. Here was the mode of transmission. The Isolation Tent was moved a further five miles from the rest of the hospital, and there were no more outbreaks of smallpox. For his devoted nursing with complete disregard for his own safety, the Sergeant SRN was mentioned in dispatches.

While Mussolini's army rested at Sidi Barrani, his troops were being very aggressive in other quarters. A surprise attack in British Somaliland gained for the Italians the port of Berbera in the Gulf of Aden. Nearer to home, an Italian army crossed from Albania into Greece, but the tough Greek fighters were more than a match for them, despite the disparity in numbers. The invaders were holed up in the northern mountains of Greece throughout the winter of 1940. In response to a plea for aid, Britain sent the few RAF squadrons that could be spared to support the Greek guerrillas, and a British Military Hospital and staff to look after their wounded.

Mussolini delayed too long at Sidi Barrani. By December 1940, Britain and the Commonwealth had a well-trained force ready to strike. The battle of Sidi Barrani was an overwhelming defeat for the Italians, who were chased back along the way they had come, leaving the POW cages overflowing. 'Five acres of officers, 200 acres of Other Ranks' was one jubilant estimate quoted by Winston Churchill.

The greater part of five enemy divisions was destroyed at Sidi Barrani and the triumphant Allied troops raced into the New Year carrying all before them across Libya. Bardia, Tobruk and Benghazi fell into their hands before Hitler sent an army under Rommel to rescue his demoralised partner.

6

The Tragedy of Greece

The 26th BGH arrived in the Greek town of Kiffissia, twelve miles north of Athens, in November 1940, their brief being to set up a hospital for the treatment of Greek casualties resulting from the guerrilla war against the Italian invaders. Three hotels were put at the service of the hospital, the 'Cecil', the 'Palace' and the 'Abergi'. Emptied of furniture, the large rooms made very adequate wards.

Although November in Kiffissia was a pleasant month, winter had already come to the mountain regions in the north. Life was hard for the Greeks fighting there and medical care had been almost non-existent until RAMC doctors and orderlies and Sisters of the QAIMNS prepared to receive them in Kiffissia. It took seven days to get the wounded down to the hospital from their strongholds in the mountains, and their condition on arrival was deplorable. Their wounds were septic, their bodies crawling with fleas and lice. Before they could be admitted to the wards, they were taken through a cleansing station to be shaved, bathed, disinfested and dressed in clean pyjamas. The filthy rags which bound up their wounds were removed and clean dressings applied.

Their appearance was quite terrifying. Black-browed, with piercing eyes and strong, rugged features, they looked like a band of brigands, but the Sisters, wary at first, soon discovered that this alarming aspect hid an endearing childlike simplicity, and they were rewarded with fulsome appreciation for everything they did.

Most of the casualties suffered from gangrene of the limbs due to frostbite, which had been dealt with on the spot by crude guillotine amputation leaving no covering skin flap. As a result, healing was impossible. The only treatment was further corrective amputation – a hard piece of logic for men who had already suffered much.

Less serious cases of frostbite, where the skin was still whole, responded to treatment with oil of turpentine, after which the affected limb was wrapped in cotton wool and gently warmed. Septic wounds were dressed twice daily with Eusol (Edinburgh University Solution of Lime) and liquid paraffin.

The Greeks made incredibly noisy patients, continually shouting at each other, laughing and singing at the tops of their voices in a manner far removed from the customary decorum of a British hospital. Sister Joan Wilson TANS sought help from an English-speaking Greek girl.

'What is Greek for "Be quiet"?'

'Do you mean "Be quiet" very weak or "Be quiet" very strong?' asked the girl.

'"Be quiet" very strong,' said Joan Wilson firmly.

'Then you say *SKARSI*,' said the girl. 'That is "Be quiet" very, very strong.'

That night, Sister Wilson went on duty fully prepared. As she began her round of the wards, she was greeted by the usual bedlam. 'Sister, I have a pain!' ... 'Sister, I want a drink!' ... 'Sister, I want more blankets!' ... Walking into the middle of the ward, she clapped her hands and called out '*SKARSI!*' loud and clear. The effect was electric. There was sudden, total silence. Much gratified, she proceeded on her round. Tonight the treatments were carried out without interruption and she got through the work in record time. From under their blankets, her subdued patients watched her closely as she went from bed to bed. Finally, one who spoke more English than the rest whispered tearfully,

'Sister, where you get that "*SKARSI*"? No good, Sister. No good.'

There was no need for Joan Wilson to pursue the translation. The point had been made.

The people of Kiffissia showed their gratitude for what was being done for their injured soldiers by showering the British Sisters with hospitality, and Christmas 1940 was a time of celebration and rejoicing. The Italians were taking a beating not only in northern Greece but also in the North African desert. Within two short months, however, all this was to change.

German troops sent to stiffen the Italian line in Libya halted the Allied advance there, and, in February 1941, turned it into a retreat. In March, German forces crossed Bulgaria and took up menacing positions on the Greek and Yugoslav borders, where they proceeded to assemble all the men and mechanised armour necessary for an invasion.

This was an enemy far out-classing any troops the Greeks could field. Britain sent 58,000 men from Egypt to her aid and a Polish Brigade from Palestine, even though every man was needed in the desert war – the loss of Greece would add to the imbalance of power in the Mediterranean and was to be avoided at all costs.

If Germany invaded Greece, much would depend on the strength of Yugoslav resistance, since the British forces covering the long, meandering Greek border with Bulgaria were dangerously over-stretched. In the event, Yugoslavia was unable to halt Hitler's armies when they poured across her borders on 6th April, 1941, simultaneously with the invasion of Greece.

Yugoslavian troops fell back and the British flank was exposed. All forward units were hastily pulled back to avoid encirclement. To old soldiers who had been through Dunkirk, it must have looked uncomfortably like 'the mixture as before'.

Events moved fast. Hitler overran Yugoslavia and headed for Athens down the coastal road from Thessalonika. The 1st New Zealand General Hospital, newly arrived on the scene and operating at Larissa, halfway between Thessalonika and Athens, was forced to evacuate after only three weeks in such a hurry that equipment had to be abandoned and blown up. The enemy was almost upon them.

The 2nd/5th Australian General Hospital (AGH) was also in Greece but all its equipment had been lost en route. Consequently, at this time, when the stability of the whole Greek peninsula had been suddenly turned upside down, the 26th BGH was the only functioning hospital. Another Australian hospital, the 2nd/6th AGH, was on its way and would need to arrive soon if it was to be of any use: the future of Greece, and of the Allied soldiers sent to help her, had begun to look increasingly grim.

Bedspace was becoming scarce at the 26th BGH. Unavoidably, Greek patients had to be farmed out amongst the townsfolk, and tents were erected in the hotel grounds to serve as extra wards. These were far from convenient. They had neither water supply nor sluices. Bedpans and bottles had to be carried to and from the hotel, along with every drop of water used.

Orderlies were in short supply. Joan Wilson and one other QA ran a busy ward between them in one of the tents with no extra help. They worked like machines, admitting patients, preparing them for surgery, washing, feeding and evacuating them, until one patient could bear to stay in bed no longer and insisted upon getting up to help them. Louis MacPherson was an Australian, a member of an Australian Field Ambulance. He had been admitted with influenza and dysentery but refused to stay in bed after the second day and appointed himself unofficial orderly to the two overworked Sisters. He was well trained and his help was invaluable. When, a few days later, the 2nd/6th AGH arrived in Greece, all Australian patients were transferred from the British hospital, but MacPherson somehow contrived to be left behind. By that time, he had become part of the team.

Air attacks on the Thessalonika–Athens road increased, and the sound of guns drew nearer to Kiffissia. Casualties brought disturbing tales of German paratroopers, dressed in the uniforms of dead British soldiers, spreading rumour and panic behind the Allied lines. Wounded German prisoners being nursed under guard in a tent on a hill some distance away from the rest of the hospital grew more cheerful every day, as each new arrival brought good news of the German advance.

When Yugoslavia capitulated on 17th April, the Greek guerrillas, brave as they were, lost heart. They were a spent force. In order to save the country from further devastation, the Greek Government suggested that British forces should withdraw without delay. On that day, half of all the medical officers and orderlies at the 26th BGH were ordered to leave. Louis MacPherson, Sister Wilson's unofficial orderly, refused point-blank to go, although he knew that to stay probably meant years of imprisonment.

'He told our Commanding Officer that his own Field Ambulance had been wiped out and that, if British women were going to stay, he certainly would not leave them. The Colonel told him that he remained at his own risk, which he did,' Joan Wilson reported.

There was now a greatly reduced staff at the 26th BGH to look after a rapidly increasing number of patients. The Matron, Miss Clarke, worked on the wards, helping to lay out the dead. The Home Sister and the Greek serving girls made huge jugs of soup and carried them to the men who lay everywhere, dirty and unshaven. Stretcher-bearers, panting with fatigue, laid the wounded wherever they could find a place. The doctors who had remained operated day and night and wore their revolvers at all times.

Some New Zealand orderlies who no longer had a hospital of their own came to lend assistance, but no extra help was sent to the lone Sister in charge of the POWs. For her, the situation went from bad to worse. First the guard was removed, and then her orderlies. She was left to cope alone with a tent full of arrogant Germans, who were aggressively confident of their imminent release. They were not so short-sighted, however, as to ignore the fact that they would be in an uncomfortable position without her. There were many amongst them who were seriously wounded, and so, lest she should be tempted to follow her orderlies, they tried to bribe her with promises of silk stockings, French perfume and even a post-war holiday in Vienna. They need not have worried. There were as yet no plans to evacuate the Sisters.

On 24th April, 1941, the King of Greece abdicated and the nation surrendered. It was now imperative to get Allied troops and casualties out of the country without delay.

On 25th April, Miss Clarke called her nursing staff together. An Australian destroyer was standing by to evacuate the New Zealand Sisters and some of the Australians. There was room for twelve British women to accompany them. Names were asked for.

It was a hateful decision to have to make. 'If we stayed,' says Joan Wilson, 'we would, for a certainty, be taken prisoner. The Germans even then were almost surrounding us. We all felt quite sick at heart. Four said they would go and four of the older ones were persuaded to go. That made eight.'

Within half an hour, those who were leaving were on their way south along the coastal road making for the port of Argos in the Peloponnese, but Germany was determined that no 'Dunkirk fleet' would snatch this army to safety, and every port was closely watched. The charred wrecks of ships, some still smoking, littered the blue bays of the Aegean while the casualties they would have embarked huddled patiently and hopelessly on the beaches, waiting for a miracle.

The original RAF squadrons had all been destroyed, fighting against overwhelming odds, and, as the convoy carrying the Sisters wound southwards, unopposed German bombers attacked again and again, sending the occupants of the trucks scuttling into the barley fields for cover. One particularly sustained attack had the Sisters holed up in a cemetery for several hours while machine-gun bullets skipped amongst the tombstones.

Not until darkness had fallen could they emerge from their shelter and the convoy continue, crossing the Corinth Canal just before the bridge was blown. One mile from the Bay of Argos, the trucks were halted and the last part of the journey was made on foot, in total darkness and complete silence, smoking and talking forbidden. A sloop waited in the harbour to ferry the troops to the Australian destroyer

Voyager lying off-shore, and there was no time to be lost. Both vessels had to be away by daybreak. The orders were: keep marching, even if attacked.

'Bloody funny troops, these,' exclaimed a crew member of the *Voyager* who had caught an attaché case thrown on board by one of the Sisters. There were alarms on the way, but the ship reached Suda Bay in Crete without mishap.

Forty Sisters of the QAIMNS still remained at the 26th BGH at Kiffissia and about the same number of Australian Sisters at Dafni. There seemed little hope of escape for them.

'The Commanding Officer told us it was only a matter of time before the Germans would arrive, and he asked us to remain calm,' writes Joan Wilson, adding, 'we were much too busy to worry about the Germans.'

The solitary Sister at her post in the POW tent on the hill wrote in her report, 'A batch of one hundred wounded German prisoners has just arrived and I am compelled to order some of the more able patients to help me with the dressings. There is no doctor here to order morphia so I give it at my own discretion to those in extreme pain. We have not enough equipment to cope with this fresh intake and so they have to eat their food with their fingers.'

They were soon to be rescued, for their own troops were scarcely thirty miles away. On the morning of 25th April, Sister Wilson was instructed to prepare all walking wounded in her ward for evacuation. A ship was standing by to pick them up that afternoon.

'Of the thirty-nine men in my tent,' she writes, 'only nineteen were fit to go. Before lunch, Mac and I rushed around with the dressing trolley, re-dressing wounds, checking plasters and making those who were going as comfortable as possible, then I went for my lunch. When I returned, I found thirty-one men up and dressed, some with extensive lacerations, some with fractured legs. I was horrified and ordered them back to bed at once but they pleaded with me to let them go. "Sister, give us a chance to get out. If we stay here, the Jerries will have us. Once we get to Egypt, the MOs will fix us up and we can have another crack at the blighters."

'I hadn't the heart to deny them the chance. I think we all now realised that it was a case of every man for himself. I put those who were fairly fit in charge of those who could scarcely walk, and a convoy of ambulances took them away along with our Commanding Officer and the Registrar who had been ordered to get out while they could.'

Forty Sisters were left with a handful of medical officers, the padre and a few orderlies. The convoy of wounded had not long been gone when waves of enemy planes came over. Fearful for the safety of their departed patients, the hospital staff listened to the sound of nearby explosions with a heavy heart. Their worst fears were soon confirmed. The long line of trucks and ambulances had been too good a target to miss and enemy dive-bombers had wrought havoc. Two hours later, the survivors were brought back to the hospital, many wounded a second time. One young Australian who had walked out that afternoon had both legs blown off.

'He was distraught in case his girl friend would no longer love him,' wrote Joan Wilson, 'but we told him about Squadron Leader Bader and how the Germans had to lock up his artificial legs to stop him escaping from prison camp and he thought this a huge joke. It cheered him up immensely.'

The Commanding Officer of the hospital had been wounded in the head, but after immediate operation, he left again that night with the Registrar. The Australian Colonel who had accompanied him on the first trip had been killed outright.

A strange quiet now fell over the hospital, for the Allied guns had gone. Only a rearguard delaying force now stood between the hospital and the Germans. The staff worked on in an atmosphere taut with suspense. Around midnight, a truck drew up and an Australian Sergeant, his arm in a sling, walked into the reception tent with a party of walking wounded. At the sight of the Sisters, he stopped in amazement.

'What the hell are you girls doing here! Don't you know the Germans are only a mile or two away?' He turned to his companions, all wounded, all needing attention. 'Come on, men. We're going back up the line to tell them there's a bunch of British nurses here. We'll keep the buggers back a bit longer somehow.'

In spite of the Sisters' pleading that they should at least have their wounds dressed and take a hot drink, the men turned about, climbed back into the truck which had brought them and drove up the line into the darkness.

When it seemed almost too late, the order came for the Sisters to leave within the hour. Greek nurses and nuns had offered to take their places and care for the remaining patients. The Sister in the POW tent gave one last quarter grain of morphia to those who needed it then joined her colleagues for a final meal in the Mess. The medical officers and the padre, who were to stay, sat looking inexpressibly weary. All weapons had been handed in.

'There was little for us to say but "Goodbye",' writes Joan Wilson. 'We had worked well together. It had been a good team. I went to the ward entrance and I shall never, never forget the expression on the faces of the men. A few whispered, "Goodbye, Sister. Good luck." I could not speak. We would all willingly have stayed but we had to obey orders. I would never do it again and we all said the same thing.

'I said goodbye to Mac, the Australian orderly. Although a patient himself, he had worked from six o'clock in the morning till twelve at night. He was always kind and gentle with the men and of invaluable assistance to me.' (Sister Wilson received a letter from MacPherson several weeks later. He had escaped and was working in an Australian hospital in Palestine.)

As the Sisters climbed on board the waiting truck, the Greek nurses who were to take over their work crowded round to say goodbye, promising to look after the wounded with the same care as their own men had been given at the start of the campaign.

There was no time to be lost. At breakneck speed and with only a pinpoint of light showing through his blacked-out headlights, the driver made for Dafni to pick up the last of the Australian Sisters, who were waiting by the roadside, then on to rendezvous with a ship in Megara Bay.

The freighter anchored there was already crowded with 3,000 wounded, and more troops were being taken out by launch. The women were directed to await their turn in the shelter of a ditch. In total darkness, company after company of men went by in silence, perceptible only by the crunch of their boots on gravel. When it was the turn of the nurses, they scrambled from the ditch and made their way to the jetty, where a launch was waiting to take them to the freighter.

At 3 am, the ship sailed with a Royal Naval escort, but as soon as day broke the freighter was sighted and attacked by enemy dive-bombers. There were heavy casualties amongst the exposed men crowded on the open decks, but the vessel was undamaged and she made safe anchorage in Suda Bay, in Crete. The Sisters joined their colleagues who had arrived earlier and went on duty at once in Number 7 BGH, which had been operating in Crete for some time with an entirely male staff. The wounded continued to arrive from Greece in a variety of craft until there was no room left in the tented wards and the nurses gave up their own accommodation and slept in the open with their possessions under their beds.

The men and women who had been working under strain for weeks on end found a temporary haven in Crete. Patients and hospital staff as well as the troops joined in a Service of Thanksgiving for their deliverance, held in the open, with a rock draped in a Union Jack as the altar, on which stood a simple cross flanked by two jam-jars filled with wild flowers. Patients carried outside in their beds, men who had been close to death and had seen many of their comrades die, and the doctors and nurses who cared for them, all joined in the heartfelt singing of 'Oh God our Help in Ages Past'.

The choice of hymn was apt, for His help was going to be needed again in the very near future. The swastika now flew over the Acropolis and Crete was next in line for attack. On their second night on the island, the Sisters were awakened and told to be ready to leave at daybreak. Once more they prepared the walking wounded for evacuation, bade goodbye to those who were too ill to be moved, and then made their way down to the harbour.

There they found their transport, an ancient vessel named the *Iona* and a despairing Greek Captain without a crew. His sailors had had enough of being bombed at sea and had bolted into the Cretan mountains. The day was saved by two Australian soldiers who volunteered to stoke for the Captain, and the *Iona* put to sea, making for Alexandria with 160 women on board.

The voyage took three days, during which the little cockleshell of a ship survived several air attacks without damage. Those on board lived on bully beef and biscuits. Tea was made in kerosene drums and drunk from cigarette tins. There was no water to spare for washing, and it was a dirty, bedraggled crowd who eventually arrived at Alexandria. Incredible as it seemed to many of those involved, all the nurses who served in Greece were successfully evacuated, which is more than can be said for the troops and the wounded. Hundreds never left Crete.

7

The Siege of Malta

With Greece, Crete and long stretches of the North African coast now in German hands, the Allies had to face the fact that the Mediterranean was an almost totally hostile sea. From airfields in Italy, German planes could range at will, threatening the important British bases of Malta and Gibraltar. If the pro-German Vichy Government of Syria were to allow similar facilities to the Luftwaffe, the Suez Canal would be directly threatened from the rear. To forestall any such arrangement, and while Crete was still being evacuated, an Allied force of British, Dominion and Free French troops took control of Syria.

The campaign was short, sharp and successful, but casualties were heavy on both sides. The open terrain over which fighting took place made the retrieving of the wounded a precarious task for stretcher-bearers, and injured men lay for several days before being picked up. By that time, chest infections due to prolonged immobility frequently aggravated the original condition.

Arthur Roden Cutler of the 2nd/5th Field Regiment, Australian Imperial Forces, later Sir Roden Cutler, Governor of New South Wales, was seriously injured in the action during which he earned his Victoria Cross. Advancing under heavy machine-gun fire, he destroyed the enemy's gun position but fell, badly wounded in the leg, and lay unable to move for several days before being picked up. After the initial amputation of his leg at the 2nd/3rd Australian CCS, he needed further surgery to drain his chest.

Allied wounded who fell into enemy hands in Syria received scant, if any, medical treatment and were in a shocking condition when repatriated to their own lines after the armistice. Untreated malaria produced in them such rigors and sweating that pools of water collected beneath their dripping mattresses in the hospital wards. This lack of concern on the part of the Vichy-French caused many needless deaths.

Their sacrifice, however, was not in vain. This campaign, added to equally successful action in Iraq and Iran to safeguard oil supply routes, did much to restore confidence in the Eastern Mediterranean. No such hopeful portents hovered over Malta, however, unhappily

placed as she was between the Luftwaffe's air bases in Sicily and
Rommel's bombers in North Africa.

Rommel demanded the destruction of the island. As long as British
planes and ships could operate from there, his supply lines to North
Africa were under threat. Its docks and air-strips would be of great
advantage to the German offensive in the Western Desert, and so the
siege of Malta began. The rocky island was incapable of producing
more than a fraction of the food needed to support even its local
population and, in addition, it was now garrisoned with troops. A
blockade of all supply ships, accompanied by an intense bombing
campaign from the air, was therefore confidently expected to bring
about a speedy surrender.

Alice Elliott, a trained nurse working for the Soldiers', Sailors' and
Airmen's Families Association (SSAFA), was walking with a friend on
the hill behind Grand Harbour when the first enemy planes appeared
at the end of 1940:

'... like nasty black flies, dropping their eggs on Valetta. The sky
was full of flak and the noise was dreadful; and all the while,
above our heads, eight Hurricanes circled around and around like
desperate birds. We wondered why they kept so far away from the
harbour and also what so few could hope to do against so many. Later,
we learned that there were no more planes to send up and that
the Hurricanes had taken to the air simply to escape destruction on the
ground.'

Miss Elliott had gone to Malta just before the outbreak of war to
look after the dependents of servicemen on the island. Although British
civilians were evacuated in 1939, the population of the island had not
dropped as their places had been taken by Maltese workers returning
from Italy when that country declared war on Britain. These families
had no homes to go to nor any means of support. For their own safety,
they were housed by the Government in the ancient underground
granaries on the island. Alice Elliott was one of a small team of civilian
nurses and one English civilian doctor who were responsible for their
health and welfare.

3,000 people were packed below ground with scant privacy. Measles,
chicken pox and whooping cough swept through those families with
children and even the best intentioned mother had difficulty in keeping
her children clean, as water was in very short supply. Once the air
raids began in earnest, however, in January 1941, there were no com-

plaints. Conditions underground lacked comfort but they were reasonably safe.

The raids came two and three times every day, and after each one
fewer houses were left standing above ground. More shelters had to
be found. Recesses were scooped out of the deep stone walls which
had been built in earlier times as town defences. The dungeons of
Coradin Prison, when equipped with toilets and running water, could
each house one family. Miss Elliott's district, which she covered by
bicycle, ranged far and wide, above and below ground, and frequently
involved considerable risk.

One evening, she was detained by an air raid at the home of a
Maltese patient, and night had fallen before the All Clear sounded to
allow her to set off for home on her bicycle.

'There was a strong wind blowing against me all the way and I had
to take great care for the road was full of bomb craters which were
difficult to spot by the permissible pin-prick of light from my bicycle
lamp. I had not gone far when the Alert sounded again and I made
for the nearest shelter. Our ack-ack guns opened up with a terrific
noise, firing at enemy planes overhead. Searchlights swung over my
head and sickly yellow flares were dropping all around me. Suddenly,
one of the enemy planes dived down and seemed to come straight at
me. I was so scared, I could not even get out of the way. He dropped
his load of bombs but he missed me and I lived to tell the tale.'

Extra planes were flown in from the decks of the aircraft carrier
Eagle to bring the total number of Hurricanes on the island to 124.
Enemy raiders no longer escaped unscathed. Morale was good and the
population adapted to almost continual air raids with fortitude, accept-
ing without complaint an early curfew imposed for their own safety.
As the period between raids lessened, it was the Maltese mothers who
were subjected to the greatest strain, as they had to hurry from the
shelters between Alerts to tend their children and prepare meals. Tem-
peramental and volatile by nature, they nevertheless displayed a stead-
fast stoicism.

When Alice Elliott's contract with SSAFA expired in 1941, she was
drafted into the Territorial Army Nursing Service and directed to
serve on the Families' Wing of the 90th BGH at Imtarfa. Here she
attended the confinements of the Maltese wives of British troops and
their good spirits amazed and delighted her. After a night of raids, she
wrote home to her family:

'We have had one hell of a night. Raiders visited us from ten o'clock last night to five this morning. Some bombs fell not far away, but the patients were wonderful. One woman in labour just laughed at me when I suggested she should go down to the cellar, and another expectant mother slept through it all. They are marvellous patients and so grateful for everything we do.' She added a postscript: 'Since the night raids, we have had two more this morning and it isn't nine o'clock yet.'

A little while later, the Families' Wing and the Sisters' Mess were hit, and three QAs were seriously wounded. One opened the door to the Matron's office to check whether Miss Buckingham was unhurt and stepped straight into space. After this, maternity cases were nursed in the basement.

In addition to the 90th BGH at Imtarfa, there was a Royal Naval Hospital at Bighi and a small RAF Sick Bay at Calafrana. Two more British Military Hospitals came out from Britain to help with the mounting casualties, the 45th BGH which moved into St David's Barracks and the 39th BGH at St Paul's Hutments.

'We all went about our work as though the constant bombing was no more than a nuisance to be endured, although deaths from air raids were rising fast and whole families were wiped out at a time,' wrote Miss Elliott. 'We would watch, fascinated, when an enemy plane was caught in the searchlights and brought down. At first, we used to feel sorry for the men in the spinning, burning plane, but as the agony of the island increased, so did our sympathies die. Before long, we were cheering wildly whenever a German plane was hit.'

Ruined churches and houses now sprawled over Malta's hills and her streets were choked with rubble. Even the sunken granaries suffered damage and some of the occupants were killed. Despite careful rationing, food supplies were being rapidly exhausted and could not easily be replenished. Convoys carrying provisions and ammunition came under attack as soon as they set sail from Gibraltar or Alexandria.

In January 1941, the sacrifices being made on their behalf were brought home to the watching crowds when the newly-commissioned aircraft carrier *Illustrious* struggled into Grand Harbour, still under attack from enemy planes and on fire. The planes continued to dive-bomb even as casualties were taken off the ship to waiting ambulances. Burned seamen filled the wards and corridors of the 90th BGH, and the medical staff worked non-stop for forty-eight hours until the emergency was contained.

Throughout 1941, the island's resources dwindled, boosted very occasionally by a lucky shipment which had beaten the blockade. But the real agony was reserved for 1942, when convoy after convoy of life-saving supplies was dispatched to the bottom of the Mediterranean. By February 1942, after three merchantmen and the cruiser *Naiad* had been sunk, the garrison faced starvation.

Inevitably, the health of everyone on the island was suffering through constant strain and malnutrition, and the medical authorities were haunted by the possible effects of an outbreak of serious disease. Their worst fears were realised when several cases of poliomyelitis were reported. Prophylactic serum for this disease was not then invented, and chances of survival were poor for those whose respiratory muscles became paralysed, since there were no 'iron lungs' on the island. Doctors, nurses and orderlies worked in relays, giving ten-minute spells of artificial respiration to these cases, a service which had to be continued for days, sometimes weeks, with the knowledge that if it ceased, the patient would die.

Working from a diagram drawn by the medical officers, a Royal Engineer unit under the command of Lt Colonel Douglas Tanner constructed an iron lung from materials salvaged from bomb sites on the docks. To their great credit, the finished machine worked perfectly, and two more were immediately put under construction. A pair of bellows, bought by Captain Gilbert Lee RE from a Maltese farmer for five shillings, was kept in reserve for the frequent occasions when power was cut by enemy action.

As the months went by with little hope of relief, a crisis arose with regard to infant feeding, for teats and baby food had long since disappeared from the shops. Nurses experimented with pasteurised goats' milk, but this quickly turned sour in hot weather; the only solution for babies whose mothers were unable to breast-feed was to introduce them to solid food at the earliest possible opportunity. The mortality among the new-born was distressingly high.

For the rest of the community, kitchen centres were set up so that everyone could have at least one hot meal a day – which, in the end, was no more than a bowl of soup.

'Hunger became an obsession,' reports Alice Elliott. 'We in the hospitals were given our individual rations daily and small they were, too. By the time the next meal came along, we had hunger pains which we tried to ease with a hot-water bottle laid against the stomach. Serving the patients' meals was a dreaded task. My orderly came to me in great distress one day. "Sister," he said, "I can hardly keep my hands off the boys' food when I carry it to them."'

In March the *Clan Campbell* (Clan Line) and the *Breconshire* (Bibby Line) were sunk only eight miles from the harbour, within sight of the hungry population waiting on the hill. Two other merchantmen managed to slip through the submarines and the dive-bombers and entered the harbour safely, but were sunk before they could be unloaded. The glee of Hitler's pilots and submariners must have been unbounded. Of a total of 26,000 tons of stores sent to Malta in March 1942, only 5,000 tons got through, enough to sustain the island for no more than three months.

The punishing raids on the island continued unabated. When the 39th BGH at St Paul's Hutments was totally demolished under a direct hit, its theatre staff moved into a cave and continued to operate there. The Royal Naval Hospital and the RAF Sick Bay closed down, transferring staff and patients to the 90th BGH at Imtarfa, but the 45th BGH at St David's Barracks, though damaged, was still able to function. No matter how many enemy planes were shot down, they were instantly replaced, while the task of replenishing the island's Spitfires and Hurricanes grew ever more difficult.

'We were told to expect the worst,' wrote Miss Elliott, 'to make our wills and warn relatives that they might not hear from us for some time. We were given iron rations to keep for an emergency but every day was an emergency and we ate them there and then. We could still laugh, however. I remember a night at the cinema, which still managed to put on a show in spite of air raids. A field of wheat was shown in an advertisement followed by thousands and thousands of loaves of bread. The house was full of troops and a great roar went up from the audience at the sight of so much food.'

The next convoy to attempt to run the blockade was in August 1942. The August Malta convoy will be remembered by sailors of all times for its splendid, hopeless sacrifice. Nine merchant ships and escorting naval vessels were sunk, as well as the aircraft carrier *Eagle* and the cruisers *Manchester* and *Cairo*. Against this heavy toll was the saving grace of three merchant ships, the *Port Chalmers* (Port Line), the *Rochester Castle* (Union Castle Line) and the *Melbourne Star* (Blue

Star Line). By brave endeavour, these three ships reached Valetta undamaged and safely discharged their cargo, saving the islanders from certain starvation.

All through the following day, crippled ships from the convoy entered the harbour. Silent crowds watched from the hill behind the docks, tears coursing openly down their faces as they reviewed the awful cost of their salvation. The American tanker *Ohio*, under tow and listing heavily, was one of the casualties, for the United States was by now fully committed to the war.

At this most desperate point, there was a shift in the fortunes of Malta. The delivery of food renewed the spirit of the people, as did the new consignment of Spitfires flown in from the decks of the American aircraft carrier *Wasp*. Fresh pilots with new planes went out to meet the enemy raiders before they could reach Malta and forced them to jettison their bombs in the sea. More and more enemy planes fell out of the skies. When the next convoy set out for Malta from Gibraltar in November, it survived the voyage without incident and was allowed to unload unmolested. The people of Malta realised that they had triumphed; their trial of strength was over.

A few raiding planes came over from time to time and a sizeable formation appeared on New Year's Eve. An undaunted population, British troops and Maltese villagers, left the shelters to shout defiance at them. Regardless of bombs, they jeered and railed at the circling Messerschmidts, and in the morning a surprisingly small amount of damage was evident. As though by intent, all the bombs had been dropped in the valley where they could do the least damage.

Excitement and joy at their miraculous salvation were heady emotions to control and caused strong reactions in the people who had survived the siege. The strain under which they had lived for so long was not easily dispelled, and Alice Elliott was not immune to the sudden weakness of spirit experienced by so many who were no longer called upon to show an example of courage.

After a short leave in Cairo, Alice was sent to serve on the hospital ship *Oranje,* a fine vessel donated by the Dutch Government in 1940. She was at once plagued by persistent, uncontrollable sea-sickness. Even on calm days, she was prostrate and quite unable to work. The Matron in charge, not fully understanding the rigours recently endured by Alice, was of the opinion that she needed only to 'pull herself together' to conquer her malaise. When, reluctantly, she had to

concede that Alice was so sick she could scarcely stand upright, the
Matron allowed Alice to retire to her bunk but, lest she be over-
indulged, poor Alice was made to do the ship's mending while she was
incapacitated.

Hurt by the total lack of any understanding and weighed down by
a black mood of deep depression, Alice made her way to the stern of
the ship. If she were to jump into the sea, she told herself, not a soul
in the world would grieve for her. She had been away from home too
long for anyone to miss her. Only one thing made her hesitate. Years
earlier, an Egyptian fortune teller had predicted that she would live to
be ninety years old. If that were so, it followed that she would be
rescued if she threw herself overboard now.

'And I couldn't bear that,' she told herself. 'Back to the sick bay,
Matron's scorn and more mending.'

A medical officer crossing the boat deck happened to look down at
that moment and caught sight of the forlorn figure at the stern rail.
Reacting intuitively, he raced down the companionway to her side and
laid a restraining hand on her arm.

'What's the matter, nurse? Come and tell me about it.'

From that alert doctor, Alice received the sympathy she had failed
to find elsewhere and went on to recover her spirits completely. She
did not need help for long, but she was crying out for it during her
spell on the *Oranje* For the rest of the war she pursued a useful career,
then cared for displaced persons in post-war Germany.

The Egyptian fortune teller was a few years out. Alice died in her
eighty-first year, after a contented retirement in her beloved cottage
on the heights of Hebden Bridge in Yorkshire, with a lifetime of
devoted service behind her.

8

Gibraltar

Everyone serving in Gibraltar was involved in Malta's struggle. Battered convoys were patched up in the Naval Repair Yards, and it was to the British Military Hospital on the Rock that survivors from attacked convoys were brought. From the heights above their hospital, Sisters of the QAIMNS could watch the brave lines of ships set out and sometimes witnessed their end.

There were few women left in the garrison. British families were evacuated in 1939 and Gibraltarian women had been given alternative accommodation in either Morocco or Britain, at their own choice. A group of WRNS cyphers at the Naval base, twelve QAs at the Military Hospital and a few Sisters of the Colonial Service working in the small civilian medical unit constituted the entire female population who were expected to do their bit towards keeping up the morale of Admiral Somerville's Force 'H' based at Gibraltar.

The ships were lavish with their hospitality, and none had closer ties with the QAs than the aircraft carrier *Ark Royal*. Every time she was in dock, they were invited on board for cards or deck tennis, to dine and to dance, invitations which they always accepted even though there were times when they felt tired or disinclined. 'Part of my team', the Captain of the *Ark Royal* called them.

When the Ark was sunk in November 1941 there were many sad hearts in the Sisters' Mess. After she was struck by a torpedo, an attempt was made to tow her into Gibraltar harbour but she turned on her side and sank when no more than twenty-five miles from the shore. Fortunately, only one life was lost but the proud service of a much-loved ship was ended.

Most survivors from shipwreck suffered from burns to a lesser or greater degree. That most painful of injuries was almost as distressing for the nurse who was responsible for the dressings as for the patient. Before the discovery of penicillin, some sepsis was almost inevitable, and dressings needed to be changed daily, whether they were of sulphonamide powder and vaseline gauze, acriflavine and liquid paraffin, or saline packs. All stuck to the burned area and could not be removed without causing intense pain.

At the Gibraltar Military Hospital, Sister Zena Potter was responsible for the burn dressings in her ward and dreaded the daily round.

'It used to break my heart to see the anxiety in the patients' eyes when I was two beds away with my trolley.'

Forty years on, she still grieves. Top marks must go to her for ingenuity, however. A cargo of champagne had been salvaged from a sunken Italian ship and Zena was allowed to put her special therapy into practice.

'I gave each man a glass of champagne when I reached him and that cheered him up. I gave him another when the dressing was finished and it sent him to sleep. The system was a real success.'

In the event of a large-scale disaster at sea, the small staff at the hospital would be placed under considerable pressure. There were no auxiliary nurses, no VADs, no Red Cross Welfare officers, all of whom played an important part in the running of a busy hospital. Neither were there any cleaners, since the departure of the Gibraltarian and Spanish women. Great reliance was placed on the RAMC orderlies who, as always, responded magnificently to any trust placed in them, and certain likely Gibraltarian men were trained in simple tasks about the wards. A detailed plan to deal with an emergency was worked out and every member of the staff was briefed as to his or her exact duties. Sister Potter, who was becoming something of an expert in the nursing of burns, was put in charge of this department.

The test came with the disastrous August convoy of 1942 when the survivors from the wrecked aircraft carrier *Eagle* were brought to the hospital. Sister Potter was given a ward full of severely burned men and allowed to choose her orderly.

'Miss Caister, the Matron, was considerably surprised when I asked for Private Brown. Private Brown was a rogue who was in jail at that moment on a charge of theft, but he had worked with me before and I knew that he was a good worker and that he would be kind to my patients. When Matron saw that I really meant it, she had him out of the jail and onto my ward in half an hour. I was also given one Gibraltarian man to train and I spent half an hour teaching him to do one thing, the cleansing of the eyes of men with burnt faces.

'I showed him how to sterilise everything and told him he was not to stop doing the eyes upon any account whatsoever. When he went off duty, I would relieve him. "It doesn't matter who tells you to go for a parade or anything," I told him. "You are to say you cannot leave your patients. If you have any trouble, refer them to me." I am proud to say that of all those terribly burned men, not one lost his eyesight.

'Miss Condon, a Sister very much my senior, joined me on the ward but said she did not wish to take over, only to help in any way. I asked her to relieve me of the responsibility of injections and medicines and anything which needed a signature. Sister Organ QAIMNS/R joined us and was a tower of strength, getting the patients ready for the theatre and receiving them on their return.

'None of the patients could feed themselves. Come meal times, Miss Caister would breeze into the ward with a cheery word, having collected all the office staff and the Quartermaster's staff to assist with the feeding. My ward was served last from the kitchens so that orderlies from other wards could come to me when they had served their own patients. It was quite something. Almost jolly. A lot of joking went on, and the patients got a hot meal and sympathetic attention. The Home Sister, Miss Jaggard QAIMNS/R, brought the Sisters' meals to the ward, as we did not have time to leave.

'We nursed a lot of seamen, for whom we had the greatest regard and admiration. They deserved the best we could give them, but sometimes that was not enough. Some did not survive. Penicillin would have made a great difference, but it was not available then.

'One man had become the father of twins whom he had not yet seen. He was terribly burned. The only unaffected parts were the soles of his feet, his armpits and his hair. Tin hats always saved the hair. One evening he said to me, "Sister, I'm not going to make it."

'I went away and prayed for inspiration. After a while, a thought occurred to me. If we could get him upright, even for a short time, it would benefit his circulation but, even more important, it would boost him psychologically. I went back to him. "Would you like to stand up for a moment?"

' "You must be joking," he said, "but it would be good."

'My method of lifting men so badly burned was, literally, by the hair. A helper would get his hands under the armpits to take all the weight. I would grasp his hair and we would hoist together. We got our sailor onto the unburned soles of his feet and supported his weight. We told him how proud his twins would be of their father, and held

him just for a few moments until a fresh bed was prepared for him.
We got him back with little trouble, manoeuvring the bed rather than
the patient. I pinned the photograph of his twins to his top sheet, for
he could hold nothing in his hands, He went to sleep looking at it and
from that time on he began to make progress and eventually recovered
completely.

'It was a busy time for all of us, but when the pressure eased a little
we would read the men's letters to them and write replies, sort out
their love affairs for them and try to find out if anything at home was
worrying them.'

Gibraltar was a model of organisation in many respects. Although
there were air attacks from time to time, they were never on a large
scale. Nevertheless, a complete hospital was built deep inside the Rock
itself by a team of Canadian tunnelling Engineers. Should the hospital
above ground be demolished, all the patients could be accommodated
here. A large cavern formed a ward, equipped with beds and warmed
by electric fires. There were bathrooms with flush toilets, an operating
theatre superior to the one above ground, since it was equipped by
courtesy of American Lend-Lease, and an excellent recovery room.
There was a Sisters' Mess and sitting-room, kitchens and a NAAFI
store. Water was collected from rock drippings and filtered. Good
ventilation had been installed, as well as an efficient means of disposing
of dressings and excreta. Every morning, without fail, a full dress-
rehearsal of the transfer of patients took place, until the whole exercise
could be completed in seven minutes.

There was every reason for these precautions. From the time of
France's capitulation, invasion from Spain was a very real possibility:
that country's sympathies were more likely to lie with the Axis partners
rather than with the Allies. Even after she had declared her neutrality,
there was the danger that she might permit access for German or
Italian troops. In either of these events, Gibraltar's function as a
working garrison would be short-lived. A few set pieces of heavy
artillery placed on Spain's dominating mountains could destroy everything on the Rock within a short time. Siege was another possibility.
Accordingly, large areas were set aside as water catchments and every
household was equipped with a rainwater tank.

On the highest point of the Rock was Lieutenant Deakin's Radar
Grid, in a top security area behind wire barricades. Under conditions
of strict secrecy, he had assembled the whole from components shipped

out from Britain. Few of those living on the garrison understood the significance of the strange construction at the top of the hill, and a mystified enemy kept up a series of reconnaissance flights. There were spies on the ground, too, of both persuasions. With Spain acting as a vast listening post, espionage and counter-espionage ran through the little community like veins through Stilton. In 'Spider' Deakin's head were the much-sought-after secrets of radar, and a most careful surveillance was undertaken of all who associated with him. These included Sister Zena Potter.

She had first noticed him when his late arrival on board the *Scythia* had delayed her sailing from the Clyde in September 1939. Since landing in Gibraltar, they had seen a great deal of each other and, as a result, Zena was subject to close scrutiny from British Intelligence to determine how much she knew of Lt Deakin's work. They had no cause for alarm on Zena's account. She was neither inquisitive nor a gossip. Realising that Spider's work was important, she decided that she had better know nothing about it. If she happened to be with him on the several occasions when he was approached by Admiral Somerville or by Brigadier Learmont, a senior British officer of the garrison, she would immediately leave him and go to the other side of the room. Nevertheless, constant investigation of Zena continued. Invitations to various functions always led to her being taken aside by someone of importance and faced with a number of leading questions about Spider's work. Becoming thoroughly impatient with the continual questioning, she began to turn down these invitations.

One such was to dine at the house of a very prominent citizen in the company of another QA, Daphne Stevens. Zena flatly turned down this invitation.

'I knew it would be another case of answering questions after dinner, but when the reply came back, bribing us with a freshwater bath, I could resist no longer and we went. There were a number of important people there, including a Mr Fleming, who took me aside and started asking me all the usual questions. "Oh dear," I said. "Let's get this quite straight. I do not know what Spider is doing. I do not want to know, and so, I cannot tell you." After that, we had a pleasant evening, and I discovered later that my interrogator was Ian Fleming, secret agent and later very successful writer. I also discovered that on that particular night I was being checked out for an event which was about to take place.

'About a week later, Spider said to me, "Would you like a trip to Tangiers?"

' "It's been closed," I said. The area, being Spanish and therefore neutral, had been open in the early days but was now prohibited. Spider insisted, however, that Daphne Stevens and I would be allowed to accompany a group of officers who were going there and that we should seek permission from our matron. This was promptly refused by the new Matron, and just as promptly countermanded by the Governor of Gibraltar who said we must be allowed to go. It was at this point that I began to suspect this was no ordinary jaunt.

'We could not wear uniform because of Tangiers' neutral state, but I took the precaution of inscribing the letters QAIMNS and my personal number on the back of a gold cross which I wore around my neck in the manner of the Gibraltarian women. I had no wish to be shot as a spy. The other officers who were to accompany us on this trip turned out to be quite senior, which again alerted me to the importance of the expedition.

'We made the crossing standing up in an old-fashioned fishing boat, but halfway over three enemy submarines were sighted and Daphne and I were told to crouch down low in the bottom of the boat. In that position, I occupied my mind in trying to decide which was the nearest coast to swim to if we were attacked, Gibraltar or Morocco, but we were allowed to proceed unmolested.

'Rooms had been booked for us in the magnificent El Minza Hotel in Tangiers, which seemed to be milling with important-looking people. I caught a glimpse of Ian Fleming, but Spider warned me that I must on no account show recognition unless he made the first move. Spider seemed to know a number of people there and we joined them for lunch. Halfway through the meal, he suddenly felt unwell and excused himself. I grew anxious when he failed to appear, for we had planned to swim that afternoon in beautiful Cape Spartel and, after waiting a little longer, I telephoned his room. There was no response so I decided to investigate.

'I found him collapsed on the bed, almost out for the count. I tried to rouse him by sponging his face with cold water but he was very dopey.

'"Somebody's slipped me a Mickey Finn," he said. "Take my money and my papers. Go off to the beach and don't tell a soul about me."

'He gave me his things and I left him to sleep off whatever drug he had been given and went off to Cape Spartel with Daphne. He was quite recovered when I returned. But when I went to my room, I surprised someone there going through my belongings. As I entered the room, whoever it was escaped through the window, and it remains the biggest mystery of my life that there was no sign of him when I rushed to the window. The outside wall went straight down to the water and he must have been quickly hauled up or down.

'By now, of course, I realised that Spider had come to do an es-pionage job. He went on his own the following morning and got the information he sought, after which we returned to Gibraltar. Daphne and I were included in the exercise merely to give credibility to the men's presence, and were no more involved than that.

'Sadly, our new Matron never learned the truth of the Tangiers weekend and put a more basic construction on it. Because of that, I am convinced that I was subsequently given an adverse report.'

If this was so, it was an undeserved codicil to a career of integrity and dedication.

Gibraltar had many mysterious visitors. They came and went in secrecy, dressed in shabby coats and caps which were belied by their educated speech. Occasionally, they needed medical care. Having no doubt shown by this time that she was capable of keeping her own counsel, Zena Potter was put in charge of the five small rooms set aside for these shadowy patients. Only she and her relief Sister were allowed to make contact with them. Important visitors made sudden, unexplained appearances. On one occasion, the Duke of Gloucester arrived at the bedside of an agent who was desperately ill with cancer of the throat and who was flown home shortly afterwards by flying boat. Gibraltar had no proper runway, and ordinary aircraft used the hockey pitch or racecourse at great risk. As she prepared the sick man for the flight, Zena was offered a handful of gold sovereigns – but she asked instead for the more professionally acceptable gift of the patient's vase of dark red roses.

Another nameless patient had fractured his heel as he jumped from a ship. He was bored to tears by his enforced confinement, so Zena gave him the job of censoring the hospital mail. She never asked questions, but her curiosity was roused one day when she caught sight of a woman flitting from one of the rooms and disappearing at great speed along the corridor. Knowing that there were now no other

women on Gibraltar but the nurses, for the WRNS had been evacuated, this unexplained visitor continued to puzzle Zena Potter, until
long after the war she read in the autobiography of the French Resistance heroine, Odette Sanson, that she had visited a patient at the
Gibraltar Military Hospital in 1942.

In November of that year, Zena returned to England and married
her Spider. To see them today, gracefully growing old amongst their
boisterous grandchildren, one would imagine that no more dramatic
event than the Harvest Festival had ever featured on their calendar.

'I know that a lot of people were doing exactly as I was,' says Zena,
'but now that I am old, I find the memory of Gibraltar gives me
pleasure and satisfaction.'

When the combined British–American invasion of North Africa took
place in November 1942, Gibraltar's role was that of a static aircraft
carrier and supply depot for the forces involved. Rubble from the
tunnelling explorations was used to construct an air-strip extension
from the racecourse into Gibraltar Bay and on the eve of the invasion,
fourteen squadrons of fighter planes assembled there. As General
Eisenhower wrote in his book *Crusade in Europe*: 'Britain's Gibraltar
made possible the invasion of North West Africa.'

9

Nurses on the Home Front

By 1940, the 'phony war' with its dusty leaflets and boring rehearsals was a thing of the past. The fire drill and the rescue squads were for real as one city in Britain after another was devastated by bombs.

London hospitals never ceased to function, although many were badly damaged. Beds for emergencies and maternity cases were always available because of a system of continuous evacuation of patients to country mansions and castles now acting as convalescent centres. Here, too, were brought casualties from Greece, Crete, Palestine and North Africa. Ancestral portraits in stately homes looked down on rows of neat, white army beds. Soldiers dressed in their blue 'sick suits' loped by on crutches.

Young women who chose to join the auxiliary nursing services as their war work could not have made a better choice. They were needed as never before. Nevertheless, the transition from a commercial career to the discipline of a hospital ward was not easy for these newcomers to nursing.

Joyce Atkins (later Robertson), a secretary in peace time, writes of her first weeks as a trainee assistant-nurse at the Royal Bradford Infirmary.

'I felt clumsy and in everyone's way. Whatever I did seemed to produce an effect like an H. E. Bateman cartoon. "Don't let Sister see you do THAT!" echoed in my ears all day long. The sights and the smells of the ward sickened me so that I could not eat, and Oh! how my feet hurt and how desperately tired I was when I came off duty at last. "I'll never stick this!" I told myself.'

She regretted more than once her decision to enrol in the Civil Nursing Reserve, and she kicked at the irksome discipline, the seemingly pointless exactitudes demanded of such banal tasks as the folding of a counterpane. She was always on the point of giving up, but she never did.

'I remember the first air raid. We had to get up in the middle of the night and go to a long tunnel leading from the Nurses' Home where bunks had been installed so that we could rest. I expect we were all pretty scared. I know I was, because I had no idea what might

happen. As we lay there, listening to the sound of planes overhead and
wondering if the next moment would be our last, Matron walked
slowly through the shelter in uniform. She was a handsome woman,
tall and erect and somehow just the sight of her had a tremendous
effect on our morale. One felt that no German would dare to drop a
bomb within miles of the hospital where this regal lady was in charge.
I believed at that time that hospital discipline was too strict, but I
doubt if the Matron would have had such an effect had we not passed
our days in mortal fear of her wrath, or had she slouched through the
shelter in mufti with her hands in her pockets.'

Later, Joyce Atkins surprised herself by finding immense satisfaction, even exhilaration, in the work she had chosen to do 'for the
duration'.

As the blitz gathered momentum, a night uninterrupted by air raids
became a rare event. Not all nurses had such comfortable shelter
arrangements as the Bradford Royal. The stone floor of the boiler
room was the best that could be done in some hospitals, with fearful
possibilities should the building be hit. VADs at the Naval Hospital
in Portsmouth were accommodated in a basement washroom where
the only furniture was a narrow wooden shelf and two rows of wash-
basins. The shelf was shunned by all. To lie there in one position for
many hours without room to manoeuvre was sheer agony, and the
tightly packed recumbent bodies on the floor below prevented any
escape until the 'All Clear' brought relief. Infinitely preferable were the
wash-basins. The VADs found that by wedging the hips in one basin
and the shoulders in another, short periods of sleep were possible.

Land and sea mines, oil bombs and incendiaries rained down on
Britain, gouging out great holes in the cities and trailing a necklace of
symmetrical waterholes over the fields for the convenience of surviving
cattle, for bombers were frequently off-target. A land mine intended
for Ellesmere Port in a daytime raid on Liverpool fell instead on
Moston Hall Military Hospital, several miles away. The hutted wards
collapsed like a pack of cards. Every nail in their construction had
been wrenched from its socket by the magnetic action of the mine,
every tubular steel chair twisted out of recognition. Because of the
hospital's light construction, however, the loss of life was not great.
Patients received sufficient protection from falling timber by being
placed under their beds. Had the building been of bricks and mortar,
the casualties would have been much greater.

Three sea mines were dropped on Bournemouth, wiping out whole streets at a time. Anyone who owned a car joined the ambulances in picking up the victims and rushing them to the Royal Victoria and West Hants Hospital. The injured were laid side by side on the floor of the Casualty department, men, women and children, the dead beside the living. Policemen, Air Raid Wardens and ordinary people of the town came into the hospital to offer their help to the nurses.

These were commonplace scenes in every city in England. Every night, the Theatre Sister at Hull Infirmary laid out her 'general set' of instruments in readiness for the surgery which would inevitably follow the raids, and every night she offered up a little prayer that a bomb would not drop on the hospital's sole liver-suture needle.

When their hospitals were bombed, when whole wards collapsed, when the roofs fell in and fire threatened their helpless patients, the nurses were not lacking in courage. Students as well as Matrons put their own lives at risk to save the sick and wounded people who were in their charge. The fifteen George Medals awarded to civilian nurses between 1940 and 1942 are testimony to their bravery, and in their citations is embodied a splendid tribute to the nursing profession (see Appendix B).

The disruption of gas, water and electricity in hospitals due to enemy action was a recurring problem. Every operating theatre had its own emergency lighting system for such a crisis, but even this failed to respond on one occasion when, during a daylight raid, the theatre at the Billericay annexe of the London Hospital was plunged into darkness while an operation was in progress. The surgeon would have been reduced to continuing by candlelight but for the ingenuity of a medical student who was present.

None of the bright sunshine of that summer day reached the operating theatre, as the window had been bricked up for safety's sake. In the adjoining small sterilising room, however, a small aperture had been left uncovered to allow for the escape of steam. With the clever use of two polished steel trays, the student deflected this beam of sunlight from the sterilising room onto the operation, which was then safely concluded.

The blitz was intended to destroy the morale of the population but, as the war went on, this theory was proved by both sides to be a fallacy. People became more dogged in their resistance in direct relationship to the pressures brought to bear upon them. Damaged

factories might hold up the production of guns and planes, bombed
railway tracks bedevilled communications, sunken ships reduced the
food ration but never, at any time, was public feeling less than aggressively buoyant.

A great comradeship was engendered in the air raid shelters and on
fire-watching duties on the roof-tops. Complete strangers became good
neighbours to the homeless. The courage of casualties astonished their
nurses. In a ward full of women who had been injured in a devastating
raid on Portsmouth, the patient who radiated cheerfulness and supported them all was a middle-aged woman who had lost both legs.
Even when a raid was in progress, battered old men watched the ward
clock and reached for their headphones when Tommy Handley came
on the air. ITMA meant more to them than anything Hitler could do.

After a night of raids, the wards would be full of the clothing and
possessions of the injured. One old man was brought to hospital clutch-
ing a frying pan. 'Well, I had to save something, didn't I?' Characters
like these relieved the ever-present tragedy of the wards. They were
also well known to the district nurse. She met them in their homes as
she went on her daily round.

There was a Birmingham munitions worker who, before he left for
the factory every morning, carried his paralysed wife from her bed to
a chair by the kitchen fire. Here she sat, alone, throughout the day-
long raids, in patient resignation. From a bucket of coal placed near
her chair, she kept the fire going, but her aim was not always true and
there would be lumps of coal all over the floor when the district nurse
arrived to give her a much-needed bath and make her a hot drink. At
night, the woman's devoted husband made her evening meal and carried her back to bed again. The next day followed the same pattern.
He did not complain, and neither did she.

The task of the district nurse was not made easier by the fact that
well-known landmarks frequently disappeared overnight in a bombing
raid. Looking for a certain address, she might find a hole where her
patient used to live, or sometimes a note pinned to a wrecked door
('Gone to me sisters'); sometimes the rescue squad was still searching.

The provision of a car for a nurse was unthinkable in those days. In
any case, there would have been no petrol to spare for her. She dodged
through the rubble on her bicycle with her bag of dressings and
instruments strapped on behind, past roped-off holes where unex-
ploded bombs still lay, to give injections to diabetics waiting for their

breakfast, to bring in the new-born and comfort the dying. She was allowed to take a mid-morning break, for which she was allowed six-pence for a cup of tea and a bun.

Night calls were especially hazardous. With no more than the per-mitted pinprick of light from her bicycle lamp, she must avoid the potholes in the road and keep her wavering front wheel out of the tramlines, while above her searchlights tracking enemy planes de-scribed the night sky in dazzling geometry. Many a distraught father-to-be, unable to get his wife to a hospital during an air raid, thought a halo more fitting than the old-fashioned cap worn by the district nurse, and would have put her worth above a twopenny bun.

Unlike other towns on the Luftwaffe's hit-list, Dover had the unen-viable distinction of being shelled as well as bombed, and it was fast becoming a place of boarded-up shops and houses. A few of the inhabitants moved away, but most chose to stay and sent their children elsewhere to school. They came flocking back in the holidays to be with their parents, and found Dover a treasure trove of shrapnel sou-venirs. Indistinguishable amongst the debris were anti-personnel mines dropped by enemy planes on dark nights, strangely fashioned metal objects of great interest to little boys. Curiosity killed not only the cats of Dover.

Sited in a fold of the land, the Dover EMS Hospital was fortunately inaccessible to any projectory arc the gunners of Calais might devise and was never damaged. On a clear day, however, from her billets on top of the hill behind the hospital, Theatre Sister Dorothy Brown (later Larsen, OBE) could almost discern with her naked eye the gun emplacement on the other side of the Channel. She never lost the feeling that telescopes were trained on her as she hurried, tin-hatted and with a gas mask slung around her neck, down to the hospital below, for her appearance on the exposed slopes invariably had the disturbing effect of triggering off another round of shelling.

Fortunately for the inhabitants of Dover, the Calais gun had to be serviced at regular intervals, which provided a welcome respite before shelling began once more. The hospital staff had a few days in which to replenish their sterile supplies. Wool swabs had to be made by hand, gauze packs had to be folded and tied in packs of ten, all had to be sterilised. The laundry staff worked overtime to produce clean theatre gowns and towels for autoclaving, for once the gun was back in service, operating was non-stop.

The total nursing staff at Dover EMS Hospital consisted of four trained nurses of the Civil Nursing Reserve, one VAD and one assistant nurse. Later, RAMC orderlies were sent to help but, in the early years, the arrival of an extra assistant nurse was greeted with joy.

She was welcomed, but her stay was brief. An airman patient overheard her speaking of a subject which he knew to be top security, and about which she should have had no knowledge. She was removed by the Military Police.

Spies were about. The Government poster depicting a sinking ship above the caption 'Careless Talk Costs Lives' was no idle warning, and nurses, with access to the medical notes of servicemen, could provide useful material for the enemy. A certain amiable woman ambulance driver was a frequent visitor to the Sisters' Mess of the Naval Hospital near Glasgow. She usually dropped in around coffee time and never failed to bring a contribution of homemade cakes or biscuits, a rare treat in those days of strict rationing. Suspicions were alerted, however, when she began to manoeuvre the conversation towards the identity of the ships then in the Clyde. Some of their crews were patients in the hospital, and the Sisters were privy to a considerable amount of information about them. The police were alerted and that particular driver was not seen at the hospital again.

Despite the upheaval of war, the training of student nurses went on unchanged. Standards of nursing were upheld and no concessions made to the difficulties of the times. Whether they had been on duty all night long or dozing fitfully in an air raid shelter, the students were expected to attend lectures the following morning. Occasionally the lecturer's patience would evaporate in an explosion of wrath when a nurse at the end of a row, unsupported by her colleagues, tumbled to the floor, fast asleep. It did not occur to any of these members of the medical profession to enquire why nurses at their lectures were so tired. Even on night duty, midwifery students were required to attend afternoon ante-natal clinics in the town. During the long night that followed, they would take it in turn to cat-nap on the laundry shelves between the official ward rounds.

Today's profession appears featherbedded by comparison. A first-year student earned £25 per annum and her keep. A sixty-three-hour working week was not uncommon. Discipline was tough, and sometimes unreasonable. In Redlands Hospital near Glasgow, junior nurses were required to serve meals to their seniors before sitting down to their own, but were expected to leave as soon as the Matron was ready, which usually meant indigestion or an unfinished meal for themselves.

These were young women with healthy appetites who were on their feet for most of a ten-hour day. In many cases, ration books were lodged with the hospital authority, so nurses were unable to buy food in the shops, and their meagre salaries did not rise to restaurant prices. Any parents living near the hospital dutifully accepted responsibility for their daughter's hungry friends and spread their own rations even more thinly.

Conditions varied from hospital to hospital, but some authorities were pathologically blind to the needs of their nurses. One night in a hostel for student midwives, the ration of one sausage each had been served to the twelve nurses at supper. One lone sausage remained on the plate, the focus of all eyes.

'Who would like this last sausage?' asked the Matron, and misunderstood the polite silence which followed. Twelve pairs of eyes watched the tasty morsel being carried back to the kitchen.

'Food must not be wasted,' the Matron scolded. 'We must remember the boys fighting overseas.'

Night nurses at Southmead Hospital Bristol took matters into their own hands. A piece of wasteland adjoining the hospital had been converted into allotments following the Government's injunction to grow more food and 'Dig for Victory'. Prime vegetables raising their heads on the other side of the hospital fence did not pass unnoticed. On the darkest nights, when all the patients were asleep and the Night Superintendent was safely in her office after the last round before morning, cloaked figures armed with wooden spoons for digging climbed the fence into the allotments. They were not greedy, taking only thinnings of young vegetables and perhaps relieving a grower of a glut of lettuce. They learned to lift potato plants and replace them with such skill that no-one would suspect that half the baby potatoes had been picked off. The frustrated gardeners no doubt pondered this pillage at length, but they were unlikely ever to have suspected a watch of nightingales from next door.

Above all else, a student nurse needed 'stickability'. Through the long nights of continuous Alerts, junior probationers collected specimens, emptied sputum mugs, heated up the 'anti-phlo' for poultices and cooked the porridge for breakfast. The junior theatre nurse at Woolwich Hospital climbed the stairs all night long from the emergency theatre in the basement to the sterilising room above, with her arms full of jugs, bowls and instruments as one operation followed another. When the 'All Clear' sounded with the coming of the dawn, she took down the black-out screens and opened the window of the upper room where the surgeons had their coffee. Stars were fading from the lightening sky, and the big ack-ack guns were silent at last. Ambulances and rescue squads were tidying up the city's gently smoking wounds.

'There,' she told herself, 'that's another night we've got through.'

Some student nurses gave up – the work was too hard, the conditions too grim and the responsibility awesome – but the majority soldiered on. After the first year, the situation improved. Ways and means were found to circumnavigate the more repressive rules which, instead of producing a company of sad-sacks, made athletes of them all. Scaling a six-foot fence in an evening dress was no mean feat, but it was the only solution when 'Lights Out' in the Nurses' Home was at half-past ten.

Above everything, there was a close, fulfilling companionship which tided them over the bad patches. Many a probationer emerged from the lavatory, her only refuge on the ward, with red-rimmed eyes, but the peaks of achievement towered over the depressions and remained in the mind long after the injustices were forgotten.

In the spring of 1942, a lecturer at St Mary's Hospital, Paddington, addressed a class of student nurses. He broke off to enquire how far advanced they were on their course.

'Second year,' replied their Tutor.

'Then perhaps you can forget all I have said. By the time you qualify, there will have been a revolution in the treatment of infection.'

On an upper floor of the same building, Professor Fleming was at that time working on his discovery of penicillin.

10

War with Japan

There were few credits on the balance sheet of 1941 that the Allies could set against the accumulation of disasters. In England, the blitz on cities continued unabated and food rationing grew tighter as the tonnage of merchant vessels sunk by the enemy increased. Inasmuch as anyone who was against Hitler was a friend of Britain's, Russia unexpectedly materialised as an ally after being invaded by her one-time partner, but advantages from this new relationship did not appear until later.

Greece and Crete were lost, with heavy casualties, and the North African campaign had turned into a series of defeats at the hands of Rommel's Afrika Korps. In November, however, fortunes in the desert war changed. Rommel was stopped at the very borders of Egypt, his troops forced back along their critically extended lines of communication. The 'Desert Rats' of the Eighth Army who had stood so recently with their backs to the wall now pressed forward to relieve Tobruk and recapture Benghazi. Christmas 1941 was a time for rejoicing after all.

That December brought more than Christmas. It brought for Britain a new and powerful ally, and a new enemy. When Japan bombed the American Fleet in Pearl Harbor on 7th December, the United States entered fully into the war. Britain immediately declared war on Japan in a gesture of solidarity. As a result, the British garrisons of both Hong Kong and Singapore came under attack from the Japanese within a few hours. A whole new zone of warfare opened up.

Shanghai, the most isolated of the British garrisons in the Far East, had been evacuated in 1940. The small party of QAIMNS Sisters stationed in the Shanghai Military Hospital was posted elsewhere, some to Britain, some to Singapore and some, like New Zealander Kathleen Thomson, to Hong Kong.

There was never any question of evacuating Hong Kong. In the unlikely event of an attack, the colony would be expected to stand fast and look after itself. Nothing beyond a couple of Canadian battalions could be spared by Britain to boost its defence. Until Japan entered the war, however, trouble in the Far East was not anticipated; although some families of servicemen had left Hong Kong for Australia at the onset of war with Germany, most of the civilian wives who had no obligations other than to look after their husbands chose to stay. Far away from Europe's agony and under no sense of urgency, they joined the Hong Kong Volunteer Defence Corps as VADs and helped in the Bowen Road Military Hospital and in the smaller Naval establishment at Wanchai. Once Japan entered the war, Hong Kong's role was dramatically changed. Nothing was predictable any more.

Bowen Road Military Hospital, standing on a hill on Hong Kong Island, was equipped with two hundred beds and had a nursing staff of twelve QAIMNS Sisters, two Canadian Army Nursing Sisters, RAMC orderlies and local VADs. It was unusually busy in December 1941 due to a particularly virulent form of malaria which was incapacitating large numbers of garrison troops, so there were few empty beds.

Upon her transfer from Shanghai the previous year, Kathleen Thomson had been appointed Theatre Sister at Bowen Road. When she went to answer a phone call in the early hours of 8th December, she anticipated a request to open the theatre for an emergency operation. Her sole anxiety was over the shortage of beds in the hospital. When she lifted the receiver, however, the voice of the duty sergeant passed on a different message.

'The CO's compliments, Sister, and Great Britain has declared war on Japan.'

Within hours, Japanese planes attacked the RAF airfield on the mainland, destroying every plane on the ground but one. They followed this with an attack on Hong Kong Island, and their first bomb demolished the kitchens of Bowen Road Hospital. Before alternative cooking arrangements could be made, casualties from the attack began to arrive.

Such an emergency had been prepared for and medical supplies were already stored in the cellars of St Albert's Convent on Rosary Hill in readiness for its possible use as an auxiliary hospital. This was now opened under the command of Lt Colonel Rudolph RAMC, with Kathleen Thomson as Matron and a staff of three QAs, some local VADs and members of the Chinese St John Ambulance Brigade. No time was lost in fetching beds and linen from the basement and equipping the large, airy rooms as wards. An upper room was put into use as an operating theatre straight away.

With no RAF planes left to challenge them, the Japanese began to bomb the island indiscriminately. Any hope that rescue might come from the sea was dashed when the two great ships of the Royal Navy, the *Repulse* and the *Prince of Wales* were sunk on 10th December while attempting to head off a Japanese landing in Malaya. American ships at sea in the Philippines hastily made for the shelter of the Australian coast. Within the space of a few days, Japan dominated all the seas in the Far East.

Hong Kong accepted the inevitability of its own demise and bravely resolved to inflict in its passing as much damage as possible on the enemy. As Japanese troops streamed into the New Territories, they were met by the Hong Kong Volunteer Defence Corps, composed of business and professional men, armed and marching with the garrison troops, but this little David had no chance against the Japanese Goliath.

Nothing could stop the Japanese advance down the mainland. Once Kowloon was reached, the island of Hong Kong came within shelling range, and further destruction was added to that caused by continual air raids. After patients at St Albert's were injured by flying glass, the windows were shuttered for protection, and from then onwards the wards were in semi-darkness, lit by hurricane lamps. When these had to be abandoned for safety reasons, doctors and nurses worked on with the aid of pocket torches.

Additional hospitals were opened in St Stephen's Boys' School at Stanley, on the south coast, in the Hong Kong Hotel, the University and the Jockey Club. Each unit was staffed by one or two doctors, two or three QAs and a small group of local VADs and orderlies. To the surprise of the trained nurses, the VADs responded magnificently to the heavy demands made upon them. Mostly young women who had led a very sheltered life in the colony until now, they worked hard and put up with all manner of discomfort without complaint. Even when their own husbands, fathers and brothers were amongst the wounded brought to the hospital, they stood up to the stress and carried on with their work. Mothers and daughters were not separated. QA Mary Currie (RRC, later Davies), like most of the Sisters, was a realist.

'I felt, in my heart of hearts, that we would all be captured. I knew that we few Sisters would not be able to cope with everyone and, when that time came, it would be better for mothers and daughters to help each other.'

There was never time for the medical staff to take shelter during air raids or shelling attacks. More beds always had to be made up for the wounded, who were left on their stretchers in all kinds of unlikely places by harassed stretcher-bearers before they hurried away for more. Somehow, each patient was washed and fed, his wounds dressed, and prepared for operation. Sometimes when a stick of bombs fell uncomfortably close it was not entirely clear as to who was comforting whom between patient and nurse.

An old Chinese house in the grounds of St Albert's had been taken over for the Sisters' Mess. There, Home Sister Brenda Morgan contrived to produce hot meals for her hard-working colleagues when they came off the wards. Kathleen Thomson was visiting her one day when a random shell demolished the building, killing Brenda Morgan and seriously injuring Kathleen. Sister Morgan, a vivacious, Lancashire lass recently engaged to be married, was buried that night. Her fiancé, a young officer in the Royal Engineers, was killed a few days later while defending the Wong Nei Chong Gap. Miss Thomson was taken to the civilian Queen Mary's Hospital on the other side of the island for operation and her place at St Albert's was taken by Mary Currie from Bowen Road.

On 18th December, Japanese troops crossed from the mainland and landed on Hong Kong Island. They captured the main reservoir and cut off water supplies. They overran the medical supply base, killing the ten RAMC men who stood guard. Nursing in the darkened wards became a nightmare. With restricted water and a dwindling supply of dressings, aseptic conditions became impossible to maintain. The upper floors at St Albert's were no longer safe, and patients were carried to the already congested lower floors where there was scarcely room to move between stretchers and beds. The dead were buried each night, in quicklime, in the nearest shellhole.

An incident now occurred at St Albert's which was to have far-reaching consequences. A seriously wounded Japanese General was brought in. Half his buttocks had been shot away and, though he was given transfusions, he did not survive. The young VAD who was laying out the body turned to Sister Currie (now acting-Matron) for advice.

'Are there any special traditions with regard to Japanese dead?'

Her timely query sparked off in Mary Currie's mind a barely remembered childhood tale of a Japanese warrior killed in battle. His comrades, she recalled, wrapped his body in his national flag. Acting upon impulse, she opened the General's pack and there discovered the neatly rolled-up flag of the Rising Sun. Consequently, when the body was washed and the wound dressed, the two nurses wrapped it in the flag and pinned the insignia of rank and medals on the chest. Having shown the dead soldier every respect, they left the body to await burial.

The next day was 23rd December, and everyone at St Albert's knew that the enemy was not far away. An operation had just been completed in the theatre when a doctor came in.

'The Japs are here,' he announced quietly.

Mary Currie, who had been assisting the surgeon, pulled off her rubber gloves and reached for her tin hat. The medical officer laid a restraining hand on her arm as she went towards the door. 'Where do you think you're going?'

'There are young nurses downstairs,' she told him. 'I must go to them.'

'The Japs'll kill you ...' but Mary was already halfway down the stairs. The MO quickly followed and they went down into the hall together, into a mass of Japanese soldiers running about with fixed bayonets. They were immediately grabbed, their hands tied behind their backs with telephone wire, then pushed outside to sit on the grass. After working for so long in the darkened wards, the sunshine hit them like a golden benefaction, lessening the tension of the moment.

'I don't know why,' said Mary, 'but I wasn't frightened.'

Japanese soldiers were overrunning the hospital grounds with the intensity of ants. One, tripping over Mary Currie's long legs, dealt her a vicious swipe with his rifle butt which, instead of intimidating her, roused her to fury. Angrily, she railed at the uncomprehending soldier about the treatment of prisoners of war as laid down in the Geneva Conventions. Captured medical personnel, she told him, should be treated with consideration.

'For God's sake shut up,' groaned the MO at her side. 'You'll get us both shot.'

A Japanese officer, attracted by the commotion, stood over them. 'Who is speaking of the Geneva Conventions?' he demanded. 'I speak English. I was educated at Oxford University.'

'Then you should know better than to let your soldiers behave in this way,' Mary retorted, 'especially since this hospital has been at some pains to honour Japanese dead.'

Japan was not a signatory to the Geneva Conventions. In the eyes of the Japanese, a POW is without honour or privilege, an object of shame, but this reference to Japanese dead put the officer instantly on the alert.

'One of your officers died of wounds yesterday,' Mary explained. 'We did everything possible to save him.'

'Show me,' ordered the officer. She was hoisted to her feet. With a bayonet pricking her between the shoulder blades and still wearing her tin hat, she led the way to the mortuary through a file of curious Japanese soldiers.

Confronted with the carefully tended body of his General, the Japanese officer was nonplussed.

'If you lived in England,' Mary said shortly, 'you should know how civilised people behave.'

The Japanese were notoriously hasty with their swords but Mary's head was never in danger. As they left the mortuary together, the long-legged QA and the short Japanese officer whom she topped by several inches, the soldier looked up curiously into the face of his prisoner.

'Do Englishwomen never cry?' he asked her.

Women were of no account in the Japanese way of life and encounters with those of Mary's calibre came as a continual surprise to them. In recognition of the respect shown to the General, the Japanese officer granted one request to Sister Currie. With cool reasoning, she asked that the English-speaking officer himself should remain in control of St Albert's, to ensure the safety of the women, and that he should accompany her on a round of the patients from time to time. To this he agreed, and in this hospital at least women were never molested. After she had first removed all dressings to prove that the men occupying the beds were really wounded, Mary was able to continue the nursing care with a certain amount of co-operation from the Japanese.

Many records are lost in wartime, particularly if a term of imprisonment intervenes to dim the memory of acts of heroism, but a number of VADs who served under Sister Currie at St Albert's at this time wrote to the Matron-in-Chief QAIMNS after the war concerning the courage displayed by this Sister.

'In the days preceding the actual capture of the hospital, the environs were infested with snipers who made every moving thing their target. Casualties filled the wards. Throughout these dangerous and arduous days, Miss Currie was untiring in her care for the patients and staff alike. Her courage and devotion were an inspiration to us all. Following the capture of the hospital by Japanese troops on 23rd December, 1941, all were called upon to endure the most terrifying experiences and, in our opinion, the cool leadership of Miss Currie contributed in great part to the high standard of morale that was maintained throughout.'

This was signed by members of the Nursing Detachment of the Hong Kong Volunteer Defence Corps. Miss Currie was awarded the Royal Red Cross medal.

On Christmas Eve, Canadian troops mounted machine guns in the grounds of St Stephen's Hospital at Stanley for a last stand. The end was near for the few surviving defenders. The last pockets of resistance were being systematically wiped out. Hospitals were filled with the dead and the dying. Japanese troops, exhilarated with victory, broke into the liquor stores and embarked on a drunken progress of looting, rape and murder.

Watched by grim-faced medical officers, they came reeling down the hill towards St Stephen's Hospital, stopping in their drunkenness to vomit by the roadside. The sixty-five-year-old civilian medical superintendent, Dr George Black, who courageously forbade them entrance to the wards, was at once shot through the heart at point-blank range, then bayoneted. Captain Whitney, RAMC, second in command, was dispatched in the same fashion before the soldiers stormed through the hospital. In front of horrified nurses, they ripped dressings and bandages from patients and bayoneted them as they lay helpless in bed. One nurse attempted to protect a patient by throwing herself on top of him, and the two were bayoneted together. In thirty-five minutes, fifty-six people were hacked to death.

A few escaped by hiding in cupboards. Lance-Corporal Harding of the Middlesex Regiment, badly injured in both legs, was bundled by the nurses into a large wicker laundry basket, from which hiding-place he was forced to witness their violation. In white uniforms now spattered with blood, they were locked in a room and taken away whenever a Japanese soldier wanted a woman. Throughout Christmas Day and the following night, they were repeatedly raped. Three VADs of the Hong Kong Volunteer Defence Corps and all the female members of the Chinese St John Ambulance Brigade were massacred. On the day following this orgy, the survivors, numb with misery, asked to be allowed to return to work, and they made their own way to Bowen Road Hospital which had been spared the atrocities of St Stephen's.

The surviving staff and patients at St Stephen's were ordered to make a huge bonfire in the hospital grounds. Desks and chairs which had been the furnishings of the original boys' school were broken up for firewood and heaped on the blaze until it was fierce enough to consume all the bodies and their blood-soaked mattresses. So ended Christmas Day at St Stephen's.

The rest of the garrison now saw clearly the character of their conquerors. Liquor stocks throughout the island were destroyed except for one bottle of brandy, labelled 'EUSOL', kept for emergencies in the operating theatre at Bowen Road Hospital. The rest was poured down the city's drains and gutters. Hong Kong stank of death and alcohol. At 0045 hours on 26th December, bloody, humiliated and unable to fight any longer, the colony surrendered to the Japanese.

Matron Kathleen Thomson, recovering from her wounds in Queen Mary's Hospital, watched the arrival of Japanese troops at the hospital gates.

'I shall never forget my first sight of our Japanese conquerors; grubby little men on bicycles, in dirty khaki uniform and white tennis shoes, wearing tin hats trailing vines of hibiscus. Surely, I thought, a British garrison cannot have surrendered to men like these?'

Every able-bodied man, and many who were not, had fought to defend the colony beyond the expectation of duty, but the cause was lost before the first shot was fired.

11

Hong Kong after the Surrender

The guns were silent, all weapons handed in. Hong Kong smouldered and smoked. Piles of unburied dead marked the last outposts of gallant fighting. Of the wounded defenders, only the seriously injured were allowed medical treatment. They were packed into trucks and delivered to the already hopelessly overcrowded hospitals. The remainder were sent to the POW camp at Shamshuipo.

Outrages against women continued for some time until discipline was enforced by the Japanese administration. The auxiliary hospital at the Jockey Club suffered similar treatment to St Stephen's, and a repetition at the Naval Hospital was only avoided by the quick thinking of the medical officer on duty. When Japanese soldiers arrived at midnight demanding to be taken to the women's quarters, the MO contrived to send a warning to Matron Miss Franklin telling her to take her two Sisters and the VADs to a place of safety. Meanwhile, pretending to have misunderstood the soldiers' request, the doctor led them to the quarters of the Sick Bay Attendants, the male orderlies of the Naval medical service. Once there, the Japanese were diverted from their original intentions by the opportunity to rob the sailors of watches, rings and fountain pens.

After this incident was reported to the Japanese authorities, all hospitals were provided with a guard of Japanese soldiers, but these men were themselves the cause of much uneasiness amongst the women they were meant to protect. Moving soundlessly in their felt boots, they would appear and disappear without warning during the course of the day and night.

QA Freda Davies (RRC, later Brown) was sitting at her desk in the ward one night writing her report by the light of a hurricane lamp. The rest of the ward was in darkness. Wounded men flitting in and out of restless sleep moaned softly from time to time, underlining Sister Davies' sense of frustration, for she had few drugs with which to ease their pain. Her orderly came to the desk, standing over her like a bulky nursemaid in his white theatre gown over khaki uniform.

'Don't look round, Sister.' His whisper was urgent. 'There's one right behind you.'

As she lowered her eyes to the book in front of her, Freda Davies caught the glint of steel at her side. For a space of time which seemed like an eternity, the two men stood motionless over her. There was no sound but the scratching of her pen and the quickened breathing of an RAMC orderly transfigured by his nobility. The moment passed. The bright blade was gone. The soldier had disappeared as quietly as he had come.

Even on the damaged top floors where they slept, the women were not free from these silent visitations, but they were comforted by the knowledge that these troops were too highly disciplined to harm them. The men offered no more offensive provocation than their unwavering stares of curiosity.

When the Naval Hospital at Wanchai was commandeered for Japanese wounded and the staff and patients were transferred to St Albert's, overcrowding there and shortage of dressings became acute. The wards were already filled with wounded and, in addition, a tented Indian hospital had been set up in the grounds of the old convent.

Although a certain amount of fresh water was now being circulated, no fresh food was available. There were large stocks of stale bread which, fried in peanut oil, provided the patients' breakfast and, for as long as the supply of tinned food lasted, a meal later in the day of stew with vegetables was possible. After that, the hospital authorities had to rely on the Japanese for food. Deliveries were unpredictable. A sack of rice would arrive, with no indication as to how long it must be made to last before another was allocated.

For a while, however, the hospitals were allowed to function undisturbed under the overall command of the Japanese Director of Medical Services for the area, Major Saito. (Saito was condemned to death as a war criminal in Hong Kong in 1946, a sentence which was first commuted to twenty years' imprisonment and later to fifteen: see *Captive Surgeon in Hong Kong* by Colonel Donald Bowie, RAMC.)

There was still access to world news through a hidden radio at Bowen Road Hospital, the responsibility of Corporal Carter of the Royal Signals. Cleverly disguised as part of the record relay system to the wards, it aroused no suspicions on the part of the Japanese guards until one day the switch was inadvertently turned to 'ward relay' just before the forbidden broadcast was due. The sound of Big Ben booming out its prelude to the nine o'clock news electrified patients and staff, and Corporal Carter broke all records to reach the controls before the measured tones of Alvar Liddell in London completely blew the cover.

The news for which they risked so much was little solace to the survivors of Hong Kong's great fight for survival. They could be forgiven for thinking that the rest of the world neither knew nor cared about their plight. Not a single reference was made to the recent struggle nor of the now evident domination of the Far East by Japan. 'Fighting continues in Malaya' was the extent of Far Eastern news.

The British Government, however, was well aware of the appalling events which had taken place in the colony. Cabinet paper 66 for the year 1942, number 22, item 82 contains the following entry for 29th January, relating to a letter sent to the Foreign Office from Miss P. Harrap, Office of Commissioner of Police, Colonial Secretary, Hong Kong. Miss Harrap escaped after the surrender to Macao, from which refuge she wrote her letter.

'One entire Chinese district declared a brothel, regardless of classes of residents. Many European women raped, some afterwards shot and bayoneted.'

This was not made public in Britain until two and a half months later, when a shocked House of Commons heard Mr Anthony Eden's statement.

In February, the Japanese announced that they intended to take over St Albert's for their own use. The British staff and patients were to be distributed amongst remaining hospitals. Miss Kathleen Thomson, who had returned to her post as Matron as soon as she had recovered from her shrapnel wounds, was now to be sent with her nursing staff to take over the care of wounded POWs from the French nuns in St Theresa's Convent on the mainland. Since the nuns would be taking all their equipment with them when they left, Miss Thomson was given three trucks and one hour in which to pack everything she would need from St Albert's.

Squads of RAMC men were hastily organised to collect linen and medical supplies and load them into the trucks. Blankets and mattresses were thrown from the open windows as the minutes ticked away. Patients were prepared for transfer. Precisely at the end of one hour, the operation was halted. Miss Thomson and her nurses were taken by coal barge to Kowloon on the mainland and herded with other POWs into a wire pen. Here they stood, without shelter in the wind and the rain, for several hours, the butt of much amusement for Japanese nurses who came to jeer at them through the wire. Night had fallen before transport arrived to take them to St Theresa's Convent.

Their quarters were an unfurnished building in the Convent

grounds. The mattresses which they had brought with them lay piled up outside in the rain, soaking wet. There was no food provided for them that night, but one of the Sisters produced a tin of cocoa which they mixed with water and shared before rolling themselves in their damp blankets and lying down on the bare boards to sleep.

At 3 am they were awakened by a loud knocking at the door. Miss Thomson was requested to report to the hospital at once. Groping her way to the door through the darkness, she found the British Commanding Officer, Major Officer RAMC, and Sergeant Major Foster under armed escort, waiting to accompany her. (Major Officer was later transported to Japan and lost his life with 800 other POWs when the ship, the *Lisbon Maru*, was sunk by US bombers.)

Together they went to the hospital where the Japanese CO, Major Saito, proceeded to explain that, due to the wonderful goodness of Japanese people, this fine hospital was to be given over to the care of POWs. He then shook Miss Thomson by the hand and congratulated her on being appointed by Tokyo as Matron. She was dismissed and instructed to return at 6 am, when she would be allowed one hour in which to take over existing patients from the French Matron before she left.

A few hours later, Kathleen Thomson was introduced to the task which was now her responsibility.

'The French Matron was terrified of the Japanese but she did her best to give me a case history of the patients in the time available. I was appalled at their condition. They had been devotedly nursed but there were no drugs for them and very little food. All were desperately ill, emaciated with starvation, unshaven with sunken eyes and cheeks. Most were only semi-conscious.

'When, after an hour, the French Matron was whisked away, I was left wondering how we were to cope with this desperate situation. Our luggage had not yet arrived. We had no food, no equipment, no drugs, no linen except what was already on the patients' beds. I aroused the staff and assigned them to different wards, and we all set to work to sort out the patients as well as we could. Later that day, two of our lorries arrived with some medical supplies, and the Japanese brought in two sacks of rice which provided the only meal of the day.

'Our rations consisted mainly of rice, spinach, turnips and chrysanthemum leaves, a most unsuitable diet for the many cases of dysentery. We tried putting the rice through a mincer, then rolling it with a bottle and making it into a kind of gruel with water, but we had neither sugar nor salt, nor flavouring of any sort, and the patients were too ill to eat this tasteless mess. In spite of our efforts, many slipped away; we knew we could have saved most of them if only we had had sufficient food.

'Sick POWs were brought to us from Shamshuipo camp in busloads. Many of them died on the way. Many were so ill that they died shortly after arrival. It was the constant dread of the VADs that they would find amongst the dead a husband, father or brother. I had to forbid them to come to the front entrance until the dead had been carried away and identified.

'Day after day, the staff stood in two ranks with bowed heads as the coffins were carried out. The Japanese insisted on sending an ostentatious wreath, which annoyed us very much. There was a red hibiscus tree in the compound, however, which never failed to supply a spray of blooms for every funeral. It comforted us to know that each soldier went to his rest with a tribute from the British beside the despised Japanese wreath.

'As time went on, food became more scarce, until sometimes there was no food at all in the hospital. Sometimes a sack of rice would be brought in late in the afternoon, and sometimes it would not. On those occasions we had a drink of hot water and went to bed. The health of the staff deteriorated rapidly due to starvation and overwork. One VAD died, and others were unable to continue on duty. Just when we thought we had touched rock-bottom, another disaster struck us.

'Among the new arrivals from the camp one evening was a soldier with distressed breathing and, to my horror, I recognised the typical "bull-neck" of diphtheria. My heart sank, for I realised that he would soon be followed by many others and we would have an epidemic on our hands. This proved to be true. Soon the top floor of the Convent was filled with patients fighting for their lives without the aid of serum to combat this dreaded disease. We had nothing to offer, other than simple nursing. The dedication of the staff was magnificent, despite the inexperience of many of them and the knowledge that, if they caught the disease themselves, there would be no serum to help them. Watched over by Divine Providence, no member of the staff contracted the disease, despite the absence of normal protective measures. We had no disinfectants and no protective clothing. We unpicked the hems of our white uniforms and made masks out of them. Whenever possible, we used the sun as a disinfectant. Every day, I presented myself at the Japanese office and begged for serum, and every day I was refused. We knew they had it. We could see piles of boxes of it through the windows of the house next door, where it had been stacked after being removed from various British hospitals.

'One evening, I was told that Major Saito wanted me at the front gate and I went down immediately. He threw a package over the gate to me.

' "There you are," he shouted, "there's your serum. Don't ever ask me for more or I will have you shot."

'Inside the package was enough serum for eight patients. The task of deciding who should have it was a hard one but we were able to save eight lives.'

In August, St Theresa's Hospital was closed down. Doctors and orderlies were to be interned with the patients in Shamshuipo Camp. The nurses were informed that they were to proceed to Stanley Internment Camp on Hong Kong island, from where they would be repatriated. Any relief they might have felt at their own apparent good fortune was overshadowed by their anxiety over their patients, many of whom, especially the diphtheria cases, were much too ill to be moved. Everyone knew that medical facilities at the camp were practically non-existent and it was with heavy hearts that the nurses prepared their patients for the journey.

With the utmost care, RAMC orderlies carried the diphtheria cases down from the top floor of the Convent and laid their stretchers gently on the floor of the trucks waiting in the shade, hoping in this way to dispense with unnecessary handling – but the Japanese guard ordered the trucks to be unloaded again. All patients were to be assembled in the centre of the compound. Here, with no shelter from the blazing sun, desperately ill men lay on their stretchers for several hours until the drivers were ready to move off. Doctors, nurses and orderlies could only watch helplessly as all their good work was undone.

On the following day, the nurses bade farewell to the rest of the medical staff and climbed into the truck which was to take them to Kowloon en route for Hong Kong island. As they drove through the gates of the Convent, they were astonished to see a Japanese officer come smartly to the salute as they passed. Their amazement increased when they recognised Major Saito.

'At first,' says Miss Thomson, 'the Japanese treated us with the same contempt as they had for their own women, but when they saw how we stood up to hardship and the dedication with which the nurses cared for their patients, they began to show a grudging admiration. Major Saito, with his parting salute, acknowledged this.'

Before they were allowed to leave the mainland, the nurses were thoroughly searched. The Japanese were acutely sensitive about written records of any kind, a fact which had given Miss Thomson sleepless nights.

'From the time when we first went to St Theresa's Convent, I carefully recorded the names and addresses of the next of kin of all those who died there, hoping that, if ever we got back to England, I would be able to get in touch with them and let them know that their dear ones had been looked after by Army Sisters in their last illness. When we left St Theresa's we were forbidden to take with us any notes or writing of any sort, so I gave each member of the staff several addresses to memorise, intending to re-write them when we reached our destination. But because of the effects of starvation, we found it impossible to remember them, so some other way had to be found. I had a talcum powder tin with a lid on the bottom for refilling purposes. The powder had long since gone but I had kept the tin because the spray of pink lilac on the label reminded me of better times. I removed the lid now and refilled the tin with french chalk from the operating theatre, wrote the names and addresses in very small writing on the thinnest paper I could find, poked the roll of paper into the bottom of the tin and replaced the lid and the label. My luggage was searched but nothing unusual was found.

'Years later, when we returned to England, I wrote letters to each of the next of kin and met with a wonderful response. Relatives had received no news other than the War Office telegram stating that their dear ones had died in a POW camp and they were so grateful to know the details of their last days and particularly to know that they had had a Christian burial with a service conducted by an Army Padre.'

There was no repatriation for the British Sisters. They became part of a community of 2,000 men, women and children confined in Stanley Internment Camp for three and a half years.

In 1943, May Waters and Kay G. Christie, the two Canadian Army Sisters who had worked from the beginning alongside the QAs in Bowen Road Hospital, were repatriated. When pressed by the Canadian Government to hasten the repatriation of the eleven British Army Sisters and three British Naval Sisters still in the camp, Mr Anthony

Eden, then Secretary of State for Foreign Affairs, stated that for
reasons he was unable to divulge, negotiations regarding the repatriation of British nurses had broken down.

There was an exchange of prisoners, but on a purely official level;
the relevant Foreign Office Paper, entitled 'Restriction of Repatriation
from Stanley Camp', K 8874/587/210, has been lost or destroyed.

12

The Fall of Singapore

Singapore was dreaming of things other than war when Kit Woodman was posted there in 1941. After escaping from France in 1940, she had helped in the evacuation of expatriates from Egypt to South Africa when the Canal came under threat. The dislocation of everyday life which accompanies war was well known to her, but she was totally unprepared for Singapore. Introspective and complacent, the island was out of step with embattled Europe.

At a time when mothers in Britain hurried to the shelters every night with their children, Singapore's preoccupation with golf, cricket and the afternoon siesta continued undisturbed. Slightly incredulous, Kit was introduced to the comfortable Sisters' Mess at the Alexandra Military Hospital, five miles from the city of Singapore, where the provision of one Amah to every three Sisters ensured a high degree of comfort. The hospital was busy enough with the tropical diseases which affected the garrison troops and with traffic accidents, but a lively social calendar for the staff made war seem remote indeed. Kit was posted to the 1st Malayan General Hospital on the mainland at Johore a few days before Japan attacked Pearl Harbor.

On the morning following the declaration of war by Britain, Japan bombed Singapore. Black-out restrictions on the island had not then been enforced and the city lay, a brilliantly illuminated target, beneath the raiders. No warning sirens were sounded and casualties were heavy in the densely populated Chinese residential district. On that same day, 8th December, Japanese assault troops landed at three points in northern Malaya near Kota Bahru.

None of this caused undue alarm in Singapore. Kota Bahru was 400 miles away across land overgrown with impenetrable jungle. There was nothing to fear from that quarter, especially from the Japanese, who were considered to be ill-equipped and so short-sighted they could not shoot straight. The whole Malay peninsula was well invested with British, Australian and Indian troops; strong coastal defences looked out to sea, and Singapore's Naval Dockyard was the envy of the world. In such circumstances, the Civil and Military Authorities saw no reason for concern. They sent troops to deal with the invaders in northern Malaya, and enforced black-out and ARP restrictions. Businessmen received instruction in the Malayan Volunteer Defence Force after office hours. Meanwhile, two giants of the Royal Navy, the *Repulse* and the *Prince of Wales*, steamed north to intercept any further attempts on the part of the Japanese to land troops.

Within the next few days everything that could go wrong did so. On 10th December, the *Prince of Wales* and the *Repulse* were sunk by the Japanese, with a loss of 1,000 officers and men. To a population accustomed to regarding the Royal Navy as invincible, this news was scarcely credible. There was more of the same sort. The jungle, far from being an insurmountable obstacle, presented the Japanese with no difficulties. By the simple expedient of a compass strapped to each man's wrist, they were able to run rings around the hopelessly disorientated British and Dominion troops. 'Fifth Columnists' spread rumour and confusion. Men were encircled, cut off from their units and wiped out.

Casualties began to arrive at the Alor Star Hospital in the far north of Malaya, but amongst the ambulances on the roads were trucks full of retreating troops. Dejected and demoralised, they reported that the jungle was swarming with the Japanese: '... useless trying to stop them'.

Then the refugees began to stream south in their cars, carts, rickshaws and bicycles, blocking the way for relief troops trying to reach the Front. Forward medical units such as the 2nd/4th Australian CCS began to pull back and, as the sound of artillery drew nearer, the staff of the Alor Star Hospital knew that it was only a matter of time before they, too, must pack up and go. On 12th December, the message 'Curtain Fallen' informed them that the moment of departure had come.

Phyllis Briggs, one of the four Colonial Service Sisters who made up the trained staff of the hospital, helped to load patients on to an ambulance train, then, with another nurse as passenger in her little car, took to the road herself and made for the town of Kulim, further south. Here, amongst the confusion of troops and refugees, she caught sight of a familiar face. Tony Cochrane, a peacetime engineer employed by the Colonial Government and her dancing partner on many occasions, was on his way to the Front with a party of the Malayan Volunteer Defence Force as troop replacements. There was time for only a quick word of greeting before they moved off in opposite directions.

More enemy landings followed on the east and west coasts of Malaya. Troops, some untrained, were hastily sent to plug the gaps, and were wiped out at once. Some of the Australian companies involved had not seen active service before and were ill-equipped to deal with a situation which grew more desperate every day. Men of the Norfolk, Suffolk and Cambridgeshire Regiments were thrown into battle as soon as they stepped ashore after a three-month voyage in a troopship from England. Without a period of retraining or instruction in jungle warfare, they were pitchforked into battle and almost annihilated. "Sister, I never even *saw* a Jap!" was the bewildered cry of the wounded.

Within a few days, every hospital on the mainland was on the move with its patients. After only one night in Kulim, Phyllis Briggs' hospital was ordered to move on to Kuala Lumpur. They passed through the town of Ipoh, then a heap of smoking ruins after continuous raids the day before, and Sister Briggs was lucky enough to get a free tank full of petrol from a garage owner who was giving his supply away rather than let it fall into the hands of the Japanese.

Kuala Lumpur was quiet and far enough away from the fighting for reports of defeat in the jungle to be dismissed as exaggeration, but the wounded had to be believed.

Finally, Kit Woodman and her hospital in Johore joined in the retreat over the water to the island of Singapore. As the ambulances and ships tried to find safety for their wounded they were not spared by the dive-bombers who followed the lines of vehicles. The red crosses clearly marked on ambulances and ships meant nothing to Japanese pilots. No grace was shown to a small ship embarking casualties, and the wounded were wounded again as stretcher-bearers carried them on board. Throughout the perilous embarkation, QA Mary Brand ran a makeshift operating theatre for emergency surgery and, still under fire, rigged up a small tent on board so that the work could continue as the ship set sail. But the planes meant to destroy the little ship and did not cease attacking until they had done so.

'When they lifted Mary Brand from the water,' states an eye-witness, 'her body was as full of shell splinters as she was of courage.' She died of her wounds a few days later.

In spite of increasing air raids on Singapore, strenuous efforts were made to maintain a semblance of normality. Businessmen still sold insurance. Estate agents negotiated the letting of holiday homes. Bank clerks and shipping agents worked at their desks through the day and took over ARP duties at night. There were as yet no plans to evacuate non-essential civilians. As in Hong Kong, the wives and daughters of British residents undertook a short course of nursing instruction and helped in the hospitals as VADs. Husbands were relieved to think that their womenfolk were under the umbrella of the Military, but they were not to know that it was full of holes.

The air raids were stoically borne. Singapore Island, soon to come under siege, swarmed with non-essential personnel and their families, the 'bouches inutiles' of a military strategist's nightmare. There were as yet no defences constructed on the vulnerable north-west aspect of the island, for fear of shaking public morale by the admission that invasion from that direction was a possibility.

In order to free more beds in the hospitals, the first evacuation of convalescent patients took place on New Year's Eve, when 114 Australian casualties sailed for home accompanied by some of their own nurses. The only hospital ship for this region, a one-time river boat named the *Wu Sueh*, began to ferry parties of wounded to Java. Convalescent depots were set up in several places on Singapore Island to relieve the pressure on the hospitals.

The Alexandra Hospital was a changed place now. The once serene and tidy wards were filled with the bustle of casualties coming and going, being documented, transfused and sent to the theatre. Drip stands and oxygen cylinders stood by most of the beds. In scenes like this, where every doctor and nurse was working to save life, there was no place for the casual visitor of calmer days. The wife of the Minister of State for the Far East had been a welcome visitor in less stressful times and was unable to appreciate the fact that her presence was out of place in a ward of acutely ill men. She was not pleased.

'Do you know who I am?' she asked the young Irish QA. 'I am Lady Diana Cooper.'

'And I am Sister Mary Cooper,' came the swift retort, 'and you still can't come in. The men are too ill.' Mary Cooper's bright fire was extinguished three years later when she died of beri-beri in a Japanese internment camp.

Throughout January, the retreat down the Malayan peninsula continued in front of a seemingly unstoppable force of Japanese. No-one now spoke of their alleged defective vision. Their aim with the tommy-guns they carried was deadly. The military hospitals from the mainland settled into new positions. Number 1 Malayan General Hospital took over Selarang Barracks at Changi and established a unit with 3,000 beds there within twenty-four hours of moving in. Kit Woodman was appointed Night Superintendent and struggled with the 'bed-state' at midnight with the Wardmaster. The 'ins' and 'outs' must tally, no matter how many casualties had been received, had died or been sent to convalescent depots.

The 2nd/4th Australian CCS under Senior Sister Kathleen Kinsella opened a 200-bed unit at Bukit Panjang. The 2nd/10th Australian General Hospital under Matron Miss Paschke and the 2nd/13th under Matron Miss Drummond took over Oldham Hall School and St Patrick's School, and began admitting patients at once. The local Red Cross Society provided hot meals until working kitchens could be arranged. The 17th Combined British/Indian General Hospital under Matron Miss Russell moved into Changi Barracks, and the 20th Combined British/Indian General Hospital under Matron Miss Spedding took over Gilman Barracks in Keppel Harbour, occupied so briefly by the ill-fated Norfolks. Here a psychiatric wing was opened to cope with the increasing number of men suffering from what had been called 'shell-shock' in the First World War, and was called 'battle fatigue' in the Second. These men, exhausted by continual fighting without proper food or rest, needed time before they could go back into the fighting. Some would never return.

The last hospital to be evacuated from the mainland was the pride and joy of the Sultan of Johore, a modern building furnished with the latest equipment. Most of the native patients there chose to return to their own kampongs rather than transfer to the island, but the European patients with their Colonial Service Sisters moved into Tan Tock Sen Hospital in the north of Singapore Island.

The last person to leave the building was the Resident Physician to the Ladies of the Household of the Sultan of Johore. She stayed until the increasing noise of gunfire could no longer be ignored and then she, too, reluctantly crossed the Causeway. Australian Dr Marjorie Lyon had been the most highly qualified woman doctor in her country when she became Fellow of the Royal College of Surgeons (Edinburgh), Member of the Royal College of Obstetricians and Gynaecology (London), and followed this with a degree in tropical medicine. In the troubled times ahead, many people would have cause to be grateful for her skills.

No-one who had experienced the retreat down the mainland was

under any illusions as to the gravity of the situation, yet no arrangements were made for the evacuation of women and children until the
end of January. Recently discharged supply ships were then available
for those who wished to leave, but still no official directives were
issued. The choice of staying or leaving was left to the individual. A
Government order would have made this appallingly difficult decision
unnecessary.

In the markets and in the clubs, the talk amongst European women
was on this one subject. 'Are you going?', and sometimes, more coldly,
'You're not going, are you?', as if the act of leaving was disloyal and
cowardly. Wives were loath to leave husbands who were now fully
committed to the fighting forces and so, rather than be accused of
running away, they stayed, thereby becoming an added embarrassment
for the military leaders.

Four ships, however, left Singapore on 30th January, taking civilian
women and children to India where they were to pick up an escort of
Army Sisters to accompany them for the remainder of the voyage
home. The *Westpoint*, the *Wakefield*, the *Duchess of Bedford* and, un-
funnily enough, the *Empress of Japan* carried to safety many women
who would not see their husbands again.

The escort of QAIMNS Sisters awaiting them in India could sum-
mon little enthusiasm for this new role of nursemaid. Senior Sister
Esther Somerville was one of them.

'I had to leave my darling TB boys in Deolali in order to change
babies' nappies for a bunch of perfectly capable women, thirty-seven
of whom were trained nurses.'

The duty was discharged, however, and Singapore rid herself of
some of the 'useless mouths'. Those who were left prepared themselves
for a long siege and kept up their spirits with such diversions as the
cinema and dancing at Raffles Hotel. They were in good heart, having
before them the example of Tobruk, which had held out for seven
months before being relieved. Singapore was surely in better shape to
withstand a siege than Tobruk, since there were two good reservoirs
on the island and plentiful supplies of food. A 'Dig for Victory' campaign was launched and all spare plots of land were dug over and sown
with maize.

What the population did not realise was that Japan had virtual
mastery of the air, and that on the vitally important landward aspect
of the island no defences of even the simplest construction had yet

been built. There was little beyond a strip of water a mile wide to deter the enemy from overrunning Singapore.

The retreat down the Malayan peninsula by weary troops came to an end on the night of 31st January, 1942. The remnants of the Argyll and Sutherland Highlanders, 880 men strong one month earlier and now reduced to ninety men, piped the last man over the Causeway, then blew it up. Believing that they were now safe within the garrison, the exhausted men sought only a place to lay their heads. A company of Ghurkas, who had been fighting for days without a break, marched into one of the hospitals, lay down in the corridor and went to sleep.

Daylight brought disillusionment. The island was no fortress. The troops themselves had to take picks and shovels to dig gun emplacements and slit trenches even as the Japanese moved their artillery into position on the other side of the Straits of Johore. The British Army had been out-manoeuvred by nimble men on bicycles who could exist on a handful of rice a day and carried no unnecessary gear. These very much underrated men were now in a position to shell the island of Singapore.

One of the first shells landed on the Tan Tock Sen civilian hospital. 120 stewards who had survived the sinking of the *Empress of Asia* two days earlier helped to rescue the patients, then stayed on at the hospital as orderlies and cooks.

The full might of the Japanese Air Force was now turned on the island. Against 530 fast, modern planes the RAF could muster no more than 138 machines, of which twenty-four were obsolete Wildebeestes. The small but valiant defending air force was continually at a disadvantage.

Bombs and shells could hardly fail to inflict a great deal of harm on the large numbers of troops and civilians now concentrated within the confines of the island. Civilians who had staunchly accepted the inevitability of a siege were stunned by the extent of the carnage. When news of the Hong Kong atrocities reached them, men who still had their wives with them crowded the shipping offices seeking berths on any ship to take the women to safety.

Other stories were beginning to filter through, of the rape and murder of Chinese women on the mainland and of the summary execution of POWs. One Australian soldier with a terrible neck wound was the sole survivor of a party of prisoners beheaded in cold blood.

Three ships, the *Devonshire*, the *Plancius* and the *Felix Roussel*, assembled in the harbour on 8th February to evacuate as many women and children as they could hold. They left only hours before a terrifying bombardment of shells dwarfed anything that had gone before, and which proved to be the prelude to a landing on the island itself. Without too much difficulty, Japanese troops landed on the north-west coast and began their advance across country towards Singapore city.

At this moment when panic hovered, when some sort of reassurance was needed by the defenders, the Naval base was fired and abandoned. A shocked population watched in disbelief as thick black smoke poured from the oil terminals. The great dockyard, which many believed to be the *raison d'être* of Singapore, was deserted, the machinery sheds unmanned. 'The Navy's gone' was the chilling message.

Among the many women still on the island were hundreds of nurses, civilian as well as Services, European, Australian, Indian and Asiatic. In addition to the three civilian hospitals, Tan Tock Sen, Singapore General and Kandang Kerbau Maternity Hospital, there were now the 12th, 19th, 27th and 40th Indian General Hospitals, the 1st Malayan General, the 17th and 20th Combined British/Indian Hospitals, the 2nd/10th and 2nd/13th Australian General Hospitals and the base British Alexandra Hospital. They were all working at full effort to keep pace with the rising number of air raid victims, and were themselves the target of many raids.

200 patients and staff died when the 12th Indian General at Tyersall was bombed and set on fire. Stretcher-bearers attempting to carry the survivors into the building of the Registrar of Vehicles were themselves machine-gunned at close range. When the village of Bukit Tanjong was burnt to the ground, the 2nd/4th Australian CCS moved to the Singapore Rifle Club.

On 10th February the last RAF squadron, number 232, departed for the safety of Sumatra. It had remained behind to inflict as much damage on the enemy as possible long after the other planes had gone. Now, it too took its leave. The population understood now that it was being thrown to the lions.

General Percival, Commanding Officer of the Garrison, thoroughly alarmed for the safety of the women in his charge, made strenuous efforts to evacuate as many as possible while there was still time. On 10th February, twenty civilian nurses and local VADs accompanying 306 casualties were safely evacuated to Java on the little hospital ship

Wu Sueh; on the same day, six Australian Sisters got away in a small boat with forty-seven patients. Hundreds of nurses remained, however, and the Japanese were not far away, despite heroic efforts to delay them by scattered parties of defenders.

On 11th February, General Percival ordered that half of all the nurses on the island and as many of the other women as possible must sail on the *Empire Star*, a cargo vessel of the Blue Star Line. With great reluctance, Principal Matron QAIMNS Miss Jones called her staff together at the Alexandra Hospital and asked for volunteers. Getting none, she made an arbitrary choice. No-one wanted to leave. Those who did go knew that they might never see their friends again.

On finding two sick Sisters of the 20th Combined General Hospital who were on the embarkation list but unable to get to the docks through lack of transport, Captain Dick Phillips, the Australian Red Cross Officer attached to the hospital, promptly commandeered a jeep and drove them there himself, through burning streets choked with rubble. Having seen them safely on board, he set off to return to the hospital, but he was intercepted by a Japanese patrol and spent the next three and a half years in captivity.

2,150 people were packed on the *Empire Star*, women and children in the holds once used for refrigerated meat, Government officials, key technicians and certain troops on the open decks. Unwilling to risk the minefields in the dark, her Captain lay out in the roads all night and sailed in the early hours of 12th February. She was soon spotted and attacked by a force of fifty-seven Japanese bombers. Men on the exposed decks were machine-gunned without mercy. The nurses rigged up three sick bays in different parts of the ship and did what they could for the injured, but there were few facilities and those men with serious abdominal or chest wounds did not survive.

Captain Capon adopted a zig-zag course for his ship but even so suffered three direct hits. Nevertheless, despite a great gaping hole in her side just above the water mark, he took her safely into harbour at Batavia later on that same day. (Captain Capon went down with the *Empire Star* three months later when she was torpedoed in the Atlantic.)

The nightmare quality of life on Singapore Island intensified. Enemy landings at several points along the coastline confused an already chaotic military picture. Snipers and Fifth Columnists spread fear and bewilderment and nowhere were conditions more strained than in the hospitals, where a reduced staff of nurses were faced with mounting numbers of casualties. To add to their difficulties, all the servants except the loyal Chinese had abandoned their posts, leaving the nurses to organise the catering as well as their other duties.

Colonial Sister Phyllis Briggs was now working at the Kandang Kerbau Maternity Hospital. Injured Chinese, Malays and Indians were taken there straight from the streets. 'The entrance hall was filled with people patiently waiting to have their wounds dressed. The stairs were sticky with blood but there was no time to clean them. Our doctors, Mr Laurie, Mr Eliot-Fisher and Dr Shields operated day and night, but many cases were so bad that we could only give them morphia to ease their pain. There were never enough beds and eventually we put men, women and children in the same room, wherever there was a space.'

Tony Cochrane, the civil-engineer-turned-soldier, found her there, in the resuscitation department, and proposed to her amongst the blood transfusions and the trauma. Then they parted, with a tryst to meet in Australia, some time, somehow. He went to join his men in the tumult of the streets, while she was left to comfort the wretched victims of the bombs for whom there was no salvation.

When the wards were damaged, the wounded were carried from place to place in search of a bed. Sister Netta Smith of the Colonial Service discovered an undamaged schoolhouse and was about to move her party of patients there when the roof was·blown off. When the 1st Malayan General was forced to move from Selarang Barracks on the exposed north coast, Kit Woodman was sent with a party of Sisters to the once hallowed Cricket Club which was now full of casualties.

'It was as I imagine wards must have looked like in the Crimean War. There were wounded men everywhere with scarcely room to walk between them. One section had been rigged up as a resuscitation area and an operating theatre was going full blast. In a side ward, two heavily bandaged officers were making terrible noises. They had attempted suicide by turning their revolvers to their own heads.'

The 2nd/10th Australian Hospital overflowed into the Cathay Buildings and then had to put up tents. The 2nd/9th Australian Field Ambulance opened an operating theatre in the Adelphi Hotel, and the 43rd Indian Field Ambulance moved into the ballroom at Raffles Hotel. In one day, 200 operations under general anaesthetic were carried out by five surgical teams in the Victoria Hall. In the days preceding 11th February, the Singapore General Hospital admitted 15,000 casualties.

After that date records could not be kept, as there were no more admission forms left on the island.

These were the terrible last days of Singapore. Snipers were everywhere. Terror-stricken troops running through the streets without aim or purpose were a liability to the many brave companies of men who steadfastly held their positions. Men drove their new cars to the end of the wharf and pushed them into the harbour rather than leave them for the Japanese. All the water mains were damaged and the smell of inefficient sanitation seeped along the streets.

On 12th February, a fleet of eighty vessels of every description assembled in Singapore harbour for an eleventh-hour evacuation. There were gun-boats, motor launches, river boats, coastal steamers, tugs, yachts, dinghies, rowing boats and sampans. It was now or never for those who wanted to get away.

Sixty-five Sisters of the Australian Army Nursing Service who were still on the island were ordered to board the *Vyner-Brooke*, a once elegant craft belonging to the Rajah of Sarawak, now a dirty, neglected tub. They joined the large crowd of women and children on the wharf and were awaiting their turn to go on board when one of their own doctors, Colonel Glyn White of the Australian Army Medical Service, came up to enquire where they were going.

Mavis Hannah (later Allgrove) of the 2nd/4th Australian CCS and ultimately its only survivor, explained that they had been ordered to leave on the *Vyner-Brooke*. He was horrified.

'Oh no, you're not!' he said firmly. 'You haven't got a hope in hell of getting away. Wait there.' He stormed off to confront those in charge of sailing arrangements.

But he came back a few minutes later. 'I'm sorry, Mavis,' he said dejectedly. 'They've overruled me. You've got to go.'

That night, 12th February, the *Vyner-Brooke* sailed straight into a minefield and was forced to anchor there until daylight, losing valuable time. She proceeded the next day without interference until the evening when she was spotted by a Japanese scout plane. She was not attacked, however, until the following morning, when she received three direct hits and sank. Among the many who were drowned were twelve of the Australian Sisters.

Friday 13th lived up to its evil reputation. All the remaining nurses on Singapore were ordered to leave. Service nurses had no choice but to obey, but some fifty civilian nurses and local VADs elected to stay on at the Singapore General Hospital and worked right through the final stages of Singapore's collapse.

The scene at the docks was chaotic. Three small coastal steamers, the *Tien Kwang*, *Mata Hari* and *Kuala*, frantically embarked passengers under the guns of dive-bombing Japanese planes, for the story of Dunkirk was well-known, even to the Japanese, and they had resolved that no-one was to escape this net. Nurses already on board the ships immediately set up sick bays to help the wounded, but many of those waiting hopefully to sail were killed, among them Colonial Sister Mac-Farlane.

500 souls, including 100 nurses and their Matrons, were packed on board the *Kuala* along with Government officials and some servicemen. One small case each was all the luggage allowed but when embarkation was almost complete and the vessel ready to sail, one lonely dressing case labelled K. Woodman QAIMNS, remained on the empty wharf.

At the Cricket Club, its owner was just waking from a few hours' sleep snatched before going on night duty. Furious with her colleagues for forgetting about her, Kit dressed and resolutely went on duty, to be met in the hall by an astonished Brigadier.

'What the devil are you doing here!' he exploded, and hustled her into his jeep. At breakneck speed he drove her to the docks, and shouldered a way for her through the long queues of desperate people clamouring at the dock gates.

'There on the empty wharf was my case, which I had packed for just such an emergency. The Brig whistled up a rowing boat from somewhere, and I was taken out to the *Kuala* by a simply huge man. When we came alongside, he just lifted me up and threw me on board, and my case after me. My uniform was crumpled, my hair all over the place. Miss Jones, Principal Matron QAIMNS, looked me over and said coldly, "You girls will have to smarten yourselves up before we reach Java." She should have seen us when we *did* land,' Kit adds grimly.

As the three ships pulled away from the shore, Kit stood by the rail for a last look at Singapore. The once green paradise island now lay charred and smoking in a sump of foul oil. Flames and gun-flashes lit up the evening sky.

'My last thoughts were of my orderlies, left behind with the patients. Excellent men, all of them. What would happen to them now?'

Unknown to those who left by that last panicky exodus, the enemy had just launched a seaborne invasion against Sumatra. The escaping vessels sailed straight into the path of a destroyer flotilla with its extensive air cover. Their chances of avoiding discovery were practically nil.

By first light on Saturday, 14th February, the *Tien Kwang* and the *Kuala* had put no more than 100 miles between themselves and Singapore, and their Captains decided to hide in the lee of one of the many islands during the hours of daylight and to resume their journey after nightfall. Contact with the *Mata Hari* had been lost during the night. Accordingly, the two ships dropped anchor near the island of Pompong in the Luigga Archipelago, and sent forage parties ashore for branches of trees to be used as camouflage. The nurses were asked to change their white dresses for less conspicuous garments.

In addition to Miss Jones, Principal Matron QAIMNS, on board the *Kuala* there were also Matrons Miss Spedding of the 20th CGH, Miss West of the 1st Malayan and Miss Russell of the 17th CGH, civilian Matrons Miss Brebner of the Singapore General Hospital and Mrs Cherry, the organiser of the Malayan Auxiliary Nursing Services. All these outstanding women were conferring on the treatment of the many wounded on the ship when Japanese dive-bombers attacked. The cabin where the Matrons were meeting was demolished. Miss Jones, Miss West, Miss Brebner and Mrs Cherry were killed outright. Miss Spedding was seriously wounded in the chest by shrapnel. Two QAs, Lorna Symondson and Helen Montgomerie, had just gone up to the top deck and were killed by the bomb which hit the part of the ship occupied by Eurasian and Chinese nurses. The carnage was terrible.

As fire broke out, survivors of the attack leapt into the water. There had not been enough lifejackets for everyone, but those without proved to be the more fortunate. When the dive-bombing planes returned to strafe the survivors in the water with machine guns, those wearing lifejackets were unable to submerge and were killed. The fourth QA Matron, Miss Russell, died then, as did Colonial Sister Mary Gentles, who had accompanied Phyllis Briggs on her drive south from Alor Star. She had put up her purple umbrella inside Phyllis' little car because the roof leaked. Her friend was somewhere else, on the *Mata Hari*, when Mary Gentles was drowned. Eighteen QAs, five TANS, as well as a number of Colonial Sisters and members of the Indian Military Service died in the warm green waters off Pompong Island on 14th February, 1942.

On the night of 13th February, Japanese troops reached the
Alexandra Hospital and were met by Lt Weston, RAMC. He was
carrying a white flag, by which token he hoped to ensure the safety of
his patients. This was not to be one of the rare occasions when the
Japanese respected the Red Cross or the white flag, perhaps because
a party of Sikhs had mounted a gun on the hospital roof. Lt Weston
and his fellow officers were bayoneted to death and Japanese troops
ran berserk through the hospital, bayoneting the patients in their beds.
Even an unconscious patient on the operating table was not spared. It
was a repeat of the tragedy at St Stephen's Hospital in Hong Kong
and, had the nurses still been there, they would surely have suffered
the same fate.

Patients who survived the initial butchery were led away in small
parties during the night and executed. Ten officers and seventy-three
Other Ranks are recorded 'Missing' at the time of this incident, but
their fate has never been in doubt. Only a lucky few escaped to tell
the tale.

The take-over of the Alexandra Hospital by the Japanese left only
two hospitals now operating for the defenders, the Singapore General
and the Kandang Kerbau. Both were now augmented by staff from
Australian and Indian medical teams. Both were overwhelmed with
casualties from the hand-to-hand fighting of these final days.

Miss Katie Stewart, a Scottish nurse who had been Assistant
Matron at Tan Tock Sen Hospital, was now in charge of the nursing
at 'the General', and contrived some sort of care for the wounded
with the aid of staunch helpers, Miss Mollie Hill, Miss I. D. Brown
and Miss S. Osborn. There was a staff of forty-five female nurses and
VADs.

Fractured mains meant that there was no water to spare for making
plaster of paris, and its use had to be discontinued. What little water
there was had to be carried to the wards in buckets, and excreta
removed in the same way. The nurses and surgeons worked in continual danger to themselves. Three Colonial Service Sisters, Nell
McMillan, Grace Logan and Agnes Sim were killed by shrapnel as
they went about their work.

700 casualties were admitted in a day. They lay side by side in beds
and stretchers, under beds, in cupboards, in corridors and even on the
stairs. The dead were pulled out from among the living to be buried at
night in quicklime in pits dug in the once immaculate hospital grounds.

When the colony surrendered, on Sunday, 15th February, 9,000 wounded were among the prisoners of war, 3,400 of whom were at 'the General'. The Japanese ordered it to be cleared and handed over, complete with all stocks of food, medicines and equipment, within twenty-four hours. A mental institution which had been stripped of everything but the bare walls and where Japanese troops had already commandeered the kitchen, was provided in its place.

In the course of time, the fifty civilian nurses working here were sent to Changi internment camp with 300 other women and their children. With hindsight, it is tempting to say that it might have been wiser to allow all nurses to stay on the island, once the time for safe evacuation had passed. A very high price was paid by those who obeyed the instruction to leave on 12th and 13th February. Only fifteen escaped. The others were killed in bombing attacks, drowned, shot by the Japanese in cold blood or imprisoned in camps where many died from malnutrition.

Sister Mavis Hannah of the Australian Army Nursing Service speaks for them all.

'It was too late to try to escape, they should have let us stay and take our chance with the rest of the medical staff. I know they were thinking of Hong Kong, but which is worse – what happened to us or what happened to the nurses of Hong Kong?'

13

Shipwreck and Capture

Almost all of the eighty vessels which left Singapore on 13th February were sunk or captured by the Japanese, or blown up in minefields. Blazing crippled ships were scattered widely over the Java Sea. Their smoke stained every horizon and, for a while, the ocean teemed with men, women and children, until they either drowned or found an island to clamber upon. In ones and twos and in lifeboat loads, they landed on the myriad tropical islands of the Malay Archipelago, many of which were uninhabited. Where there was no water, the castaways perished. Where the Japanese were already in control, as in Banka Island off the Sumatran coast, they had no alternative but to give themselves up.

The *Vyner-Brooke* sank in fifteen minutes following the attack by Japanese planes on the morning of Saturday, 14th February. Her decks were a shambles, but Matron Paschke of the 2nd/10th Australian General Hospital had the satisfaction of seeing her nurses carry out her instructions to help the wounded and the civilians off the ship before leaving themselves. Then she, too, kicked off her shoes. 'Keep an eye on me, girls,' she called. 'I can't swim.' And she climbed down the rope ladder into the sea, into the flotsam of shipwreck, where the dead bumped against the living in a mess of barrels, crates, luggage, planks, galley refuse and thousands of dead fish. Amongst the many drowned that day was Kathleen Kinsella, Senior Sister of the 2nd/4th Australian CCS which had done so much good work at Bukit Panjong, Bukit Timah Road and later in the Rifle Club.

Survivors clinging to rafts and bits of wreckage were grateful for the strong currents which bore them towards the distant hill of Banka Island, and could also be thankful that exploding bombs had scared away the sharks which infest these waters. A boatload of wounded under the care of Matron Drummond of the 2nd/13th AGH and some of her Sisters covered the ten miles to the island without mishap. They immediately lit a fire on the darkening beach to serve as a guide to those still in the water. But at this point, the drag of the tide changed. The notoriously capricious currents common to this part of the world proceeded to make havoc of all further attempts to reach the shore. When the rafts and spars with their clinging cargoes were no more than three-quarters of a mile from the beach, they were whipped out to sea again, brought back and swept away once more in a cruel titillation by the sea, until the bright fire on the beach began to seem like some unattainable mirage to the hapless survivors in the water.

Mavis Hannah was one of sixteen people with a precarious handhold on a raft meant for two. She could not swim and was tugged to and fro in this fashion for two days before setting foot on dry land. A raft carrying Matron Paschke and some of her Sisters came within reach of the shore three times, only to be swept out to sea again. On the fourth run-in, Sister Betty Jeffrey and Sister Iole Harper slipped off to lighten the load and swam alongside. This time, it seemed a landing must be made. All were confidently borne forward until the voices of those ashore could be plainly heard, but the currents were not yet done with them. With deliverance so close at hand, the raft was swept out to sea once more and this time did not return.

Matron Paschke and her fellow Australians, Sisters Trennery, McDonald, Dorsch, Clarke and Ennis, the last-named with two small children on her lap, were swallowed up in the darkness of the night and not seen again.

The two swimmers, Betty Jeffrey and Iole Harper, were also carried away from the welcoming fire, and they were eventually washed into the midst of a mangrove swamp in another part of the island. Spiked roots tore at their arms and legs. Mosquitoes descended on them in clouds and nowhere would the swamps give a foothold. All night long, they swam in and out of muddy creeks seeking solid ground. Day came and then another night. They snatched at sleep, supported by branches. Desperate for fresh water, they struggled further into the depths of the swamps and, by the third day, were beginning to hallu- cinate when they were rescued by Malay fishermen who fed them and gave them shelter. After they were rested, however, their rescuers advised them to give themselves up. The Japanese already occupied the island and were known to deal savagely with any natives who helped the enemy.

Meanwhile, the party on the beach grew as more survivors came in from the sea, many of them wounded. Almost all suffered to some extent from blast due to the underwater explosions while they were in the sea, a condition which produced intense abdominal pain and fre- quently resulted in death at a later stage due to internal haemorrhage.

Women wearing elasticated girdles were noticeably less affected than men.

A spring of good water had been found and, with medical supplies brought from the ship, the nurses did their best for the wounded. Nevertheless, it was obvious by the second day that the more seriously injured would not survive without hospital treatment. Because of this and the fact that there was no food other than a few ship's biscuits, a decision was reached to surrender to the Japanese, who, according to local Malays, occupied the nearby town of Muntok.

A Naval officer in the party volunteered to approach them and surrender on behalf of them all, requesting that stretchers be brought for the seriously wounded. After he had gone, the elderly, accompanied by the walking wounded and all the civilian women except one who offered to stay behind to help the nurses, set off to walk through the scrub to Muntok at their own pace. Once there, they were interned in Muntok jail.

Left behind on the beach with the wounded, Miss Drummond and her party prepared themselves for their first encounter with the Japanese. When their envoy returned with an escort of Japanese soldiers and no stretchers, their anxiety sharpened; justifiably, it transpired.

All the men, wounded or otherwise, were ordered over the brow of a dune and there they were bayoneted to death. The soldiers reappeared, wiping the blood from their weapons as they came, and ordered the women to walk into the sea. They then proceeded to machine-gun them from behind. Only one of the twenty-two women survived. Sister Vivian Bullwinkel (ARRC, MBE, later Statham) of the 2nd/13th Australian General Hospital was shot through the left side. The bullet passed through her body above the hip without doing a great deal of harm, but it caused her to lose consciousness so that she fell into the water as if dead like the rest of her colleagues. The soldiers marched away, leaving the tide to carry ashore the victims of their incomprehensible barbarity.

Other survivors met with better treatment on surrendering and were sent to join the growing company in Muntok jail. Possibly the Japanese considered that severely wounded men were not worth saving and, having killed them, had to remove the witnesses.

The *Mata Hari*, which had left Singapore at the same time as the *Kuala* and the *Tien Kwang*, escaped detection from the air and had almost reached Banka Island, not knowing that it was already in the hands of the Japanese, when she was captured by an enemy ship. Armed only with one obsolete gun and carrying more than 300 women, her Captain had no option but to surrender. Phyllis Briggs and five of her Colonial Service colleagues were amongst those on board.

'A Japanese Naval officer came on board followed by two sailors carrying swords and was met by our Captain, standing at the salute, calm and polite, in immaculate uniform although he had not slept since leaving Singapore two days earlier. There was a moment of complete silence and I remember feeling icy cold despite the heat on deck. We women were told we could take one suitcase ashore. I could see one of the guards removing watches and rings so I knotted what jewellery I had into a scarf and tied it about my head. We spent the rest of the day and the following night on the jetty, without food or water. We had several wounded with us, including one man who had been severely injured when the *Prince of Wales* went down, but there was little we could do for them. It was almost noon the next day when we were ordered to walk to the jail, in the hottest part of the day. Once there, we were given a bucket of water to share amongst us, but no food.'

The coolie jail now put aside for prisoners of war was a collection of tin-roofed dormitories enclosing a concrete quadrangle. Truckloads of shipwrecked survivors arrived over the next few days, having been picked up on different parts of the island. Soon the building which had been designed to house 200 coolies held 600 men, women and children.

Irish QA Mary Cooper, who had argued the toss with Lady Diana Cooper, was here, with hands badly lacerated from sliding down a ship's rope. Australian Sisters from the wreck of the *Vyner-Brooke* began to arrive in ones and twos as they were picked up by the Japanese; Veronica Clancy, unabashed in a man's greatcoat over her corsets for she had used her uniform as a sail to bring her raft to shore, and Iole Harper and Betty Jeffrey, with hands and legs badly infected by mangrove thorns. Thirty-four of the original sixty-five who had sailed on the *Vyner-Brooke* were still unaccounted for when Vivian Bullwinkel arrived, holding a water bottle to her side to hide a telltale bullet hole in her shirt. From her the fate of Matron Drummond and twenty Sisters was learned.

The hole in the shirt was quickly patched and the story not

mentioned again, for fear of putting Vivian's life at risk. The Japanese would scarcely cherish a living witness to their depravity. She was the last Australian Sister to make an appearance. The remaining twelve had drowned.

As well as this considerable number of nurses in the jail, there were five doctors, two of them women. They took over an old guard room as a surgery and endeavoured to treat the wounded. No assistance was forthcoming from the Japanese and the doctors had no equipment or drugs other than their personal emergency kits.

When permission was refused to send RAF officer Armstrong to the native hospital for amputation of his gangrenous foot, the only course open to the doctors was to operate themselves in the far from satisfactory conditions at the jail. The man's life depended on immediate operation and the doctors requested instruments and anaesthetic from the Japanese, both of which were refused. Since there was no alternative, the operation was carried out without anaesthetic using a saw contrived from an old kitchen knife. Fortunately the patient was too ill to be aware of much that was going on but when, a few days later, the other foot had to be amputated under similar conditions, he did not survive.

Incidents like this brought home to the medical staff the fact that they were dealing with people whose traditions included no compassion for the weak and the wounded. This was confirmed in the case of a man who lay on the floor of the surgery waiting to have his abdominal injury dressed by the nurses. A passing guard casually ground his heel in the open wound. These were the men who would wield the power of life and death over thousands of captive men and women in a future which looked more grim with every day that passed. There were some exceptions to this inherent cruelty, but not many.

The vexatious currents which had so bedevilled the survivors of the *Vyner-Brooke* brought the same confusion to the numerous wrecks over the Java Sea. The *Kuala* was fortunately near the island of Pompong when she sank, and most of her survivors managed to struggle ashore. QA Naomi Davies, however, holding on to a wooden box, was in danger of being swept out to the open sea when she was hauled on board a crowded lifeboat. At the oars were Mr Arthur Ross of the Malayan Government Service and Dr Margaret Thomson, who had been severely injured in the previous day's bombing attacks. With every stroke of the oars the deep sutures inserted in her thigh by Dr

Lyon could be seen to cut through the flesh, but the stoic doctor kept to her post. Swept far away from Pompong, the boat made a landing late that night on the uninhabited island of Kebat and the party of thirty-nine, many of whom were wounded, thankfully went ashore. Dr Thomson and Sister Davies did what they could for the injured before settling down for the night on the beach. Close by Sister Davies' side lay an unattended little girl of eight years old.

Jean Duncan's Scottish father had stayed to fight for Singapore when the child was put on board the *Kuala*. In the confusion of the shipwreck, Jean had become separated from her Chinese mother and two baby sisters. Arthur Ross pulled her from the water and Naomi Davies took upon herself responsibility for the child, a trust she was to keep until the end of the war.

Next day, the grim discovery that there was no fresh water on the island was made. A two-gallon keg from the lifeboat was the sole supply for more than forty people, for survivors from other wrecks were being washed ashore, some of whom had been gravely wounded in the Japanese attacks.

Amongst them was D. H. Kleinman, one-time tennis champion of Malaya. When he died of his wounds, Naomi Davies reclaimed the slacks that she had lent him to replace his own trousers, which had been lost during the shipwreck. He had been the second recipient. The first, a sailor from the *Prince of Wales*, had also died of wounds. Three years later, Naomi sold the slacks over the fence of an internment camp for an egg.

Pompong Island, small, uninhabited and covered in dense jungle, offered not so much as a coconut in the way of food to the 600 men and women who were castaways there, but there was at least a good spring of water. Dr Marjorie Lyon's first priorities were the wounded. She had swum ashore supporting her wounded colleague, Dr Elsie Crowe, and now, with the help of those nurses who had survived the attack, she set up a sick bay under the shelter of some trees at the edge of the beach.

Using branches of trees as poles, the nurses improvised stretchers from their elasticated roll-on girdles and waded into the shallows to carry the wounded in from the sea. Matron Spedding was among them. Kit Woodman had managed to swim safely to the island, despite the fact that two lengths of the swimming pool back home had previously been the extent of her prowess. With the other nurses, she was now doing what she could for the injured. A few medical supplies had been brought from the ship and strips torn from their uniforms served as bandages. They all carried morphia, so at least the agony of the dying could be eased. The men and women treated by Dr Lyon with such skill were unaware of their good fortune to be in the hands of such an experienced surgeon. She amputated the leg of a young woman in a lifeboat, and carried out much essential surgery on the beach.

On this small island, no more than a quarter of a mile wide, were gathered hundreds of men, women and children from different races and different walks of life, uprooted from their homes and fearful for the future. Dissensions quickly arose. Selfishness surmounted any consideration for the common good when the small amount of food rescued from the ship was rationed out. In an atmosphere of growing tension, the threat of crowd hysteria and the break-down of order was very real. Some of the more responsible in this shipwrecked community were forced to take control.

Group Captain Nunn of the Malayan Volunteer Air Force had somehow managed to retain his revolver.

'I'll shoot the first bugger who panics,' said the man who, a few short weeks ago, had been the Director of Public Works in Malaya. With the support of Squadron-Leader Farwell RAF, the heat was taken out of the situation.

'What a sorry sight we are without the trappings of civilisation,' was Kit Woodman's unspoken thought.

With assistance from certain of the Malay Police Force who were still free and of loyal islanders, survivors who had access to a craft of any kind lost no time in organising an escape route to the west coast of Sumatra, where it was still possible to pick up a passing British ship. The large island of Sinkep, which was still in Dutch hands, was chosen as a staging point before crossing the open sea to Sumatra. To this end, every available vessel was put into use and the islands in the area searched for survivors.

The arrival at Pompong of the rescue ship, the *Tanjong Penang*, was greeted with relief. Silently, under cover of darkness, for Japanese scout planes patrolled the daytime skies, the island trader crept up to the island. 150 women and children were already on board, picked up from another island, but she was prepared to take all of Pompong's wounded who could be moved, in addition to a further 250 women and children. Jean Duncan's mother and her two little sisters were amongst those who thankfully went on board. That grieving mother would never know that her eldest daughter had survived the wreck of the *Kuala*.

Embarking the wounded in pitch darkness was a difficult operation and the Captain requested that some nurses travel on the ship with the patients. Sister Margot Turner QAIMNS (DBE, RRC, later Matron-in-Chief QARANC) and Sister Beatrice Le Blanc Smith QAIMNS were two who sailed. After bedding down their patients in the hold, the nurses found space for themselves on the crowded decks as the *Tanjong Penang* pulled up anchor and slid silently away into the dark night.

The thought uppermost in the minds of all those who were left on Pompong was that they had just said goodbye to their only chance of escape. Yet, before morning, the rescue ship had joined the other vessels at the bottom of the Java Sea and most of those who had sailed away with such hope were dead, including the family of Jean Duncan.

Japanese planes had attacked at dawn. The ship's hold containing all the wounded and most of the women was totally destroyed. As the vessel burst into flames and rolled over on her side, Sister Turner and Sister Le Blanc Smith slid into the sea, shipwrecked for the second time in three days.

Darkness added extra terror to this disaster, for those in need could only be traced by their cries. Although wounded in the attack, Beatrice Le Blanc Smith helped Margot Turner to tie two rafts together and shepherd fourteen people to them, of whom six were children and two mere babies. By putting four women back to back on the rafts with children on their knees, the remainder of the party had space to hold on to the ropes.

The two Sisters swam around their charges, encouraging them to hang on, but when daylight came, two were found to have slipped away. Beatrice Le Blanc Smith was more seriously wounded than she had allowed. Alarmed at the deterioration in her friend's condition, Sister Turner insisted she take a place on the raft. She was found to have a massive wound of the buttock and died that afternoon.

The following day brought no sign of rescue nor of any other survivors. The raft was now alone on an empty sea without shelter from a blazing sun. By the end of the second day, all six children had died, totally deranged by the sun, and the last of the women holding to the ropes drifted away. By the third day, only Sister Turner and one other woman remained, sitting back to back on the raft. When this last companion overbalanced and was swept away by the vicious currents, Sister Turner was alone. Rain fell during the third night and she was able to catch a few drops in the lid of her powder compact. She ate a few strands of seaweed which came within her reach but when she was rescued on the fourth day by a Japanese destroyer, she was too weak to move. Burnt by the sun and totally dehydrated, she was hoisted on board more dead than alive.

There are certain acts of kindness performed by the Japanese which go some way to redress the list of their crimes against humanity. From the Japanese doctor on board the destroyer, Sister Turner received the greatest consideration and attention. He fed her himself with sips of water and bread soaked in milk under the shade of a deck awning, and replaced her dirty uniform with a clean pair of trousers and a shirt. When the ship tied up at Muntok pier later in the day, he carried her ashore himself.

Sister Phyllis Briggs was on duty at the surgery in the jail when this very sick woman dressed in Japanese shirt and trousers was carried in on a stretcher.

'She was burnt black by the sun, her eyes sunk deep into her head. Until she spoke, I had no idea that she was English.'

The multiple shipwrecks which befell the last exodus from Singapore obscure the fate of many. Two QAs, Sister Hervey-Murray and Sister McClelland, left a small island in a sampan. Neither they nor their native boatman were ever seen again. The Java Sea, with its sharks, fierce currents and blazing sun, was probably responsible for many of the unaccounted dead.

Soon after the departure of the ill-fated *Tanjong Penang* from Pompong, other smaller craft appeared. Loyal Malays risked their lives by ferrying survivors in relays from the smaller islands to Sinkep where a modern Dutch hospital was available in the town of Daboh. Doctors and nurses moved in, grateful for the hospital's facilities, and began to deal with urgent surgery without delay. Here the wounded could be properly rested, their wounds dressed and plasters applied, before they proceeded to Sumatra.

Arthur Ross's party of castaways on Kebat Island were rescued on the fourth day from that waterless place by a Chinese junk, and they eventually reached Sinkep after two weeks of island-hopping in different craft. Dr Thomson was able to have her injured thigh treated and encased in plaster before resuming her care of the patients.

When the last of these had passed through Daboh, it was time for the doctors and nurses to go. Arthur Ross had been assisting with the escape route until now and came to say goodbye to Dr Thomson and Sister Davies who had shared with him the ordeals of the last few weeks. Since he could not claim any immunity which, questionably, the Red Cross might afford, he would not travel with the hospital party but made his own arrangements to leave that night by native sampan.

The doctors and nurses, with the last of the patients, prepared to leave Sinkep. There was no time to be lost as Japanese troops spread over the nearby mainland and enemy scout planes were beginning to show an increasing interest in the island. British planters in the region delayed their own escape in order to help the hospital staff to safety. Five doctors, four of them women, and sixteen nurses made up of six QAs, four Colonial Sisters and six members of the Indian Military Nursing Service, and the remaining patients, split up into small parties for the trip across the open sea to Sumatra. Various small craft navigated by planters or Malays made the crossing safely, but the motor launch carrying Dr Thomson, Sister Netta Smith and patients had to turn back to Daboh with engine trouble, and found there a Japanese patrol waiting to imprison them.

The rest of the hospital party successfully navigated the River Indragiri in central Sumatra as far as the town of Tambilihan. Here the patients were allowed to rest before continuing on the next arduous stretch to the coast. Japanese troops were closing in from the north and the south, but the central route of escape was still open. Dutch colonists living in the area helped in every way possible, putting their excellent Dispensary at the service of the patients. In ones and twos and by whatever means possible, the escaping party made their way over the mountains. Kit Woodman and Canadian QA Mary Charman were given a lift by members of the Dutch Home Guard who, in a last brave and futile gesture, were on their way to confront the Japanese.

Time, however, had already run out for Kit, Mary and many more. When they reached their destination, the once busy port of Padang, the harbour was empty of ships. The docks were crowded with troops and civilians but the last ship had gone. The week before, the Naval cruiser *Danae* had made an unscheduled refuelling stop and had taken on board all 700 refugees hopefully waiting there. All who arrived after the *Danae* sailed were too late.

Resigned now to imminent capture, Kit and Mary located the

Padang Salvation Army Hospital and reported for duty. Here they found their colleagues, Sisters Naomi Davies, Lydia McLean, Louie Harley and K. M. Jenkins of the QAIMNS. Matron Miss Spedding was a patient, and Drs Lyon and Crowe were hard at work. Another woman doctor, Ethel Norris, had been among the lucky ones to escape.

There was nothing to be done now but await the arrival of Japanese troops.

When Arthur Ross eventually reached Britain, he wrote to Naomi Davies' sister in some distress:

'It seems that those left behind (in the hospital) never got away. I was very upset. Many of my friends were there and we had been through almost unbelievable experiences together. I last saw Naomi at the Daboh hospital on Sinkep Island, attending to the wounded.

'I had the honour to be leader of the party on Kebat Island and it is up to me to tell you of the courage of your sister. We had a terrible four days there with many wounded amongst us and only two gallons of water. We had no medical supplies or dressings. Bandages were made from torn-up clothing. Naomi was a tower of strength in the party, always cheerful and courageous. She helped me greatly by clearing away thorn bushes to make a camp on our arrival and when our water supply was almost finished, she *volunteered* to come out into the open with me to wave distress signals to the next passing Japanese plane. For the sake of the children amongst us, she was prepared to run the risk of being machine-gunned in cold blood. Thank God, the arrival of a Chinese junk saved us from this desperate measure.

'Unless you have heard to the contrary, Miss Davies is now a prisoner of war.

> Signed,
> Arthur Ross of the
> Malayan Government Service.'

All the nurses who did not escape were posted 'Missing' and stayed that way until two years later when, in 1944, hope was finally extinguished for some parents. For others came the good news of their daughters' survival, albeit as prisoners of the Japanese.

Kit Woodman's brother, serving in the Forces in India, repeatedly wrote home discouraging any hope that his sister might be alive. 'My mother never accepted that,' says Kit. 'She kept on making cakes for me.'

The Imperial Nipponese Army was no longer a subject to joke about. It was rapidly beginning to appear invincible as it spread with incredible speed over the islands of the Pacific and the Dutch East Indies. Landings had been made after days of severe aerial bombardment on the island of New Britain, marking the beginning of the bitter New Guinea Campaign.

Australian troops and Air Force had been pulled out of the region just before the Japanese landed in January, but the 2nd/10th Australian Field Ambulance, with six Sisters of the Australian Army Nursing Service on its staff, was left in charge of the wounded at the Mission House at Kokopo. On the morning when Japanese ships sailed into the harbour at Rabaul, the Sisters made the perplexing discovery that the two doctors of the unit and all twenty orderlies, complete with trucks, ambulances and all medical supplies, had been ordered back to the mainland during the night, leaving only the padre, John May, to face the Japanese at the Sisters' side.

Since there were no doctors in evidence, their claim to be nurses was disbelieved. 'You are here for the use of the soldiers,' the Japanese officer stated, 'and you will be shot.'

They were lined up on a verandah while a soldier with a machine gun took up a position some yards away. Lying flat on his stomach, he trained his gun upon them, manoeuvring it for a satisfactory field of fire. The nurses could only hope that their end would be quick. At this point, the execution order was postponed until the following day.

During the night that followed, the six Sisters had plenty of time to ponder their predicament, for sleep was impossible. They were aware that, even if a reprieve were granted, further ordeals would no doubt be in store for them. Each put a phial of morphia in her pocket to be used if life became too grim.

There was no execution and, although they were subjected to all manner of indecencies, the women were not molested. Large numbers of Japanese geisha girls, who had accompanied the invasion, moved into the Bishop's house and saw to the needs of the soldiers. Japanese troops took great pleasure in unbuttoning their trousers in front of the Australian women and in urinating over them, but they were otherwise left alone.

The Australian Sisters were allowed to continue their work at the hospital but with no drugs and little food, there was little they could do for their patients. Six months later, all the patients were interned in Rabaul POW camp and Sisters M. J. Anderson (ARRC), D. Keast (later McPherson), M. Cullin, E. Callaghan and I. Whyte, under their Senior Sister Kathleen Parker (ARRC, later Sly) were put on board the *Naruto Maru* for Japan, joining ten civilian nurses and sixty-five Australian officers in a filthy hold. Once in Japan, the nurses were separated from the other prisoners and put to manual labour, to cut down trees and cart firewood and coal, to sweep the streets and empty latrines, and, if their masters considered that they were not working hard enough, they were beaten. For the next three and a half years, they were the slaves of the Japanese.

The impact of this cruel and enigmatic race on the people of the western world was considerable. The fact that the Japanese were no less cruel to their own people made them no less difficult to understand.

The fall of Singapore caused terrible casualties among the hundreds of nursing staff of many different nations who were in the region. The Singapore Memorial carries the names of forty-eight Matrons and Nursing Sisters of the Queen Alexandra's Imperial Military Nursing Service and Reserve, of the Territorial Army Nursing Service, of the Indian Military Nursing Service and the Auxiliary Indian Nursing Service Reserve, who lost their lives during the fall of Singapore. Forty-one Matrons and Nursing Sisters of the Australian Army Nursing Service lost their lives, many of them machine-gunned on Banka Beach. Forty-nine Nursing Sisters of the Colonial Service lost their lives during the Malayan Campaign and are listed in the Nurses' Roll of Honour in Westminster Abbey in London (see Appendix C).

14

1942 ... Darkest before the Dawn

Before the war, Sisters of the QAIMNS did not nurse Indians. The prestigious British Military Hospitals staffed by the RAMC and the QAIMNS in such well-established bases as Poona, Quetta and Allahabad provided a high standard of care for British forces and comfortable living conditions for the staff. There were well-run Indian Military Hospitals staffed by Indian doctors and orderlies to care for Indian servicemen. Indian civilian hospitals were something else entirely, where hygiene was non-existent, where bedpans were emptied into an open drain which ran down the centre of the ward and sepsis was a built-in feature.

Sister Gwendoline Jones, QAIMNS (later RRC), was the first QA to work in an Indian Military Hospital. In 1941, she accompanied an RAMC officer to the province of Gowali, 7,000 feet up in the Himalayas, with the blessing of the Principal Matron of India and a grant of 200 rupees with which to open a hospital.

The Gowali Regiment was about to return to its depot after covering itself with glory in the North African campaign. The medical officer and Sister Jones were to arrange for the proper treatment of its wounded. Intensely proud of their regiment, the Gowali tribespeople were eager to help. A building suitable for a hospital was soon found and, within a week, Gwendoline Jones had a staff of eight volunteers, made up of Indians, Eurasians and Muslims. There were two trained nurses amongst them. The others were without experience, but became good orderlies and auxiliary nurses under supervision. Their basic kindness was of inestimable value to one overworked doctor and a QA who was Matron, Theatre Sister, Home Sister and Ward Sister all in one.

The remoteness of the area caused many difficulties. Even a simple X-ray involved the patient in a fifty-mile drive by ambulance down an indifferent road, followed by an overnight train journey. The grant of 200 rupees provided only the bare essentials, so equipment was scanty. A small generator supplied electricity for use in the theatre only, otherwise lamps were used. In all things other than actual nursing, however, the Regiment could be relied upon for help.

After this very successful Indo-British unit had been established, the line of demarcation between the two types of hospital disappeared. QAs began to serve in Indian General Hospitals (IGHs) along with trained Sisters of the Indian Military Nursing Service (IMNS) and the Combined British/Indian General Hospital (CGH) came into being.

When Japan invaded Burma, India's position in the Far Eastern arena of war leapfrogged from backwater to first line of defence. Casualties of the 17th British/Indian Division began to flow into eastern India as Japanese troops pressed northwards. With her considerable experience in nursing Indian troops, Sister Jones was sent as Assistant-Matron to the 75th IGH on the Indian side of the Brahmaputra River in north-east India. Here a handful of RAMC officers, QAs and Indian Sisters received the Indian wounded as they were brought out of the jungles of Burma. Their hospital was a collection of tents and one old Indian building infested with snakes and rats.

Orderlies and auxiliaries were drawn from the locality, but the poverty-stricken jute plains of Bengal lacked the culture of the more prosperous Gowalis. The young girls who came to work at the hospital had never seen knives and forks before, and the sepoys had never worn boots, but they all learned to look after the sick with devotion.

Hospital equipment, such as it was, was provided by the Indian Red Cross. Even basic materials like paper were in short supply, and considerable ingenuity was needed to surmount the deficiencies. Therapy charts were made from the slips of paper inside cigarette packets. Sections of cardboard cut from the packets were dyed with certain lotions obtainable from the Dispensary – Lotio Rubra, Gentian Violet and Brilliant Green – to represent different diets. After the medical officer's daily round of the wards, each patient was given a card, from the colour of which the *bheestie*, who spoke no English, would deduce the kind of food he must serve.

'We were a unit on our own,' says Miss Jones. 'We were hundreds of miles from any other British unit, and there was no-one to see if we bent the rules occasionally. During a particularly cold spell, casualties who were about to leave on stretchers for the long drive to the next hospital begged to be allowed to take their blankets with them. This was highly irregular, but we could not send them away cold. The day of reckoning came when the Quartermaster was called upon to account for the disappearance of so many of the blankets on his inventory.

Casting his eye wildly about the store in search of an explanation, he caught sight of a scurrying iguana and, in a flash of inspiration, wrote "Eaten by iguana" in the appropriate column. The change in diet of a creature normally satisfied with small insects passed unremarked at HQ.'

At this time, every encounter with the Japanese was a disaster for the retreating Burma Army. After Rangoon was lost, the trickle of casualties arriving in India from Burma swelled to a flood. Twice and sometimes thrice a week, ambulance trains brought a load of 400 wounded to the 75th IGH, all of whom had to be treated and evacuated to base hospitals as quickly as possible to prevent the system from grinding to a halt. By dedicated maintenance, a team of RASC drivers, each of whom was later 'Mentioned in Dispatches', managed to keep a fleet of twelve ambulances on the road at all times.

The catering for such large numbers of patients at the 75th IGH was, in Miss Jones' words, 'sketchy'. There were no proper ovens, but occasionally a British Tommy on the retreat, whose unit was resting nearby, would volunteer as temporary cook and contrive some sort of makeshift oven. When the soldier's unit moved on, he would some-times be left behind, to be discovered weeks later working in the hospital kitchens. Such confusion was possible in the mêlée of troops pulling out of Burma at this time. They had been fighting in difficult jungle conditions for three months and now were drawn up at the very gateway to India. Air support had been wiped out by the Japanese Air Force. Most of the tanks and guns had been destroyed in the long trek north. A last stand formed along the Imphal plains near the Burma/Assam border, but the outlook was grim and morale was at rock bottom.

No support could come from the sea, for the Bay of Bengal was now totally under Japanese control after a great sea battle at the beginning of April in which the British Far Eastern Fleet had suffered heavy losses. Its remaining ships were compelled to seek safer anchorage in East Africa.

Not all the shipping casualties of this disastrous engagement were battleships. An innocent merchantman, the *Glenshiel* of the Glen Line, carrying general cargo and a few passengers from Calcutta to Freman-tle in Western Australia, inadvertently strayed into the battle scene and found herself facing two hostile periscopes at dawn on Good Friday, 3rd April. As the first torpedo struck home, passengers clambered into the lifeboats and were winched away by the Chinese crew, but the boat which carried Sister Gibbs, QAIMNS, leaked badly as soon as it touched the water. The pump was found to be out of action and the sailors began baling with whatever came to hand. Sister Gibbs, who had some experience of handling a boat, helped to row away from the stricken ship.

'Look, Missee!' One of the Chinese sailors grabbed her arm. A torpedo was flashing towards them, just below the surface of the water. It passed directly beneath the lifeboat and set off another huge explosion in the *Glenshiel*. One of the two attacking submarines now surfaced, blazing away with its guns trained on the bridge of the sinking ship, where figures were still plainly visible. Sixteen shells passed over the heads of the terrified occupants of the lifeboat before the *Glenshiel* finally went down. Satisfied at last, the submarine submerged, leaving a few small boats milling around in a sea covered with debris.

Prospects for the survivors were not hopeful. In Sister Gibbs' party, there was one other woman, a young Chinese with a baby of a few months. The rest were government officials bound for Australia, British ship's officers and Chinese crew members. They were hundreds of miles from any land in a badly leaking boat, and so near to the equator that the limit of endurance in an open boat would be four days at the most.

As the boat took in more and more water, everything which could be spared was thrown overboard to lighten the load. A few blankets and a piece of canvas were saved to make a shelter held together with Sister Gibbs' hairpins. The baling went on, non-stop, with tin hats and with topees until they became too sodden to be of any further use. Even the attaché case of a government official was put to use after its secret documents had been torn up and scattered over the ocean. Three months of hard work in Delhi on behalf of the Australian Government were destroyed in a few minutes. Meanwhile, the men worked desperately to repair the damaged pump, but it was another twelve hours before it could be made to function.

Sister Gibbs' official report continues: 'Sharks appeared in great numbers around our boat. Fortunately, they seemed dazed by the explosions and we beat them over the head with the oars when they came too close. We hoisted our red sail and yellow flag but there was not a vestige of a breeze. We covered our heads with odd handkerchieves and towels. I had saved the top of my topee, dried it in the sun and now wore it strapped to my head with a towel.

'We shared our cigarettes and had a ration of two prunes and two ounces of water each. I made the baby's feed of Nestlé's milk and water. The young mother begged me to 'put her baby to sleep' if matters became desperate, and I gave her my word. It amazed me to see how quickly the little party became organised. Seamen are indeed wonderfully kind.'

Nevertheless, hope was wearing thin when the pump miraculously jogged into life. By this time Sister Gibbs was standing up to row, with water above her knees. Two hours later, they were rescued by a Naval destroyer, one of many searching for survivors from the 116,000 tons of shipping sunk during this battle. The survivors were taken 500 miles away to a ship which had been damaged and could take no further part in the engagement. Sister Gibbs, in a sailor's white shirt and shorts, reported to the medical officer on board for duty.

'The next day, we were told to expect more survivors. The cruisers *Dorsetshire* and *Cornwall*, the aircraft carrier *Hermes* and several merchant ships had all been sunk near the site of our disaster. We took sixty badly burned sailors on board and, as I was the only nurse, the ship's surgeon asked for volunteers to help me care for them. The Chief Steward had been in the RAMC in the First World War, and he was of great assistance. I had my emergency kit of dressings and some sedatives, and we had picric and tannic acid in the ship's medical store with which to treat the burns.

'Several days later, a tanker drew alongside and, to my dismay, I was requested to get on board. I did not want to leave the patients but I was ordered to do so. I then had to board the tanker by a terrifying walk across a plank, and we set off for Ceylon with a little corvette going back and forth across our bows until we reached Colombo on 17th April. I learned later that all the patients I had been forced to leave reached South Africa in safety.'

In 1942, a catalogue of disasters took place. In February, American ships taking shelter in Darwin harbour, Northern Australia, were pounced upon by Japanese planes. Twenty-one American and Australian ships were sunk or severely damaged, and shore installations, including two hospitals, were destroyed. A bomb went straight down the funnel of the 1st Australian hospital ship, the *Manunda*, killing ten

of the medical staff, one of whom was Sister Margaret August de
Mestre. Another Sister, Lorraine Blow, was seriously wounded.

The *Manunda* sent her lifeboats into the harbour to rescue survivors
and brought them back to her operating theatre for treatment, despite
the considerable confusion on her own decks due to the bomb. She
also took casualties from the shore, since both hospitals there were out
of action. Her staff worked right through the night. In the morning,
although disabled, she managed to sail to Fremantle for repairs, and
she was back in service within six months, in time for the New Guinea
Campaign.

This campaign brought the war into Australia's own backyard. Certain Australian Divisions, which had already proved their worth in the
Middle East, were recalled to fight in New Guinea, in some of the
most difficult fighting terrain in the world, where roads were no more
than jungle tracks. In this first encounter with the Japanese, the Australians were beaten back over the Owen Stanley mountains until the
Japanese were within a few miles of Port Moresby, the jumping-off
point for Australia.

The troops' morale was at its lowest, their valour reduced by the
incipient suspicion that the Japanese were indeed invincible. In the six
months which had passed since Pearl Harbor, these once under-
estimated men had carried all before them, sweeping aside all oppo-
sition. At this critical moment for Australia's safety, the American
Fleet attacked and scattered a Japanese invasion force heading for Port
Moresby, and the victory put fresh heart into the troops fighting on
land. The 7th Australian Division guarding Port Moresby against the
landward advances of the Japanese drew up defence lines on Imita
Ridge, some miles from the port, and allowed no further passage. The
battles that followed were long and bloody, but the Division gave no
more ground.

In the Middle East, the battles in the Libyan desert continued to
use up men and materials, without any lasting gain of territory. The
victories of late 1941 were rapidly overturned in February 1942 when
Rommel recaptured Benghazi. 'Benghazi for Christmas, Egypt for New
Year' was a bitter joke amongst men who said that the letters MEF
stood not for Middle East Forces but for Men England Forgot. They
had spent two years fighting backwards and forwards across the desert
with nothing to show but wooden crosses in the sand marking places
where their comrades had fallen.

After Benghazi, Tobruk was the next to be lost. Determined not to repeat his earlier mistake of leaving a fortified enemy port behind his lines, Rommel set his sights on taking the town. He surrounded Tobruk with armour and overlaid it with a blanket of bombs.

Inside the doomed town, the 62nd BGH and the 2nd/2nd Australian CCS were fighting a losing battle against mounting casualties. Towards the end, rank amongst doctors, nurses and orderlies was no longer considered important, as each got on with the job in hand. A sergeant who had been a bus driver in Kent before the war was in charge of the Blood Transfusion Unit. It was here that the hospital ship, the *Somersetshire*, covered herself with glory, earning the nickname of the 'Old Tobruk War-Horse' for making eleven trips from Tobruk harbour to Alexandria with casualties and under fire.

Rommel was not to be denied his victory, and the town which had so gallantly withstood a seven-month siege the previous year was forced to surrender. When the end was near, the Sisters were ordered to withdraw.

'We could not have been more distressed,' wrote Miss Dunn, Matron of the 62nd BGH, 'nor more loath to leave the hundreds of dying and wounded men in the hospital. The RAMC were left to shoulder the whole burden, with the certain prospect of becoming POWs, yet we were shown only the greatest kindness and understanding of our position by all ranks.'

The Sisters escaped by ambulance down the coast road. Two days later, Tobruk surrendered, thereby placing in Rommel's hands a rich storehouse of supplies and large stocks of petrol which were to serve him well in what he confidently hoped would be his final attack on Egypt.

At this point, the High Command of the MEF was changed. General Alexander arrived to become Commander-in-Chief and Lt General Bernard Montgomery took over the command of the Eighth Army. Their impact was as dramatic as a blood transfusion.

'There will be no withdrawals,' Montgomery stated unequivocally, and he set about building up his demoralised troops in the short time left to him before Rommel reached Egypt. Men who had spent the previous months looking over their shoulders were infected by the drive of the new leaders and reassured by the timely arrival at Suez of large shipments of tanks and armaments. Endless lines of trucks carrying reinforcement troops drove through the dust of the canal zone to take up position at El Alamein. As a last line of defence, the Nile itself was fortified and its bridges mined. With restored confidence, men prepared for the fateful battle.

All women who could be spared, some Army Nursing Sisters along with ATS, WAAFs, WRNS and FANYs, were evacuated from Egypt. Those QAs who remained would run the hospitals with the help of orderlies. They kept at hand a packed bag, in case flight became necessary. Miss Miller, Matron of Number 1 BGH, took to wearing an outsize hatpin in her head veil. 'No German,' she vowed, 'will take me without a fight.'

All through the summer of 1942, Rommel advanced towards Egypt. While elements of the Eighth Army fought a delaying action, the main body of men was being prepared for the final confrontation. There was to be nothing haphazard about this battle. The time, the place and the probable course of events had been worked out by Montgomery, whose confidence was reflected in the men who were now being asked to make further sacrifices.

The hospitals were cleared in readiness for casualties. All patients who were able to carry a gun, even those suffering from dysentery or hepatitis who were not critically ill, were sent to rejoin their units. The seriously ill were evacuated to Palestine or South Africa, many against their will. One patient with a serious leg wound, who was on the evacuation list for South Africa, pleaded to be left in Egypt.

'They might send me to England, Sister. God knows I want to see my wife and kids again, but those swine killed some of my mates at Tobruk and I want to have another go at them.'

But he had to go, and Sister Kitty O'Connor made up his bed for someone else. The next time she glanced in the direction of the Canal, she could see no funnels. All shipping had been withdrawn. It gave her a lonely feeling.

The day which would affect so many lives arrived. A solemn service of intercession was held for the troops in the Garrison Church in Cairo, after which the soldiers went to their posts, and the nurses to their empty wards, to wait. The Battle of El Alamein began on 23rd October and lasted for twelve days.

15

El Alamein and After

The guns of the great battle could be heard quite clearly in Cairo. When the pavement outside the British Embassy was seen to be littered with torn-up papers, the shop girls drew their own conclusions as to which way the fortunes of war were heading and judiciously decided to favour the winners. With arms full of flowers and gifts of cigarettes and bottles of wine, they set off to meet Rommel's conquering troops. However, the soldiers coming down the road were not Germans, but Australians in transit, who promptly relieved the girls of their presents and sent them packing with a few memorable phrases.

For several days, the outcome of this head-on confrontation between giants hung in the balance. Casualties were heavy on both sides. Ambulances driven by RAMC men, FANYs and Quaker Friends were positioned to pick up the wounded from the Advanced Dressing Stations where medical officers worked in the field. The medical staff on ambulance trains also carried out urgent treatment as they whisked their loads away from the scene of battle to the rapidly filling base hospitals.

QA Joan Wilson had been working at the 63rd BGH at Helmieh since her escape from Greece the previous year, and was now Night Superintendent there.

'It took me two hours to get round our 1,880 patients, but I made a point of seeing the very ill at least twice a night. My report for Matron was a nightmare. I generally started it about 11 pm and wrote steadily all night long until 5 am, by which time my fingers ached. The report had to contain all new admissions, listed by name, rank, age, number and unit, diagnosis and condition; all patients with a temperature over one hundred degrees or who were on the Dangerously Ill list or the Seriously Ill List; all operations and all deaths. At 5 am I would start my morning round.'

Doctors and Sisters at each hospital were on 'convoy duty' to receive casualties one night in three. Those men not in need of immediate surgery were given a hot meal. The walking wounded were sent to the bath as soon as possible, which was an indescribable comfort to men who had been caked in sweat and dust for days. Stretcher cases often fell asleep as the Sisters bathed them.

The large Up-Patients' Dining Room at the 63rd BGH made an excellent reception area where casualties were examined before being sent to the wards. The Matron, Miss Monica Johnson, was working here, helping to pull forward the stretchers of those who were to be prepared for immediate operation.

A soldier, hearing her voice, called out, 'Who's that?'

'It's the Matron,' Miss Johnson answered. 'What do you want?'

Lance Corporal Gallup had been blinded by a mine and lay on a stretcher with his head heavily bandaged. 'My friend's here somewhere, Matron,' he said. 'He's lost his hands. If we're put together, maybe we can help each other.'

Although these particular injuries would normally have been nursed in different wards, the two mates were given adjoining beds. Between them they had one pair of hands and one pair of eyes to take them to the ablutions, to the NAAFI and finally back home to England.

At the end of twelve days' fighting, the German Army fell back and a jubilant Eighth Army gave chase. The Battle of El Alamein had been won at the cost of 13,500 British and Commonwealth lives, and enough wounded to fill all the military hospitals in Egypt.

There was nothing the Sisters would not do to recompense the men for their sacrifice of life and limb. The wounded, in their turn, were unfailingly grateful for any service, as though they felt such consideration to be undeserved. For many, the sight of a Sister in some forward position was an unexpected reassurance. One wrote home to his mother, 'They took me to a hospital and there were British nurses there. This was a bit of a surprise and bucked me up considerably.'

General Montgomery was well aware of the beneficial effect of a female nurse on a wounded man's morale. He firmly believed that the presence of Sisters in forward areas calmed and comforted injured men, and gave them the assurance that they would be properly nursed.

A man who until recently has been full of health and vigour, part of the conformity of the parade ground, the canteen and the battlefield, experiences a terrible aloneness when suddenly enfeebled in a hospital bed. Without the warning afforded by civilian illness, he is transformed in an instant from manliness to an object of pity. His mates make their clumsy boots behave reverently at his bedside but clatter away in guilty relief when the time comes to go. They make the joke about the pretty nurse, try not to look at his tubes and bottles, and say they will come again. But until they, too, lose a leg or an arm, their sight or their guts, they will not understand what is meant by that word which is engraved on every war memorial: 'sacrifice'.

The mutilated man lying in his quiet bed has plenty of time for reflection. His intermediary between life as it was and how it will be in the future is his nurse. The bond between them is a kind of aphysical love. Temporarily, she is mother, wife and sister in one female image.

Her feelings towards a man reduced to helplessness through no fault of his own are masked by professionalism; nevertheless they are often deep and painful.

A wounded Desert Rat looked up from his bed at the slim figure of QA Dinah Lidster (later Taylor) as she laid a light finger on his pulse.

'Don't let go my hand, Sister,' he pleaded. 'I haven't seen a woman for two years.'

The right formula for a hospital ward is not easy to define. Beside the decorum and the gravity there is always humour.

'What do I call you?' asked the newly enlisted QA upon meeting her first Bombadier.

'Just forget about the "Bomba" bit, Sister,' came the confident reply.

This harmless fun was probably in the mind of a Tank Corps Major as he bade farewell to Sister Kitty O'Connor on being evacuated from Number 2 BGH. Kitty had been responsible for dressing the extensive burns from which he had at one time seemed likely to die. Now his stretcher was being loaded aboard a plane bound for England.

'We are all so glad you are going home,' Kitty told him. 'We have been terribly worried about you.'

'I would not have pulled through at all,' he said, 'had it not been for the marvellous musical-comedy atmosphere of the ward.'

Florence Nightingale would have understood that statement, although she might have expressed it differently, for it is exactly this environment which can make a desperately injured man want to go on living.

When the patient lost the will to live, there was little that anyone could do to help. A wife's infidelity went deeper than a bullet and could kill just as surely. Upon being reprimanded by the ward Sister

for his unco-operative behaviour, a young soldier suffering from malaria broke his habitual silence. His wife had left him for another man.
Their child was in an institution and their home up for sale.

'So you see, Sister, I don't care what happens to me now. I tried to
stop a bullet and didn't succeed. Malaria is not going to kill me.'

On discharge from hospital, he returned to the desert and was
posthumously awarded the Military Medal for bravery in the face of
the enemy.

In November 1942, Tobruk was taken once more, and for the last
time, by the Eighth Army. Still at work in his Field Dressing Station
when he was finally relieved was a long-suffering RAMC surgeon.

'No-one pays any attention to visiting times in the desert,' he complained, on being overwhelmed once more by soldiers.

British wounded who had been left behind in Tobruk Hospital when
the town surrendered were full of praise for the German General
Rommel. The 'Desert Fox' never failed to visit his seriously wounded
men every day when he was in their vicinity.

The port was in ruins, the harbour choked with the wrecks of ships,
but never again would Tobruk be fought over in this conflict. Desert
Rats in hospital in Egypt went wild with joy at the news and relived
every battle.

'Remember that banger? Blew us both into the middle of next week.'

'Aye, an' blew me ruddy leg orf, an' all.'

Rommel had met his match in the new, revitalised Eighth Army
and would never again threaten the Canal. The battle to push him out
of Africa went on, however, and casualties continued. Day after day,
week after week after week, surgeons operated for long hours at a
stretch in tents as hot as ovens, often at great personal risk, and always
with the utmost humanity.

As a civilian, Brigadier Eastwood had been an eminent orthopaedic
surgeon. He had volunteered for service overseas with the RAMC
despite having suffered a serious coronary attack. After a morning
spent operating in the desert, he collapsed and died, aged forty-three.
As his body, draped in a Union Jack, was carried through the surgical
lines, men on whom he had just operated were beginning to come
round from the anaesthetic. His convalescent patients stood in stunned
and respectful silence at the entrance to every ward.

The soldier standing by as his wounded mate was lifted on to a
stretcher was right when he said, 'You'll be all right, chum. There's

the whole of bloody Harley Street back there, waiting to fix you up.'

It was at the 63rd BGH at Helmieh that the idea of a central depot for sterile supplies was born. Until now, each medical unit had been responsible for sterilising its own dressings, theatre linen and gloves, no easy task for forward units with few facilities. The 63rd BGH now undertook to produce all sterile supplies for the area. Henceforth, there was a constant traffic of trucks arriving empty from the desert and returning loaded with sterile equipment to forward hospitals and Casualty Clearing Stations. The hospital which began in a barracks had grown over the years and was now an important medical base. In addition to its capacity for 1,800 patients, it possessed an X-ray department, a Blood Transfusion Centre and now the Central Sterile Supply.

New Zealand and South African wounded were nursed in their own hospitals, but casualties from the Australian 9th Division which fought so well at El Alamein were nursed in British hospitals as their own had been recalled for service in New Guinea. Some were admitted to the 63rd BGH and were a sore trial to Sister Joan Wilson who, after coping successfully with Greeks, Poles and Yugoslavs, found the ultimate challenge in the Australian soldier.

'They were a wild lot,' she wrote. 'Their courage and endurance were superb. Some of them suffered dreadful pain but never complained. They would lie awake for hours, perspiration pouring down their faces, gritting their teeth and never saying a word. I used to walk around the ward but they would never call me and when I asked if they needed anything, they would just shake their heads and say, "I'm as good as a box o' birds." When I thought that things had gone far enough, I would insist that they have an injection to relieve the pain, but even then many would refuse or apologise for being a nuisance.

'But - oh! - when they were up on their feet, they were perfect devils. They were the most undisciplined crowd in the camp and broke out by any means. Two of my patients got out one night, went down to the town of Helmieh and got drunk. On being challenged by the guard on their return, they punched him on the nose. This meant serious trouble. I sent for them the next morning and gave them a good talking to. They listened meekly and apologised.

'Then one said to the other, "Shall we give it to her now?" and solemnly presented me with a small parcel. "We wanted to buy all of you Sisters a little pressie," they explained, "before we go back to the desert."

'The expression on their faces was so comical that I regret to say I burst out laughing. Of course, I should have given back the dear little pendant they had bought for me but I could not bear to hurt their feelings. I asked them what they had been doing until midnight.

' "Drinking Mr Churchill's health," they answered stoutly.

' "Well, Mr Churchill can't get you out of this mess," I told them. "Go and explain to the Commanding Officer."

'The ward MO saw them later in the day and asked how they had got on.

' "We saw the Old Man," they said. "He's not a bad old bugger but we've got to leave the hospital today."

'It was good judgement on the part of the Commanding Officer. A court-martial would not have changed them and they were excellent soldiers. Men like these walked straight into a minefield to clear a path for their mates and stuck to their guns until the last round was fired. We were sorry to see them go.'

Also in November, the siege of Malta was relieved and a combined British-American force was successfully landed in north-west Africa to harass Rommel's army from behind. By a miracle of good luck, this action, code-named 'Torch', achieved complete surprise. A fleet of troop carriers sailed undetected across the Bay of Biscay. Planes took off from Gibraltar's new extended runway and landings were made at Oran, Algiers and Casablanca.

German Intelligence was aware that a landing was imminent but mistakenly believed that Dakar on the west coast of Africa was the chosen site. Consequently the waters off that coast swarmed with alerted submarines as the date of the invasion drew near, and many innocent vessels not connected in any way with the operation were attacked and sunk.

A convoy of forty-four ships left Freetown in West Africa for Britain at the end of October, dangerously under-escorted with only the four corvettes that could be spared from the force prepared for 'Torch'. Submarines attacked almost at once. Joan Hunter-Bates (later Moore) and her friend, Marjorie Lloyd, were two of the nine QAs on board the SS *Stentor* (Alfred Holt and Blue Funnel Line) who were returning to Britain after a year's service in Nigeria with the 56th BGH. Their vessel was the first to be hit. There was a huge explosion as a torpedo found the cargo of manganese and the klaxon sounded 'Abandon Ship' immediately.

At this stage of the war, everyone who travelled by sea was constantly prepared for emergencies. The passengers and crew, in lifebelts and carrying their so-called 'panic bags' of a few cherished possessions, filed in an orderly way to take up boat-stations. The consignment of palm oil in one of the holds was now seeping through the alleyways but there was no panic.

'An image of that night which will never leave me,' writes Joan Hunter-Bates, 'is of seventy-five to a hundred faces on the main staircase, stoically waiting their turn to ascend to safety or to death. There was no pushing or shoving, just the plain, solid courage of ordinary people. Amongst those waiting, I saw Dr Stopford, the late Bishop of London, with his wife and two small sons, who were going home on leave from the Gold Coast. The boys, one carried by his father, another by an Army officer, both reached a lifeboat but their mother was too late. She descended by rope from the stern and her body was later recovered from under a life raft.

'To get out onto the deck from the staircase, I had to duck through a doorway of fire, for the bridge was ablaze. She was going down bows first and, as I struggled uphill to the stern, I was joined by "Taffy" Davis, a Territorial Army Sister. When we found that our lifeboat had already been launched and that we would have to jump about thirty feet to reach it, Taffy went back to a boat amidships which had not yet been launched. I climbed on to the rail and jumped into the water. When I surfaced, covered in oil, the *Stentor* was no more and Taffy Davis was not seen again.'

Marjorie Lloyd's foot was caught in the ship's ropes when she jumped from the boat-deck and she was hauled into a lifeboat with a twisted ankle as the ship went down. Yet when the corvette *Woodruffe* came to the rescue under cover of darkness, Marjorie somehow managed to climb the scramble net. The sailor waiting on deck to heave on board the clinging figures was expecting a man's weight and flung her high into the air.

'My God!' he said. 'It's a woman.' He had almost tossed Sister Lloyd back into the sea.

'We must have smelt terrible,' she writes, 'for we were covered in palm oil, but we had a rub-down and were given some of the crew's clothes. I was a peculiar sight in the Captain's tropical shorts kept up by a bootlace, a pyjama top and long seaboot stockings. Then we learned that four of our fellow QAs were missing.'

Four Army Sisters lost their lives on the SS *Stentor*.

Every night at dusk, enemy submarines returned to attack the convoy. Eleven of the original forty-four ships were sunk and the corvettes were crowded with survivors.

There were no corvettes nearby when the SS *Ceramic* (Shaw Savill and Albion Line) was sunk on 23rd November. The U-boat commander responsible claimed that she was part of the North African invasion fleet but her position west of the Azores clearly refuted this. In fact, she was carrying 650 women and children from the bombed cities of Britain to Australia. Also on board were twenty-six Sisters of the QAIMNS. who were to tranship at Durban for the Middle East, and one solitary serviceman. After he had sunk the *Ceramic*, the U-boat commander rescued only one person from the hundreds of helpless people in the water, far from any other shipping. He picked out the one serviceman and took him back to Germany as proof that the ship was a troop-carrier. All the crew, the women and children and the twenty-six Sisters of the QAIMNS, were lost.

16

The Miracle of Penicillin

In the opening stages of any assault landing, hospital ships play a vital part. During that interim period before a foothold ashore is consolidated, there is only one route for the wounded: back to the sea, where ships equipped with surgical facilities, doctors and nurses await them.

Throughout Operation 'Torch', hospital ships *Oxfordshire* (RN) and *Newfoundland* (RAMC) picked up casualties from the wharves while the ports themselves were still being fiercely defended by Vichy French troops. From there it was only a short trip to Gibraltar where doctors and nurses waited in readiness to treat the wounded before passing them on to Britain. Survivors from HMS *Partridge* could be thankful that a hospital ship was at hand when their ship sank off Algiers. Exploding depth charges subjected the men in the water to a pressure of between one and two thousand pounds per square inch. Prompt treatment by the naval surgeons and QARNNS Sisters on board the *Oxfordshire* undoubtedly saved many lives.

This first combined British–American operation went well. By mid-November, their forces had spread eastwards along the coast of French-controlled Algeria to challenge Rommel in Tunisia. British and American hospitals now sailed from Britain to establish themselves in the newly occupied territory, but the approaches to North Africa swarmed with enemy submarines intent on redeeming themselves after their earlier failure to detect the invasion force. Much valuable equipment was sent to the bottom of the Mediterranean and many lives were lost.

At the end of November 1942, the *Strathallan* (Strath Line), with the staff of a general hospital on board, was picked off by a shadowing submarine as she dropped to the tail of a convoy before landing at Algiers. A torpedo went clean through her engine room and fire broke out at once. Some of the lifeboats were lowered in too much haste. One without a bung flooded as soon as it hit the water, floating out its occupants some of whom were drowned.

Everything was ship-shape, however, in the lifeboat where sat the Principal Matron Designate for Algiers, Miss Lucy Wane, QAIMNS. In gloves and crisp, white blouse over neatly pressed slacks, she regarded her party of Sisters with some disapproval. One in particular, who was hanging miserably over the back of the boat, came in for a sharp rebuke.

'This is no time to be sick, Sister!' Miss Wane passed her comb around the bedraggled company. 'For God's sake,' she said witheringly, 'there's no need to look like survivors.'

Not everyone had left the stricken ship, however. At the time of the impact, two QAs, Olive Stewardson and Julie Kerr, hurried below decks to the sick bay where five helpless stretcher cases lay. They prepared the men, dispatched them to safety and were about to leave themselves when the burned crew from the engine room were brought into the sick bay for treatment and the two nurses put aside all thought of leaving. As more men were carried in, three other women passengers came to help, Judith Baskott, an English nurse, and two American WAACs, L. Anderson of Denver and A. Dregmal of Wisconsin. They worked through the rest of the night. When daylight came, the *Strathallan,* though still afloat, was listing badly, but all on board were lifted to safety before she sank. Sister Stewardson and Sister Kerr were awarded the RRC. Five of their fellow QAs lost their lives.

Other hospitals, which landed without mishap, occupied sites in Algiers, Bone and Phillipville on the coast and inland on the Constantin Plateau. A visit by RAMC medical staff to one of the American hospitals was an occasion for wonder and envy. Their up-to-date equipment and plentiful staff were in sharp contrast to the British hospitals, where improvisation was the key word. This was America's first year of the war and Britain's third. America had not drained her exchequer to buy guns and ships nor had her factories been bombed to rubble. The difference showed.

When the 97th BGH at Guelma ran out of canvas, as it did every time there was a 'push' and the bed-state swelled from 1,200 to 2,000, medical officers gave up their Mess tent for use as a ward, departments were contracted to make more bed space and the wounded were nursed in the open until canvas could be erected over them. Medicines were carried on temperature boards in place of trays and, since primus stoves were always in short supply, orderlies built fireplaces between the tents so that the hot water needed for fomentations was always available. For all septic wounds, four-hourly hot fomentation was still the standard treatment.

One morning in April 1943 a stranger appeared on the wards of the 98th BGH at Sousse on the east of Tunis.

'He's wearing a panama hat and khaki shorts,' Assistant Matron Ursula Dowling reported to the Matron, 'and he hasn't got his knees brown yet.'

'That,' said Miss Thorpe, 'is Professor Florey. He has come to try out his new drug.'

A seriously ill man whose wound was infected with gas gangrene was selected for what is believed to be the first use of penicillin in the field. Until now, no-one had survived this dreaded condition. When the tell-tale bubbles could be felt beneath the tissues, the man was beyond the help of contemporary medicine. Yet, to the astonishment of the staff at 98th BGH, this man recovered.

Other reports of the amazing properties of the new drug began to come in. A patient with an appalling wound of the buttock at Number 2 BGH was selected by Professor Florey as being the man least likely to live. QA Dinah Lidster was one of the nurses in attendance.

'This man had lost so much tissue that the bone was exposed. A recovery was not reasonable, yet it happened after treatment with penicillin.'

Before the incredulous eyes of the doctors and nurses involved, miracles were worked every day on the busy surgical wards. This yellow powder with the musty smell revolutionised the treatment of wounds, and deaths from sepsis were reduced to an amazingly low level. In short supply and very expensive, it was at first reserved for Front Line troops in the Mediterranean arena of war. But when laboratories in America and Australia stepped in to help with production, this great British discovery became available to every Allied soldier on active service and played a major part in the final victory.

Although the North African campaign was now going well for the Allies, enemy submarines still dominated the Mediterranean, taking a high toll of the shipping there. QA Maureen Ferris (later Shaw), bound for India via Suez on the *Marnix Van St Aldegonde*, was taking a bath when the vessel was struck by a torpedo.

'This is no place for me,' she said to herself and dressed hurriedly. Maureen is a born survivor who finds some difficulty in taking life seriously, even when complicated by shipwreck.

'The engines and the air-conditioning stopped. There was a terrible silence then – BONK! – the whole ship turned over on its side. There was a crashing and banging of things falling. A tin trunk fell on top of one Sister and spread her nose across her face. "Well," I thought, "this is it." I didn't know then that a ship always rights herself before going down. I learned that later when I married a sailor. Up she came again, listing badly. It was getting dark and there was some confusion as the lights had gone out; there was no panic, although planes were machine-gunning the decks as we tried to reach the lifeboats. The only bit of excitement shown was by the ENSA (Entertainment National Service Association) people, who were rushing about shouting "My fiddle!" "My guitar!" and that sort of thing.

'I met one of the Dutch engineers and I told him my boat had a hole in it. "Well, Maureen," he said calmly, "You'll have to find another one, won't you?"

'I saw a boat being launched in another part of the ship and, as I sat on the rail, thinking it was a long way to jump, an English Naval officer came up from behind.

'"Come on, Sister," he said, "just like the backyard at home." He gave me a shove and over I went, into a boat already crowded with about seventy people. Another boat was crowded with QAs and WRNS and I noticed with some satisfaction that the WRNS were rowing. We had all got a bit fed up with the WRNS during the voyage, a bit too much of the "Daddy's ship" talk for us. On this occasion, the QAs gracefully conceded that the WRNS were better equipped to deal with seafaring matters and gave them the oars.

'In my boat, we were packed so tightly that we swayed back and forth with every stroke of the oars. The troops had just had their supper and one was vomiting all over my knee, but there was nothing I could do about it. After about six hours, we were rescued by an American destroyer. One of our Sisters, Adams was her name, got stuck halfway up the scramble net and hung there like a fly with her long hair spread out all over the net. In the end they had to haul up the whole net with her in it.'

The survivors were taken ashore at Phillipville and the Sisters were quartered with the General Hospital there. Their pressing need was for uniform replacements, but there were no female garments in the clothing store. Ordnance Supplies in Britain had overlooked the fact that some shipwrecked survivors might be women. All that was available were replacements for a Guards' Division which had recently

passed this way. The shirts hung below their knees, trousers concer-
tinaed round the ankles and three or four pairs of socks had to be
worn in order to fill up the boots. It was many weeks before replacements for QA uniform reached North Africa, and until then the Sisters
worked in cut-down Guards' uniform.

In this way, against the expressed wishes of their patron, Queen
Mary, the QAs came to wear trousers – which were at once seen to be
the only sensible garments for nurses in forward positions. Even the
Senior Officers' Mess in Algiers had to amend its rules forbidding
entry to any female wearing trousers when the Principal Matron of
Algiers herself arrived wearing the only clothes she possessed after
shipwreck; and when a party of high-ranking QA Matrons came from
England on an inspection tour of the North African hospitals, which
involved stepping over men on stretchers on a crowded tent floor,
they formed their own conclusions concerning a suitable dress for
Sisters.

The arrival of the shipwrecked Sisters from the *Marnix Van St
Aldergande* sorely stretched the meagre amenities of the Phillipville
hospital which offered them shelter. Water was in short supply and a
single tap in the hospital compound had to be shared by the Sisters
and all officer 'up-patients'. The problem was tackled in a very demo-
cratic way.

'The patients in their pyjamas and we in our outsize shirts and hairy
trousers formed a circle and walked around the tap,' Maureen explains.
'First time round, you got your toothbrush under the tap and went on
your way, brushing your teeth. Next time round, with one tablet of
soap between three, you went WHOOSH with your hands under the
tap and passed the soap to the next one. You had one more go at the
trickle of water and that was your morning's toilet.'

Canadian officers, hoping to find survivors from a ship which had
carried an entire hospital staff of Canadian Sisters, made several visits
to this camp but found no trace of their missing nurses.

Maureen and her colleagues from the *Marnix Van St Aldegonde*
were put on board the next ship making for Alexandria, which happened to be the *Derbyshire* (Bibby Line). She was travelling in convoy,
and the Sisters were involved in yet another submarine attack.

'As soon as the signal was received that there was a submarine in
the area, all ship's engines and blowers were stopped. We spoke in
whispers, and waited. What made things worse was a Canadian officer

who kept glaring at us and muttering that it was bad luck to carry women.' But Maureen was lucky this time. The Commodore's ship was sunk but the *Derbyshire* escaped.

Long overdue uniform replacements awaited the Sisters at Port Tewfik on the Canal. From the dusty recesses of some forgotten storehouse were produced articles of the uniform worn by the QAs of 1917 when nursing the wounded of Gallipoli. The long-skirted dresses trimmed with rows of pearl buttons were scarcely less appropriate than the boots and battledress of the Guards' Regiment. It was with a distinctly eccentric wardrobe that Maureen and her fellow QAs sailed on for India.

Later, she was to write, 'When you go to a posting in India, you take your bedding roll with you and you spend five days in a train. Someone waves you goodbye and when you get to where you're going no-one has ever heard of you, there is no transport to meet you and no-one knows you are coming.

'You usually arrive at a station in the middle of the night, hot, dusty and tired. You ask, "Where is the hospital?" "Ten miles away," is the usual airy answer, "and you won't find anything going there to-night."

'Finally, you make your own arrangements, hitching a lift on a supply truck or something similar, and when you arrive at the hospital, there is consternation. "But who are *you?*" they say. You are not expected. It is always like this in India.'

Tossed here and there by the fortunes of war over the last months, Maureen was anxious to get to grips with the job she had set out to do when she left England, to nurse the wounded. She presented herself at her new posting, the prestigious Allahabad General Hospital, in good heart. Aware that there were shortcomings in her uniform, she was nevertheless unprepared for the Matron's mild rebuke, 'You really must get yourself some evening dresses, Sister.'

This was a regular peacetime hospital with a very comfortable Mess. It was a posting generally regarded as a reward for past discomforts; the next move usually led straight back to the canvas bucket and the hole in the ground. In Maureen's case, the next move was to the borders of Burma to look after General Orde Wingate's 'Chindits'.

Three men emerged to change the scene in Burma. General Slim took charge of the 'Forgotten Fourteenth' Army and transformed it with his vigour. Admiral Mountbatten was appointed overall Commander, South-East Asia, with a brief to co-ordinate future land and sea operations; General Orde Wingate conceived a heroic role for men who were prepared to sacrifice everything, undergo the harshest of privations yet expect neither help nor pity from anyone, in order to beat the Japanese.

His men, the famous 'Chindits', were drawn from fifty-one nations. Their skins and creeds differed widely but they had three things in common. They were all volunteers, all physically A1 Plus, and they all hated the Japanese.

They were dropped by parachute behind enemy lines in deepest jungle, their mission being to disrupt enemy communications, destroy roads and bridges, blow up ammunition dumps and supply depots. They scaled mountains, forded impassable rivers and, on one expedition, trekked 450 miles through virgin jungle. They travelled light and were supplied with victuals and ammunition by air. If they missed a 'drop', or if the parachuting cannister fell into enemy hands, they starved. They carried no wounded. If a man could no longer walk, his friends dispatched him humanely rather than leave him for the Japanese to torture.

The first medical unit to receive the survivors from an expedition when they were brought from the jungle was the CCS at Silket near Imphal where Aggie McGeary, QAIMNS, was Matron at the special request of Orde Wingate himself. She had nursed him through a bad bout of typhoid during the previous year and he believed that he owed her his life. She was the kind of woman he wanted to look after his men, and his request was duly granted.

His judgement proved to be impeccable. She took on wholeheartedly the care of the Chindits and became their staunch champion. When they were brought to her, usually late at night, in a state of exhaustion and starvation, some weighing no more than four stones, she put them to bed and spoiled them with every indulgence that was possible to obtain and occasionally some that were impossible. Nothing was too much trouble for her if it could recompense these brave men for the hardships they had suffered.

'They were scarecrows,' says Maureen Ferris, 'starving, mentally and physically exhausted, but simply great men.'

Matron McGeary caused more than a flutter of discontent amongst the more regimentally minded Matrons of the QAIMNS by dispensing summarily with all red tape. 'Usual channels' were not for her. She went straight to General Wingate with her requests and was given everything she wanted. Her deceptively fragile appearance hid a woman of iron. Small and dainty, she was dynamite in a lace doily.

'All the best things go Aggie's way,' complained the long-suffering Matrons of other hospitals in the area, struggling with their unrewarding requisition forms. But the final word on 'Aggie' must come from the late Brigadier B. E. Fergusson (Lord Ballantrae, Colonel of the Black Watch, Commander 16th Infantry Brigade, Chindits) in his book *The Wild Green Earth.*

'I must mention the famous, the impish, the kindly the mutinous, the saintly, the wicked, the beloved, the Glasgow–Irish, the "always-on-the-verge-of-court-martial" Matron, Miss Agnes McGeary, MBE.

'She cheeked the Generals, scolded the doctors, she bullied me. She saved Wingate's life when he was dying of typhoid. She stole for the wounded. She brought back to health many who would otherwise have died. She raided Ordnance Stores. She embezzled "Comforts". She vamped Brigadiers. She cheered the dying.

'She wrote letters to the bereaved and when she got answers from them, she wrote again, and again, and still again. She sent me a clipper for my beard and a live goose by Dakota for my dinner. She was a darling who possessed all our hearts, and in whatever row with authority she is involved in today, she has all our wishes for a happy issue out of all the afflictions she so lightheartedly brings upon herself for the sake of others.

'I only hope that I am never under her command. Indeed, I have but one hope more fervent than that, that she is never under mine.'

Major Agnes McGeary of Mossend, Glasgow, QAIMNS, RRC, was awarded the MBE for her gallant and distinguished service on the Eastern Frontier of India. She died in 1954 of cancer of the stomach, devotedly nursed by her own nursing Sisters, one of whom, QA Helen Hiley, had served with her at the Silket CCS.

The Chindits' successes were accompanied by advances by the Fourteenth Army towards Arakan in Northern Burma and by a Chinese Army in the north-east under the command of American General Stilwell. When Japanese forces, after much preparation, led their long-expected attack on India through the plains of Imphal, they were stopped by a confident army with plentiful guns and Spitfires at its command.

At this historic battle, the Japanese were defeated and fled, leaving thousands of their dead behind. That was the moment when the fighting men in Burma knew that there would be no more retreats. The jungles they had to fight through stretched ahead to Rangoon, and after that through Malaya, but the Fourteenth Army would never march with its back to the enemy again.

Every effort was made to improve the medical services for men fighting under difficult tropical conditions. When it was discovered that, at any one time, as many as fourteen per cent of the troops were out of action due to malaria, more stringent preventative measures were adopted. Daily doses of paladrin became compulsory. Long sleeves and long trousers were obligatory after dusk and certain RAF planes were adapted for the spraying of DDT on stagnant water.

Penicillin was still in short supply and was not yet available outside the Mediterranean area but one man's life was saved with its help in a lucky chain of events.

In January 1944, Naval Sister Ann Ramsden, previously Sister Tutor at St Mary's Hospital, Paddington, and now attached to Admiral Mountbatten's HQ in Delhi, was asked to 'special' an RAMC consultant physician, Brigadier Marriott, whose condition following a routine operation for repair of hernia was causing grave concern. Septicaemia had developed when Miss Ramsden joined the nursing team, and the Brigadier was on the Dangerously Ill List.

News of his serious condition reached his friend and colleague, Brigadier Bedford of the Eighth Army, who, with Lord Moran, had recently attended Mr Churchill in Tunis when he became seriously ill with pneumonia. Penicillin was available but Lord Moran, having no clinical experience of the drug, preferred to treat his patient with sulphonamides. The Brigadier promptly dispatched the unused penicillin without delay to Delhi for the doctor who had saved hundreds of lives and was now in mortal danger himself.

A dispatch rider met the plane and delivered the precious package into Miss Ramsden's hands. 'Instructions stated that the ochre-coloured powder was to be dissolved in distilled water and given by intramuscular injection every three hours. My patient found the treatment intensely painful, but his response was immediate and he made a complete recovery.'

Miss Ramsden must have cast her mind back to that day in 1942 when, as Sister Tutor of St Mary's Hospital, Paddington, she was present at the lecturer's forecast that a new drug was being researched which would revolutionise nursing procedures. The powder which had just saved the life of her patient had its origins in her old hospital.

17

Into Italy

Rommel did not give up North Africa easily. Reinforcements of German and Italian troops and armour poured into Tunis from Sicily and the Allied armies closing in on him from west and east had to pay dearly for every yard they gained. Booby traps scattered in profusion along the path of the advancing armies effectively slowed their progress and men learned not to touch the tin hat dangling from a tree or the box of chocolates in a ditch.

There was no denying the Allies their final victory, however. When the massed Eighth and First British Armies, the Americans and the Free French converged and bore down on Rommel's last stand in the ruins of Tunis, surrender was inevitable. On 12th May, 1943, the war in North Africa was brought to an end. There was wild jubilation in the streets of Tunis, victory parades and military bands. Medals were distributed and the Free French went quite wild with parties. The long and gruelling war in the desert was over.

In some of the hospital wards, however, rejoicing seemed out of place. The celebrations meant little to crippled and disabled men contemplating an unpromising future.

'What have I to look forward to, Sister?' asked a man whose abdomen had been penetrated by a mine, who now had a permanent colostomy and no stomach. 'My job won't look at me like this.'

The women who nursed these men and gave them support during their blackest hours are unable to wipe them from their memories.

Hospitals and sick bays of the Army, Navy and Air Force now stretched from Algiers to Alexandria. VADs ran convalescent depots by the sea and in the cool of the hills. Only those patients needing long-term care were sent back to Britain. Italian and German prisoners of war were transferred in stages to camps in Britain and Canada but until then, their wounded were nursed by the QAs.

Sister Kathleen Smith, TANS, was no longer with Number 12 CCS but was stationed with the 19th BGH at Geneifa in the Canal Zone, in charge of a ward of sick Italian prisoners, most of whom were suffering from tuberculosis after years of living under poor conditions in the desert. It was a melancholy ward of sick, sad men in a drab tent on a dusty desert, and Kathleen Smith resolved to brighten it up with flowers from the nearby town of Ismailia. Her appearance in the ward with arms full of roses, carnations and chrysanthemums was greeted with cries of delight. 'Bella, bella fiori!' Those patients who were able hastened to help her arrange the blooms in jars.

Giuseppi was one who was unlikely to recover. He had already suffered several haemorrhages and was later repatriated with other very sick POWs in exchange for an equal number of invalid British soldiers in enemy hands. He made himself responsible for the pot plants and, when he left the hospital, Kathleen Smith gave him one of the cherished geraniums to take with him.

'I will make cuts,' he told her, 'and make more to grow and each one will make me think of you.'

As she bade him farewell, Sister Smith could only hope that he would live long enough to see them bloom.

There were many Italian POWs at Geneifa, all of whom willingly performed any duty asked of them. They were accommodated in a wire enclosure next to the British part of the hospital and congregated every evening to sing songs from the operas. All the recent slaughter seemed far away at these times, which bring back poignant memories for Sister Smith.

'In the stillness of the evening, after a hot and tiring day, when the air was cool and the distant mountains shimmered in all the mother-of-pearl colours, blues and mauves, pale green and deep rose, one heard this beautiful singing. The whole camp seemed to pause and listen, and our own British patients gathered on their side of the wire enjoying such old favourites as "O Sole Mio" and "La Tarantella". They loved to have a sing-song themselves, but their repertoire never rose above "Roll Out The Barrel" and "She'll Be Coming Down The Mountain".'

During this period following the end of hostilities in North Africa, forward-based hospitals in Tunisia were able to put their establishments in order. Without the immediacy of constant convoys of casualties, there was time to treat and dispatch patients without haste and to empty the wards systematically in readiness for the next campaign, the occupation of Italy.

Servicemen and women enjoyed a brief period of relaxation by the warm, golden sands of the Mediterranean, but the city of Tunis had nothing to offer. Scarcely a building had escaped damage and no shops survived. With her unspent salary burning a hole in her pocket, Sister Frankie Newton, QAIMNS/R, was about to give up an abortive shopping venture when a line of women outside a building caught her eye. Scenting a bargain and ignoring the fluster of consternation caused by her uniform, she took her place in the queue. However, when a red-faced military policeman explained that the ladies were waiting for a medical examination, in accordance with General Montgomery's recent sanctioning of brothels, she beat a hasty retreat.

There were other little gaffes when the nursing staff collided with the less well-known side of troop management, as on the occasion when rubber goods indented for a Naval destroyer unaccountably turned up at a sick bay for WRNS. The Naval Sister in Charge handed several cartons to the ship's embarrassed medical officer.

'I wondered why they'd sent me so many finger stalls,' she said equably. 'We don't have *that* many cut fingers.'

On 23rd July, the troops embarked for Sicily and were soon to be followed by the hospitals. Nurses who had grown to know the desert in all its moods would leave it forever. Like everyone else involved in the long African campaign, they belonged to a desert fraternity; especially proud were those who were entitled to wear the figure '8' on their Middle East ribbon.

The rats, bugs and more-or-less permanent 'gippy tummy' would seem less important over the years: what remained would be a memory of miraculous sunsets, of wild flowers on the Constantin Plateau, of Phillipville's luscious peaches, of a cherished tomato plant found growing in the bottom of an abandoned Italian dug-out, and, dearer than all, the comradeship of the troops themselves.

Sicily was logically the next target once North Africa had been won, and German troops were ready and waiting to give a good account of themselves as the first assault craft ploughed through the shallows. Hospital ships and the smaller hospital carriers stood by to ferry casualties to the base hospitals waiting in Tunisia.

The responsibility for transporting casualties fell solely upon the British as America's hospital ships were all in service in the Pacific arena of war. HMHS *Dorsetshire*, *Newfoundland*, *Talamba*, *Empire Clyde* and *Vasna* were all involved in the Italian campaign, in addition to the smaller hospital carriers *Leinster*, *St Andrew*, *St David*, *St Julian* and *Dinard*. Painted white according to the Geneva Conventions, with a broad green band around the hull and plainly marked with red crosses, they sailed fully lit up during the hours of darkness, presenting a sitting target to unscrupulous bombers. As those on board quickly came to realise, the decision about whether to respect or ignore the conventional immunity rested entirely with the individual Luftwaffe pilot above them at the time.

A hospital ship of the class of the *Dorsetshire* (Bibby Line) was equipped with dispensary, X-ray department and operating theatre, and could carry in comfort 500 patients. Hospital carriers, drawing a shallow draught which enabled them to go close inshore, could carry anything from 160 patients on the *Isle of Jersey* to 380 on the *Leinster*. A staff of nine QAs served on the *Leinster*, but smaller carriers managed with four.

Instead of lifeboats, the carriers were equipped with water ambulances. These were flat-bottomed so that they could be run ashore if necessary, and were fitted with stretchers so that casualties were carried with the minimum of discomfort. Davits swung them to the decks of the mother ship for ease in unloading. Larger numbers of casualties were conveyed by Landing Craft Tanks.

In the opening stages of the invasion of Sicily, staff on the *Leinster* worked through the first forty-eight hours with a break of only two hours. Surgeons left the theatre briefly when it needed to be cleaned and went to the wards to give blood transfusions. Crew members acting as assistant stretcher-bearers accompanied the orderlies ashore, frequently under fire, and brought the wounded to a reception area on the ship to be examined and classified by a doctor while Sisters stood by to give injections, renew dressings and prepare those in need of urgent surgery. Constant training resulted in smooth, speedy embarkation. With the minimum of delay, casualties were carried to the port of Bizerta in Tunisia and the ship was cleaned ready for the return journey.

The first disaster to strike the hospital ships came seven days after the initial landings, when HMHS *Talamba* was attacked and sunk while embarking casualties. The wounded were being brought to her from the shore on anything that would float; some had already been admitted to the wards. When enemy bombers scored a direct hit, the whole exercise went into reverse – with the utmost urgency, the wounded now had to be taken *off* the sinking ship.

A surgeon had just completed the amputation of a soldier's leg when the ship was rocked by explosions. Hastily binding the stump, he secured the unconscious man to a stretcher and, with a prayer for his survival, cast him into the sea. With unsuspected buoyancy, the stretcher kept the man afloat. He was rescued and subsequently made a good recovery.

Matron Violet M. Innes, QAIMNS (later OBE) shepherded all the wounded in her care into a lifeboat and got them safely away – 'without even soiling her veil', as one astonished eye-witness put it. Because of the many ships in the area able to give assistance, the total of lives lost was small. In spite of a broken leg, QA Makepeace was able to keep herself afloat for ninety minutes until she was rescued, but her colleague, Sister Maud Louise Johnson, was among the missing.

By the time Sicily had been fought over and won, the Italians had lost their appetite for war and surrendered when Allied troops prepared to invade the mainland. The Germans moved quickly to fill the gaps left in the defence by their disenchanted ally, and they were already manning Italian gun emplacements in the mountains overlooking the Bay of Salerno when the British/American Fifth Army came ashore on 8th September.

The landing beaches were under constant bombardment from enemy artillery and casualties amongst the assault troops were high. The sight of hospital carriers nosing their way into port was welcome indeed to medical units ashore who could find no place of safety for the wounded. The canvas of the wards was torn to shreds by chunks of flying mortar. A shell which landed on the operating tent of Number 14 British CCS killed the surgeon, the patient and the orderlies. For a few days, the outcome of the assault hung in the balance. The beachhead was not finally secured until 12th September, when the British Eighth Army, working up from the toe of Italy, arrived to harass the enemy.

On 13th September, 100 American nurses left Bizerta on HMHS *Newfoundland* bound for Salerno where they were to set up an evacuating hospital, the equivalent of a British Casualty Clearing Station. Unlike the British nurses, they were expected to do their own 'digging-in' on arrival and came on board the hospital ship equipped

with spades and picks for the job. It is possible that an enemy scout
plane saw the line of khaki-clad figures embarking, and, mistaking
their implements for rifles, concluded that the hospital ship was being
improperly used for the transport of troops. This would account for
the fact that, as the *Newfoundland* approached Salerno that night, she
was attacked and sunk. A bomb, landing between the funnel and the
bridge, wrecked the sleeping quarters of the ship's medical staff. The
QA Matron, Miss Agnes McInnes Cheyne, and five of her Sisters, all
five of the ship's RAMC doctors, eight orderlies and nineteen crew
were killed outright. Sister Kathleen (Jock) Neilson owed her life to
her colleague, Pat Jenkins; although badly burned herself, Pat pulled
Kathleen from under a collapsed and burning bunk. The American
nurses were quartered in a different part of the ship and escaped
unhurt.

The carriers *Leinster* and *St Andrew* hastened to the assistance of
the *Newfoundland* which was burning fiercely, every one of her port-
holes lit by flames. Rescue boats slid over the dark waters where
tongues of flame licked up the oil in which survivors floundered helplessly. Sixty badly burned men with huge serum blisters hanging from
their charred bodies walked on board the *Leinster* rather than suffer
the pain of lying on a stretcher on their untreated burns.

With a total of 460 wounded on board, the *Leinster* made for Bizerta,
but before she could tie up at the wharf, an alert was sounded. Her
staff would have preferred to remain in the harbour near other shipping
which could give aid if necessary but she was ordered out to sea again,
to cruise slowly off-shore, alone, knowing that only a few hours earlier
a hospital ship had been deliberately attacked. On this occasion, however, her immunity was respected and she was able to discharge her
patients safely later in the day.

Italy paid dearly for having thrown in her lot with Hitler in 1940.
Caught in the crossfire between armies, her farms and livestock were
blasted by shells, her country roads churned up by tanks and her cities
flattened. When the Allies entered Naples, they found within its ruins
a starving population. They found bubonic plague, typhus and fear.
The currency had collapsed and the only market was Black. Mothers
sold their daughters' favours to the troops for a packet of cigarettes
with which to buy food.

Army medical authorities set up clinics for the civilian population
and the British Red Cross Society opened food and clothing depots,

but military priorities could not be diverted from the next target, which was Italy's capital, Rome. Mount Cassino, however, from whose heights the enemy could overlook all Allied troop movements, stood in the way. From these heights, the enemy could monitor and bombard every Allied troop movement. There could be no advance until the mountain was taken. A hard decision confronted men who, even in battle, clung to civilised principles, for Mount Cassino was crowned not only with a German arsenal but also with a historic monastery. To destroy one without the other would be difficult; nevertheless, the attack began with instructions that the monastery was not to be deliberately bombed.

Winter came early in that year of 1943. First the rain, and then snow and sleet, produced wretched conditions for the fighting men, yet all that was expected of them in fair weather must be accomplished in foul. They marched in squelching boots in torrential rain and found no dry place to lay their heads. The wounded lay patiently in sodden uniform awaiting the stretcher-bearers, and pneumonia made its appearance on the wards.

General hospitals held in readiness in North Africa now came to support the CCSs and small medical units which, in conjunction with the hospital ships, had dealt with all casualties until now. Barracks, schools, cinemas, museums, even churches were disinfested by the sanitation squads and turned into hospitals. When no suitable building was available, tents were used despite the bitter weather.

A high sea was running when the ship carrying Number 1 BGH entered Salerno Bay, and the Captain was loath to try to land his women passengers in such conditions. Troops could scramble down nets over the ship's side and into the bobbing boats, but this feat was obviously beyond some of the older Sisters of the QAIMNS on board. Nevertheless, Shore Command insisted that they were urgently needed on land and must be disembarked. A New Zealand hospital near Naples was waiting to move to a forward position and could not do so until relieved by Number 1 BGH.

One of the older members on board was Miss Birch, QAIMNS/R who had been with Number 1 BGH at Kantara since 1941. She had worked through all the emergencies of the desert war, including the last, when she was one of a handful of Sisters remaining, with bags packed, as Rommel reached El Alamein. Now aged fifty, she was about to embark on another campaign.

'The crew fixed up a canvas shute from the deck to the landing craft below. They put us in at the top, gave us a push and someone caught us at the bottom. Good job we were wearing trousers.' Like everything else in Miss Birch's long life, the situation was met with good-humoured acceptance.

Another veteran was Miss Jean Mitchell, who staunchly led Number 10 CCS from Dunkirk and then to and fro across the desert for the last three years. She was now Matron of Number 2 BGH, and arrived with her hospital to occupy a barracks at Caserta as the attack on Mount Cassino began.

'Every morning, we used to hear squadrons of our planes going over to bomb the mountain. They bombed and bombed and bombed, but no-one would bomb the monastery itself until General Freyburg, the New Zealand Commander, said he would not put his men on the hill again until the monastery with its concealed artillery was bombed. He said it was suicide. We had terrible casualties. They just poured in every day.'

This astute lady, now ninety-three years old, with gentle brown eyes, has seen in her lifetime more of the world's misery than most people are able to imagine.

Top: 1. (From the left) Sarah Davidson (New Zealand), Lynette Walsh, Teddy Head, Miss Williams and Hilary Glazebrook (all from Australia) in Cape Town in 1940, en route to the Middle East. Caught in Britain in 1939, they joined the QAIMNS/R, whose grey and scarlet uniform they are wearing. Only Lynette Walsh and Teddy Head (who supplied this photo) survived the war.

Above left: 2. Frankie Newton, QAIMNS/R, with General Montgomery in North Africa in 1942. (Photo supplied by Frankie Newton.)

Above right: The first nurses to land in Normandy after the invasion. Senior Sister Iris Ogilvie MBE ARRC (LEFT) and Sister Mollie Giles MBE ARRC (RIGHT) of the Princess Mary's Royal Air Force Nursing Service.

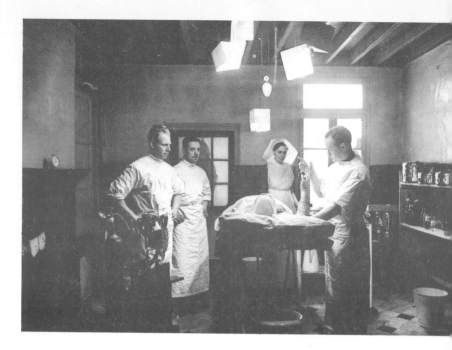

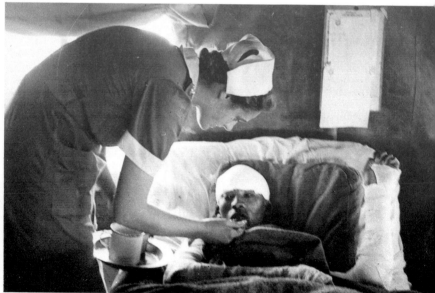

Top: 4. Number 3 CCS operating in the kitchen of a requisitioned château at Mondicourt, France, in 1939. The shadowless operating lamps were fashioned from petrol tins by the Royal Engineers. (Photo: Imperial War Museum.)
Above: 5. A Sister of the New Zealand Army Nursing Service with her Indian patient in a desert hospital. (Photo: Imperial War Museum.)

Top: 6. Sister Greaves (later Fox), QAIMNS/R, with the 15th Mobile CCS at Anzio beachhead. Sister Greaves was awarded the George Medal. (Photo: Imperial War Museum.)

Above: 7. The Second Front in Normandy: Sisters Morrison and Rodgers of the 79th GH pitching tents. Sisters had by now replaced their grey and scarlet suits with battledress trousers more suitable for the demands of front-line nursing. (Photo: QARANC Museum.)

Top left: 8. Six British Sisters of the QAIMNS/R who survived Bankinang POW camp. (Clockwise from top left) Kit Woodman, Lydia McLean, Naomi Davies, K. M. Jenkins, Louie Harley and Mary Charman. This photo (supplied by Kit Woodman) was taken about six weeks after their release, and the nurses had begun to put on weight.

Top right: 9. Belsen, 1945. One freed prisoner who was still able to walk collecting water for his fellows. (Photo supplied by Pat Stephens.)

Above: 10. Two QAs watching the burning of the filthy prison huts after the liberation of Belsen in 1945. (Photo supplied by Pat Stephens.)

18

The Battle of Mount Cassino

In January 1944, while most of the Allied troops in Italy were pitting themselves against heavily defended German positions on Mount Cassino, an American/British force made a successful landing at Anzio, south of Rome. They failed to exploit their original advantage of surprise and lost the opportunity to make a quick breakthrough to Rome. Instead, they allowed themselves to become hemmed in by German artillery, which had not been slow to move into the ring of hills overlooking the beaches and from these positions were able to command the landing area and all attempts to break out from it.

Despite this, back-up troops and supplies continued to come ashore, causing such congestion that every German shell could scarcely fail to inflict maximum damage. In a small area bounded at one end by an ammunition dump and at the other by a troop reinforcement camp, three British Casualty Clearing Stations operated, Numbers 2, 14 and 15, alongside the 93rd American Evacuating Hospital as well as several Field Ambulances. There was barely room for stretcher-bearers to manoeuvre between the tents.

Sister Sheila Greaves (GM, later Fox), who was in charge of the pre-operative ward at Number 15 CCS, describes the set-up.

'At the far end of the long ward tent, which was dug-in to a depth of two feet, was a small resuscitation annexe for four stretchers on trestles. Under these, when necessary, we used to put oil stoves to warm up badly shocked patients, a practice which would not be approved of today. The theatre and sterilisation tents led off midway down the ward and three surgical teams operated in shifts. We alternated 'take-in' periods with Number 2 CCS and these occasions were always hectic. One had to spot those in need of immediate resuscitation and/or surgery and pray that, in the dim light, someone in desperate need would not be overlooked. Wonderful people from the Friends' Ambulance Unit were attached to us. They were a non-combatant group and did magnificent work, frequently being wounded themselves. There was a Scottish boy of only seventeen who had to have his leg amputated.

'At night, one heard the lorries and tanks groaning forward. How they managed with no lights was a mystery to me – but even a struck match would produce not only a warning shout but also a quick response from the Alban Hills where the German guns had grandstand positions.'

Patients were in continual danger from flying mortar. Doctors, Sisters and orderlies all took a turn with spades and shovels to dig the tents in a further two feet, throwing up the excavated earth as protective walls. Even so, many patients were wounded a second time and five American nurses lost their lives.

For extra protection, trestles were abandoned and the stretchers were lowered to the ground with duckboards at the head and foot to prevent them from sinking into the mud. The Sisters were glad of their tough khaki trousers and gum-boots as they carried out nursing procedures on their knees. Chest and abdominal cases from all units were nursed in a small building which had been appropriated by Number 2 CCS. Here they stayed until fit enough to be moved. Otherwise, all casualties were evacuated within twenty-four hours after treatment or sooner, whenever a hospital carrier presented itself, for there was no room to hold them ashore.

Sisters Geraldine Edge and Mary Johnston, both on the nursing staff of the hospital carrier *Leinster*, describe the following incident in their book *Ships of Youth*. On 21st January, the carriers *Leinster, St Andrew* and *St David* were still loading casualties at Anzio when darkness fell. To save them from the nightly barrage of shells from the Alban Hills, Shore Command ordered the three ships out to sea, to cruise, fully lit and in close formation, until daylight.

Enemy pilots decided that this target was too good to miss and attacked immediately, despite the clearly defined category of the vessels. The *Leinster* was the first to be hit, fortunately not seriously. She was able to get the small fire under control almost at once, but the *St David* was not so lucky. She suffered a direct hit and at once began to sink. The staff had six minutes in which to get as many patients as possible from below decks to the ship's rail, where even those who had just undergone operation had to be persuaded to jump into the water. One with both eyes bandaged was put into a lifejacket and thrown into the sea, to be lifted into a water ambulance a few minutes later. Another who had just undergone major abdominal surgery and who had been receiving intensive care when the ship was struck, somehow managed to haul himself out of the water on to a raft and was later found to be in good condition.

The nursing staff were still on the ship when her bows began to rise steeply out of the water and she slid down stern first.

'Wait for the Sisters!' the Captain called as the boats pulled away from the sinking vessel and the Sisters jumped into the sea. The Captain went down with his ship and with him went the RAMC Commanding Officer, two QAs and several RAMC personnel. As the enemy planes flew off, the *Leinster* and the *St Andrew* were left to locate cries for help and take the wounded on board. An American soldier amongst the wounded, noting the Red Cross brassards worn by the QAs, remarked, 'Gee, you must be the only folks around here who still believe in God.'

The Anzio beachhead was stuck and stayed that way for three uncomfortable months. Nurses, like the troops, had to adapt to stressful, cramped conditions while carrying out their duties under shellfire. They slept in narrow trenches three feet deep and lined with blankets to prevent the sides from falling in. The women were still mindful of their appearance, despite the beetles which nightly came to a sticky end in face cream and the earth which fell in a continual dust over their hair. Sandbags stacked on a bedspring over each trench gave extra protection at the head end, but the wire mattresses presented a formidable snare for hair curlers. Once darkness had fallen, no-one left her trench for any purpose whatever and, in the morning, all the Sisters could be seen carrying their tins to the latrines in the most natural way.

These field latrines, which were in the centre of the camp, had been constructed without any thought of females using them. They were roofless, surrounded by a waist-high strip of hessian and the Sisters had to choose whether to sit it out brazenly with head and shoulders showing over the top of the hessian or to bend double and pretend they never went near the place.

Despite the discomforts, there was never any shortage of volunteers to nurse in forward positions. The Principal Matron QAIMNS at General Alexander's HQ was inundated with such requests.

The greatest deprivation at Anzio for both patients and staff was lack of sleep. The noise of gunfire was constant and danger from shelling always present, but the work of the medical staff went on, with or without sleep. Sisters on day duty started work at 0745 hours each morning and, apart from short meal breaks, worked through until 2030 hours.

The sole laboratory assistant at Number 14 CCS began his day at 0600 hours by collecting blood slides from the wards and spent the rest of the day identifying blood groups, testing for dysentery and malaria. At the end of the day, alone in his little tent which was laboratory and home, he wrapped himself in his blanket and lay down on the ground, hoping for a few hours of rest before the new day's work began all over again.

In the early hours of 14th March, enemy planes dive-bombed the reinforcement camp which lay adjacent to Number 15 CCS. Tents, men and spouting earth exploded in all directions as the planes struck and wheeled and struck again. Sister Greaves and three medical officers ran from the CCS into the midst of the confusion, treating the wounded even as the canvas above their heads was torn apart by machine-gun bullets. Time and again, they carried the wounded back to the CCS and returned for more. This QA, who confesses to being afraid of the dark, was awarded the George Medal for her courage.

After three months and much bloodshed the Anzio beach head was secured and enemy strongholds cleared from the mountains. But even then there could be no advance towards Rome until the battle of Mount Cassino had been won. Every attempt to take the fortress had so far been unsuccessful. Indian, French, American, New Zealand, Polish and British troops had hurled themselves upon its rocky slopes, only to be driven back by sustained deadly fire from above.

Enemy snipers made no concessions to the non-combatant role of stretcher-bearers; many of these dedicated men were themselves wounded or killed while carrying their comrades across the exposed face of the mountain. Recovery of the wounded was extremely difficult. Each dangerous journey to base with a casualty could take as much as eight hours while hundreds of wounded men were left behind to await their turn. Because of this, surgeons began to move their Field Dressing Stations further up the mountain, setting up their tents in any depression which could afford shelter.

Matron Miss Jean Mitchell of Number 2 BGH at Caserta was asked to provide two Sisters to accompany a Field Dressing Station and nurse those who were too seriously wounded to be moved.

'I sent two of my best girls,' she says. 'One was Sister Peck, who later married Sir Arthur Porritt RAMC, afterwards the Governor of New Zealand. These two Sisters went up the mountain and were responsible for saving the lives of many wounded men.'

QA Frankie Newton was now attached to an Indian CCS operating in a cow-shed at the base of the mountain and saw at first hand the fanatical courage of the Ghurkas. Their wounded came down the mountain unaided, sometimes with a limb almost severed, holding aloft their own blood transfusion and refusing morphia to ease the pain.

So much endeavour could not go unrewarded forever. General Anders and his intrepid Poles opened the way for another concerted attack on the summit, the fourth so far. This was more likely to succeed than previous attempts, for Allied planes now dominated the skies. All thoughts of sparing the monastery had long since been abandoned.

On the night before the planned assault, troops detailed for the attack moved into position along all routes leading to the mountain. Corporal H. E. Rolfe of the 1st Battalion East Surreys sought some rest for his Signals Unit before dawn would bring the order to attack. He wrapped himself in his blanket and, using his pack as a pillow, lay down in the open under the stars, confident in the knowledge that his men were out of reach of standard shelling by the enemy. German gunners, however, alerted to the possibility of attack, began to send long-distance shells over all the approach roads to the mountain. One of these finished off Corporal Rolfe's participation in the war.

A tremendous explosion hit him with a sledge-hammer blow. He struggled to his feet and, with a mouth full of blood and loose teeth, staggered to the Regimental Aid Post. He remembered nothing further until the sound of English nurses' voices roused him at the CCS.

'Apart from the ENSA party I had seen in Naples, these were the first Englishwomen's voices I had heard since landing in Algiers in 1942. The oh-so-sure arms of a Sister held me like a baby while I took a sip of water.'

While his unit went into action without him, Corporal Rolfe was taken to the Maxillo–Facial Unit attached to the 65th BGH in Naples to have what was left of his jaw wired together. There were many such injuries at Cassino. The rocky nature of the ground made the digging of slit trenches almost impossible and statistics for head and facial injuries were unusually high.

Corporal Rolfe continues, 'Twelve days after being wounded, the breathing tube was removed from my throat and Sister shaved me, a tricky feat because of the jagged wound running from my lower lip to what had been the cleft in my chin.' Like most wounded soldiers, he made himself useful in the ward as soon as his condition allowed.

The last battle for Cassino had been fought and won. German positions on the summit were finally overrun: the way ahead to Rome was now open. One of the most bitter battles of the Second World War had for its memorial a mountain littered with the dead and crowned by blackened ruins. When all the turmoil had ceased, Sister Kitty O'Connor from Number 2 BGH went on a visit there in the spirit of pilgrimage.

'Hardly one stone remained on top of another. The tin hats of dead soldiers lay about under dead trees where no birds sang. There was total silence. Then a poor peasant went by with a donkey pulling a cart in which sat his wife, his child and a sewing machine.'

Important army medical centres were now operating throughout that part of Italy controlled by the Allies. Specialist treatment was available for neuro-surgery, maxillo-facial, chest, genito-urinary and ophthalmic injuries. When wounded Yugoslav guerrilla fighters were brought to Italy for treatment, a maternity wing was opened at the 98th BGH at Bari for their womenfolk, many of whom were pregnant.

The Communist guerrillas were at first suspicious of the imperialist British, but their mistrust faded under the concern for their welfare shown by the doctors and nurses. Brave as lions, the women had been fighting alongside the men in the mountains of northern Yugoslavia ever since Hitler invaded their land. The first task facing QAs who admitted them to hospital was to persuade them to remove the live grenades from around their waists.

Their health was poor. Infestation by intestinal worms was a common complaint, the result of eating grass. Wounds of long standing showed no signs of healing. Surgery had been crude and many boys of fifteen or sixteen had suffered guillotine amputation of limbs. Ante was a small six-year-old who had thrown a live grenade at a bunch of chickens and almost blown off his foot.

'That's nothing,' he boasted. 'You should have seen the chickens.'

The wards represented the League of Nations. There were the Free French and the Moroccan 'Ghoums' who fought for them, Poles, Yugoslavs, Italians who were now fighting on the side of the Allies, as well as British and Dominion troops. Corporal Rolfe was now convalescent and the ward Sister's right-hand man.

'All the Sisters were hopelessly overworked and anything we comparatively well patients could do in the way of serving meals or feeding someone who could not fend for himself, we willingly did. All the different nationalities raised problems from time to time. Sister asked me to take the Indian in the next bed to the toilet. I took him along, opened the door, pointed to the seat and left him. A few minutes later, I heard a call – "Sahib!" – and there was his head showing about a foot above the doorway! I doubt if he had ever seen a western-style toilet in his life and I had to make him understand that the seat was for sitting on.'

Every effort was made to fly home all gravely ill patients, but air-lifts depended entirely on the weather and there were many un-avoidable postponements and disappointments. The slower but more reliable route was to take patients by sea to Tunis, where the Tunis-Algiers ambulance train waited to carry them to the embarkation port of Algiers.

There were nine such ambulance trains in Africa, five British and four Free French. Each British train was staffed by two RAMC medical officers, two QAs and twenty-six orderlies and could carry 300 casualties comfortably. For sick men, however, who had already been in transit from Italy over several days, the three-day journey from Tunis to Algiers was something of an ordeal.

Sisters Hilda Edwards (later Thomas) and Bernie Hughes, who staffed this train, were fully occupied during that time, renewing dressings, giving injections and medicines, washing and feeding these very sick men. The two girls were good friends and able to keep up each other's spirits, which was fortunate, for their train was often loaded with tragedy.

On one occasion the entire convoy consisted of French soldiers who had spent the winter fighting in the snows of Mount Cassino. Their feet were gangrenous from frostbite, and the great civic welcome which awaited them at Constantine could not alter the fact that their destination was the hospital for amputation of their feet.

'One of the happiest convoys we ever had,' wrote Hilda Edwards, 'was of Grenadier, Welsh and Coldstream Guards. They were so happy to be going home that they sang all the way from Tunis to Algiers; all the old favourites, "There'll Always Be An England", "Tipperary", "Roll Out The Barrel", and great was the *hiraeth* for me when the Welsh Guards sang "Ar Hyd Y Nos" (All Through The Night), and "Celon Lan" (Pure Heart).

'Yet all of these men were blind, some in one eye, some in both. One who had my unbounded admiration had lost both arms and was totally blind. I asked him one day if he would like a cigarette and, since he occupied one of the lower bunks, I sat on the floor to hold it for him. This gave him the chance to talk, which was what he needed more than anything else. His fifth child, whom he would never see, had been born while he was in Italy. I hoped that he would not detect the emotion in my voice. I admired these men so much because they had the will to live, an unconquerable spirit and a sense of dignity which even mutilation could not destroy.'

Into this bellicose spring, the fifth since the outbreak of war, crept an event of pure compassion which crossed the demarcation line between friend and foe. On 20th May, Allied POWs who were so sick or so disabled that they could never fight again were exchanged for the same number of German and Italian prisoners of war who were in the same sad category. Kathleen Smith's Giuseppi was amongst them. With Sweden as the intermediary, the exchange took place in Barcelona in neutral Spain. 900 Allied servicemen, who would be invalids for the rest of their lives, boarded the Swedish ship, the MV *Gripsholm* and sailed for Algiers.

A great reception awaited them there. Cheering crowds of servicemen and women lined the wharves as the *Gripsholm*, gay in the blue and yellow colours of Sweden, steamed slowly past the drab grey battleships of the Royal Navy. When she drew near enough for the men packed by the rails to be clearly distinguished, the military band waiting on shore struck up "There'll Always Be An England".

A solitary man on board lifted his voice to take up the melody, then wavered, needing support. 900 others drew breath and, as the gangway went down to freedom, the full-throated roar of the last poignant words rang out in moving measure:

'If England means as much to you,
As England means to me.'

The band of the British Armoured Division never had such an accompaniment as this.

The Supreme Allied Commander Mediterranean Forces, Sir Henry Maitland-Wilson, took the salute and went on board, accompanied by other dignitaries. The severely disabled and the very sick were carried ashore for treatment in the Algiers hospitals.

Hilda Edwards, as one of a number of invited Servicewomen, ATS, WAAF, WRNS, FANYs and other nurses, went on board for dinner. The men were shy at first and Hilda found conversation difficult.

'Some had been prisoners for four years and we were the first women they had spoken to during that time. But, gradually, the barriers came down and they began to speak freely of the places they had known before captivity, Abyssinia, Tobruk and Benghazi. They all wanted news of home. Was England as beautiful as ever? How was London after the bombs?'

Hilda's escort into dinner was a South African, one of the many Dominion soldiers on board. Before the war he had been a big game hunter. As he led her into dinner, this now sick and ailing man leant across the table and plucked a flower from a vase which he gravely presented to her. 'It is so long since I gave flowers to a woman.' The little tribute lies faded between the leaves of a book in Hilda's home in Dyfed today.

The reception on board the *Gripsholm* served to cushion the first brush with society for men who had been out of it for so long. Ahead of them was a difficult period of readjustment with their families, and men whose appearance was drastically changed watched with dread as well as joy as the visitors arrived for the first meeting in an English hospital. The ward with its lack of privacy was a poor setting for reunions of deep emotional significance and sometimes pitiful fragility. The euphoria of release frequently gave way to a depression which only time could heal, and some of the men had little enough of that particular balm left.

19

Prelude to Overlord

By 1943, Japan was no longer the all-powerful nation she had once appeared to be. On the contrary, she was being steadily driven from most of the territories she had appropriated. Her troops in New Guinea were being pushed back over the mountains by Australian and American forces until their only remaining foothold was the town of Lae on the northern coast. That campaign was a tough test not only for the fighting men but also for the nurses who accompanied them.

During the wet season when two to four inches of rain fell every afternoon, water rushed through the centre of the ward tents in a torrent. Even the simplest nursing treatments were complicated by having to be carried out in ankle deep mud. Collection of wounded from the dense jungle was difficult enough in the dry season, but when the searching planes were grounded by rain an injured man might lie for days before being found, with nothing over his wound but the emergency dressing he applied himself. Anyone who could walk did so, even though he might be seven or eight days on the way before coming across a jeep to take him to the nearest air-strip. When the wounded were eventually brought to the 2nd/9th Australian General Hospital, they were deeply ashamed of their condition and would protest that they were too dirty to be touched by the Sisters who bathed them, made them comfortable and dressed their wounds.

The workload of the nursing staff was heavy. In addition to medical attention, care had to be taken to protect each patient with mosquito netting every night in order to keep malaria at bay; no small task when the bed-state rose to 2,000 wounded, as it did at the 2nd/9th AGH during the Buna Gona 'push'. Matron Nell Marshall, Australian Army Nursing Service (RRC, later Williamson), pays this tribute to her staff:

'My girls were tremendous. No days off. Working in gum-boots in all that heat from six in the morning till nine at night with never a growl from any one of them.'

The operating theatre was an old tin hut, gauzed in to keep out the flies and with a permanent audience of natives at the door, watching the surgeons at work. For six weeks during the bitter Kokoda Trail campaign the operating theatre was never empty.

From the hospital, casualties were taken to Port Moresby for evacuation by hospital ship to Brisbane in Queensland. The *Manunda*, despite several narrow escapes, was in operation on this run from start to finish of the New Guinea campaign, but her sister ship, the *Centaur*, was sunk on her second voyage. She was forty miles east of Brisbane on her outward trip on 14th May, 1943, when a submarine attacked. A torpedo sliced her in two. Of the twelve Australian Sisters on board, only Ellen Savage survived. For her courageous support of fellow survivors during the thirty-six hours before they were rescued, she was awarded the George Medal.

The sea claimed the lives of many nurses during the Second World War. One of the greatest disasters took place the following year, on 12th February, 1944, when the *Khedive Ismail* (British India Navigation Company and later P & O Line) was sunk south-west of Ceylon. Bound for Colombo with troops and the entire staff of a general hospital on board, she went down with a loss of 1,300 lives, which included all forty-four Sisters of the 150th British General Hospital.

Despite these tragic losses, fortune was beginning to favour the Allies. In particular, intensive medical research was producing notable results. Chemotherapy was clearing the wards of British hospitals. Penicillin was eliminating sepsis and sulphaguanidine was reducing dysentery to a condition which no longer required hospitalisation. Nowhere was this improvement more evident than in the Far East, where malaria was being brought under control. No such benefits were available to the Japanese troops. Ill-nourished and unprotected by prophylaxis, they died like flies in the jungles of Burma. 15,000 perished during their retreat in New Guinea.

In the spring of 1944, events that boded well for an Allied victory occurred one after another. The Germans were now in full retreat across Russia, after suffering a huge defeat at the siege of Stalingrad. North Africa had been won, Italy half-won and the Italians were out of the war. The time was approaching for the long-awaited Second Front to be launched in Europe. Hope of ultimate victory at last seemed justified.

None of the good news reached the unfortunate prisoners of the Japanese who were hidden away from the rest of the world in jungle camps. Starvation and disease took their toll as one hopeless year followed another. Had they known, in 1944, that the tide had turned against the Japanese at least, they might have found the strength to hang on. In the event, the last year of imprisonment proved for many to be the straw that broke the camel's back.

In Britain, rumours that the Second Front was about to begin became more persistent, and dogged civilians set themselves to endure and to keep on enduring, for as long as they were necessary, the privations and shortages of their daily life. This meant more recipes for eking out the food ration, more clever dodges to make clothes last longer - new cuffs made from shirt tails, mittens from old socks and knickers from sub-standard parachutes. Great films full of love and glycerine tears offered escapism at two shillings for a seat in the dress circle, and when such palliatives failed, there was always a sympathetic ear and a shoulder to cry on down in the air raid shelter.

The cities were scarred and gutted by fire. Terraced houses bereft of lifelong neighbours leaned unsteadily on their scaffolding crutches and tarpaulins flapped amongst the chimney pots. All this was accepted with stoicism because things were just as bad, if not worse, in Germany. To judge by the nine o'clock news every night, nothing could possibly remain of the Dortmund-Ems Canal, and the marshalling yards at Frankfurt were regularly wiped out.

The appointment with the wireless set, kept so steadfastly through the years when nothing was offered but blood, toil and sweat, was now paying out little dividends. Alvar Liddell and Bruce Belfridge no longer reported retreats and disasters. Hitler's invading days were over and his frontiers were closing in on him.

Never before had an operation been so meticulously planned as 'Operation Overlord', the invasion of Normandy. The effort and courage needed for this huge gamble constituted the greatest demand yet made on the troops. Casualties would be high. The Germans had used their four years of occupation in Northern France to construct a formidable line of seaward defences. But the time had come when Hitler must be fought on his own ground, and the troops went into training.

They trusted that their Generals would not set them a task beyond their strength and that they would acquit themselves honourably. Although their lives were ordered for them, death was their own affair, and they must meet it as well as they could. Like everyone else, they had their ideals about freedom, but when confronted with the moment of personal accountability, when they had to face a swivelling machine gun which paid out death like tickertape, when the order was 'Clear that minefield', they were not thinking of the suffering Poles, Czechs,

Norwegians, Danes, Dutch, Belgians and French. For them, trails of glory and trumpet fanfares no longer embellished the image of war. They were too conscious of the vulnerability of their own guts for poetry to matter.

In the acute nearness of death, they were thinking not of home and country, not even of their loved ones, but of their mates and their cap badge and all the mates they had lost along the way. In his own peculiar way, the British Tommy wrapped up his embarrassment at such thoughts and made a joke of dying.

When the moon and the tides were right; when the weather was in a co-operative phase; when ample troops were ready and vast reserves of weapons and ammunition had been built up; when enough planes, tanks, amphibious vehicles, ships and landing craft had been assembled; when the Quartermasters' Stores overflowed with boots, buttons, ink and toilet paper; then 'Overlord' would begin.

Britain became a storehouse of war materials and a vast depot of troops. Uniformed men of many countries jostled long-suffering civilians in their crowded buses and trains. There was no room to walk on the pavements of Piccadilly for GI guys making for the 'Rainbow Room'. Their jeeps rattled along country lanes, and old men groused as 'them Yanks' innocently appropriated time-hallowed corners in the pubs.

Newly qualified nurses, who had begun their training in 1940 and had missed the earlier campaigns, now lost no time in applying for the Services. They were equipped and eager to play a part in the invasion of Europe.

At this stage of the war, care of the wounded had reached a high degree of efficiency. Any delays in getting an injured man to a surgical unit had been ironed out and his evacuation from there to a place of safety followed at once. Landing Ship Tanks (LSTs) and hospital carriers would take care of the first casualties from the Normandy beaches, and it was hoped that within a few hours of being wounded they would be back in an English hospital.

With memories of Dunkirk still fresh in the mind, medical authorities laid in massive banks of blood and plasma and, as the appointed day drew near, all hospitals in the south of England evacuated their patients to places further north. One immeasurable advantage would help the casualties of this campaign: penicillin was available for every wounded man.

Medical units which were to take part in the operation were alerted at the beginning of the year. Army General Hospitals, Casualty Clearing Stations and Field Dressing Stations, Naval and RAF Sick Bays, all were brought up to strength and ordered to pack their equipment. Every surgical instrument had to be greased against rust, wrapped in oiled paper, sewn in sacking and stencilled with a code. These were the days before plastic. Every enamel bowl, jug, kidney dish, every piece of operating equipment and every bedpan, urinal, drip stand, bed cradle, splint, syringe, and a Union Jack for burials, all must be wrapped and packed in tea chests, then identified with a stencil for speedy reassembly. Because of the experience gained abroad, a 1,200-bedded hospital could be operational within forty-eight hours of arriving at a selected site.

Experienced Matrons and Senior Sisters were brought back to Britain from overseas stations to accompany the hospitals and CCSs bound for France. The rest of the nursing staff was chosen with care. There are those who excel in initiative and leadership and others for whom bedside nursing is sufficient responsibility and complete fulfilment. Both types were necessary, and it was essential that square pegs were not put in round holes.

Matron Monica Johnson, now at Southern Command HQ in England, was able to advise on the choice of staff after her years of hospital administration and personal knowledge of so many Sisters. Nevertheless, she would have exchanged her present position eagerly for the opportunity to take a hospital to France once more, for she remembered the ignominy of Dunkirk, but in this campaign she was required to remain at home base.

For the first time, a programme of physical training was drawn up for Nursing Sisters. After four years of war, it was realised that they needed to be fit, able to scale a rope ladder over the side of a ship, jump from a burning deck into a heaving boat and sleep on the ground with only a hip-hole for comfort. During this spring prelude, they learned how to march, how to scramble through barbed-wire barricades and how to defend themselves from an attacker. They wore boots and men's battledress of a material specially treated to repel vermin, which was as unsympathetic to the skin as hairy cardboard. The beloved 'grey and scarlet' of the QAs and the Navy and RAF 'blues' went down to the bottom of the tin trunks, until such time when veils would take the place of tin hats once more.

The LSTs which would evacuate the first casualties from the landing beaches had a capacity for 350 stretcher cases in addition to 160
walking wounded. They would be staffed by an all-male Naval medical
team of surgeons and Sick Berth Attendants. Hospital carriers with
Sisters on board would take part in all subsequent trips.

With their superior manoeuvrability and shallow draught, the carriers were more fitted to work in the Channel than the larger hospital
ships, and a small fleet was assembled and prepared for duty in Normandy. The *Dinard* was recalled from the Mediterranean to join the
Amsterdam, the *Isle of Jersey*, the *Duke of Lancaster* and her sister ship,
the *Duke of Rothesay*. Each carried four to six Sisters of the QAIMNS,
seven or eight RAMC doctors and supporting RAMC orderlies, in
addition to the vessel's crew.

The *Duke of Rothesay*, which had started life as a railway ferry on
the Hersham-Belfast run, had been operating until now as an assault
ship. As her Captain watched the camouflage paint being replaced by
sparkling white in the docks at North Shields in Northumberland, it
is possible that he preferred her old role to the new; an unseen vessel
slipping through the darkness of the night felt much safer than this
gleaming target lit from stem to stern.

The smoking lounge of her pre-war days became the operating
theatre. All four decks were fitted with double tiers of bunks, and there
were special arrangements for spinal injuries and fractures. The
Amsterdam was a newer ship with a purpose-built interior, and QA
Molly Evershed counted herself lucky to be chosen for one of her staff.
Glad to be leaving the military hospital in Wales which had little
involvement with the forthcoming campaign, she wrote to her sister in
Cambridge, 'The *Amsterdam* is a smashing ship. At last I can make a
worthwhile contribution to the war.'

In the event, her contribution proved to be over and above the call
of duty.

By the end of May 1944, a state of readiness had been reached in
all departments of war. Troops in the peak of condition waited in
heavily guarded marshalling camps. Ships of a variety of categories
took up position in southern ports and estuaries. There was barely
time to rejoice at the fall of Rome on 4th June before the invasion of
Normandy began.

On the night of 5th June, the golden sunset in Britain was overlaid
by a veil of tiny specks rising from the land in the west and heading

south-east. The evening air throbbed. The images grew in size until they became identifiable as a great concourse of planes: 'ours' this time, not 'theirs'. People ran out of their houses into the streets, turning marvellous faces to the sky as Albemarles and Stirlings went over, towing gliders filled with troops. Every man, woman and child knew that this was the opening of the Second Front.

QA Marjorie Smith went to sleep that night on the hospital carrier *Duke of Rothesay*, berthed in the Thames estuary, and awoke in the early hours of the morning to find herself at sea surrounded by ships towing sections of the Mulberry artificial harbour destined for the coast of Normandy.

'We had sailed through the Straits of Dover in the company of the invasion fleet and were now ordered to detach ourselves and proceed to Southampton. Our sailing orders came two days later.'

Complete surprise was achieved by the assault troops. German Intelligence was aware that a landing was imminent but believed it would take place in the Pas de Calais. Even after the troops had gone ashore, some time elapsed before reports of a landing were confirmed and German reinforcements could be sent to the area. By then, the First US Army held the coastline from the base of the Cotentin peninsula eastwards to Colville-sur-Mer and the Second British Army, which incorporated the Third Canadian Division, were ashore and covering an area stretching from Arromanches to the mouth of the River Orne at the eastern extremity. The Allies had a toe-hold in Hitler's France.

20

The Second Front

As anticipated, the first casualties after the landings were back inEngland, receiving treatment at Dover EMS Hospital, within a few hours of being wounded. The capacity of that small hospital was quickly outstripped, and subsequent convoys were met by ambulance train and taken to two large receiving centres at Botley's Park near Chertsey and at Swindon. Pressure on these centres was heavy until such time as hospitals could be established ashore on the Normandy bridgehead. Convoys of 600 came twice daily, to be treated, washed, fed and passed on. Only those in need of urgent surgery were retained. The remainder were passed to the appropriate specialist hospital – Oxford for Heads, Basingstoke for Maxillo-Facials, Liphook for Chests, Stoke Mandeville for Spines and Limbs. American casualties were treated in their own hospitals in England.

Student nurses evacuated from London's St Thomas's Hospital to Botley's Park suddenly came to grips with battle casualties at first hand. There was scarcely time to change the sheets after one evacuation before the next convoy arrived.

'There was a marvellous spirit throughout the hospital,' wrote student nurse Rachel Cashmore (later Taylor). 'I doubt if the heavily financed National Health Service of today, with so many staff levels, could cope with a similar situation. We did the lot, cleaning, cooking, catering, clerical work and, of course, the nursing.'

German POWs who came in with the rest of the wounded were put down one side of the ward and Allied soldiers down the other, facing each other, sharing the same doctors, nurses, orderlies and even bedpans. The situation was too much for the Tommies' sense of humour. They picked up their crutches, 'phtt-phtting' along the row of beds opposite; their enemies, shouting '*Freund!*', flung up their arms in mock surrender. The deadliness of the recent battles was translated into pantomime.

From 8th June onwards, hospital carriers took their turn at picking up casualties from the beaches, going in to load amidst the din of bombardment from the Royal Navy standing off-shore. The wounded had received only emergency treatment from the Advanced Surgical

Units who had gone ashore with the assault troops and they came on board with intravenous drips still in position. Some were not fully round from the anaesthetic given to them in a Field Dressing Station, and many needed immediate operation by the ship's surgeons. The six Sisters on the staff of the *Duke of Rothesay* were kept busy during the two and a half hour crossing, administering drugs, checking dressings and plasters.

'What the men wanted above all else,' wrote Sister Marjorie Smith, 'was to have a wash and get into clean pyjamas. They were all given Dorothy Bags provided by the Red Cross which contained toilet articles, cigarettes, chocolates and a paperback book. All of this was much appreciated, as was the gesture on the part of the ship's officers who, of their own volition, went round the wards as barbers, shaving men who could not do it for themselves. Sadly, we never learned what became of our patients, as ambulance trains awaited them at our port of arrival in England.'

Advance parties from hospitals and Casualty Clearing Stations consisting of men only went ashore on 10th June, the Sisters following six days later. Number 32 CCS opened up in La Riviére not long after the town had been won by the East Yorks in bitter hand-to-hand fighting. Many seriously injured men urgently needed attention, and, until the Sisters of the unit arrived, RAMC surgeons did day and night duty on the wards as well as their own work in the theatre. Well-trained though the orderlies were, they could not give the intensive post-operative care that was necessary if men with serious abdominal wounds were to survive. In a ditch spiked with wooden crosses, one of the newly arrived QAs found the grave of her Commando brother.

The first nurses to land were Senior Sister Iris Ogilvie, later Bower, MBE. ARRC. and Sister Mollie Giles, later Eichenberger, MBE. ARRC. of Princess Mary's Royal Air Force Nursing Service. In pitch darkness on the night of June 12th, they were landed on Juno Red Beach and escorted inland to snatch a couple of hours sleep in a slit trench before joining their unit, the 50th RAF Mobile Field Hospital.

This unit was to carve itself a fine record in the critical days ahead, carrying out surgery and assisting in the evacuation of thousands of casualties by Dakota.

Five general hospitals, Numbers 79, 81, 84, 86 and 87, landed in Normandy on 16th and 17th June, just before a series of Channel storms of a fury unprecedented for that month. The weather put a temporary stop to the follow-up of men and supplies. The 75th BGH, sailing from Southampton on 19th June under lowering skies, was caught up by gales which wrenched mines from their moorings and sank more ships than were lost on D-Day itself. Large sections of the Mulberry Harbour were torn up and destroyed. No troop reinforcements or ammunition could be landed on the beaches. Casualties could not be evacuated. In all the once fashionable hotels along the Normandy coastline, at Gris-sur-Mer and Courseulles-sur-Mer, the wounded lay on stretchers awaiting evacuation, their numbers swelling with each day that passed, but Dakotas could not fly nor ships sail during those four days of storm. Hitler could not have engineered a better ally at this critical moment than the English Channel.

On the evening of the fourth day, the seas calmed and fifty sea-sick Sisters of the 75th BGH landed shakily at Arromanches. Their hospital was urgently needed ashore, for German reinforcements were now arriving at the invasion area in some force and every Allied advance was achieved at the cost of many casualties. There was no room for complacency over the progress of 'Overlord'. The limit of the bridge-head on 23rd June when the storm ceased was no more than thirty-five miles wide and five miles deep in the weakest area. At any time, the whole ambitious venture could be overturned and the troops pushed back into the sea.

In the British sector, the town of Caen was proving to be an unexpected obstacle. Unknown to British Intelligence, Panzer troops had moved into this area to rest just before the invasion took place and what had been detailed as a D-Day objective by the British Second Army was not captured until several weeks later after much hard fighting.

After one particularly disastrous attempt by the Canadians to take the town, the Canadian hospital was totally swamped with casualties and British units stepped in to help. Number 35 CCS took 100 of the most seriously injured cases and stopped admitting on its own account until the crisis was over.

Sister Helen Wright (RRC, later Stanger) was Senior Sister of the CCS. 'They were mostly French-Canadians and all had severe abdominal wounds. We nursed them solidly without a break. All were on intravenous drips and continual gastric lavage. The latter was a great boon for, without this emptying of the stomach, the patients would not have been permitted to take anything by mouth. As it was, we were able to keep their mouths fresh and clean, which was a great comfort to them. Thanks to the really splendid efforts on the part of the staff, we lost only six of those very ill men.'

In German hospitals, such severe injuries were judged to be too difficult to nurse under battle conditions and men with major abdominal wounds were left to die.

Safe sites for hospitals were difficult to find. Number 3 CCS at its post near 'Jerusalem Crossroads' at Bayeux became acutely vulnerable when Royal Engineers began to construct an air-strip nearby. German gunners found the range and from then onwards the tents of the CCS were exposed to continual bombardment. Of the eight or ten Sisters on the staff of a Casualty Clearing Station only one can be spared for night duty, so Sister Margaret Cromar was alone with her orderlies when shelling began and was glad of the company of one of the day Sisters who got up to help her. Sister MacLaughlin had seen active service in North Africa and knew what it was to be alone with a ward of gravely ill men during a shelling attack. With the help of orderlies, all the beds were collapsed so that patients rested on the tent floor for extra safety. This became a nightly routine, and Sister MacLaughlin never failed to give assistance – until one night the padre came in her place. She had been seriously wounded in the chest by shrapnel. The CCS was moved to a place of greater safety. Protective earth walls were thrown up around the tent which housed the abdominal cases and Sisters and orderlies came in shifts from the new site to nurse these very ill men until they were fit enough to be moved.

There was no room in Normandy for any man who could not fight, so even such minor cases as septic fingers or haemorrhoids were evacuated along with more seriously injured men. Evacuation went on by sea and by air whenever the weather permitted. Each day, the senior RAMC officer of each medical unit did a round of the hospital wards with the Company Officer in tow, marking off men for evacuation. The turnover at a 600-bedded hospital was frequently as high as 400 in and 300 out on the same day.

Inevitably, during the initial off-shore bombardment, there had been casualties amongst French civilians despite efforts on the part of the Allies to give them warning. Immediately prior to bombing attacks on strategic points, leaflets had been dropped over the villages involved.

MESSAGE URGENT DU COMMANDEMANT SUPRÊME DES FORCES, EXPÉDITIONNAIRES DES ALLIÉES AUX HABITANTS DE CETTE VILLE

Afin que l'ennemi commun soit vaincu, les Armées d'air Alliées vont attaquer tous les centres de transports ainsi que toutes les voies et moyens de communications vitaux pour l'ennemi.

Des ordres a cet effet ont été donnés. Vous qui lisez ce tract, vous vous trouvez dans ou près d'un centre essentiel à l'ennemi pour le mouvement de ses troupes et de son material.

L'objectif vital près duquel vous vous trouvez, va être attaqué incessement. Il faut, sans delai, vous éloigner avec votre famille pendant quelque jours de la zone de danger où vous vous trouvez.

N'encombrez pas les routes. Dispersez-vous dans la campagne autant que possible.

PARTEZ SUR LE CHAMP!
VOUS N'AVEZ PAS UNE MINUTE À PERDRE!

Translated, the warning reads,

URGENT MESSAGE FROM THE SUPREME COMMAND OF THE ALLIED EXPEDITIONARY FORCES TO THE INHABITANTS OF THIS VILLAGE

In order that the common enemy may be conquered, Allied Air Forces are going to attack all centres of transport as well as all the methods and means of communication vital to the enemy.

Orders to this effect have already been given. You who read this tract happen to be near a centre which is essential to the enemy for the movement of his troops and materials.

The vital target near you will soon be under incessant bombardment. You must escape at once with your family and stay out of the danger zone in which you are placed for several days.

Do not cause congestion on the roads. Scatter into the countryside as much as possible.

LEAVE IMMEDIATELY!
YOU HAVE NOT A MINUTE TO SPARE!

With few drugs and scant equipment, French authorities did their best for their casualties in the Bayeux hospital, a building which had been used by the Germans as a prison and had been left in a filthy condition. Certain QAs with a good working knowledge of French were sent to help the French nurses and were given, as assistants, women from the town whose linen caps concealed the shaven heads of collaborators. Many of the wounded died a terrible death, for the soil of Normandy is laden with the spores of tetanus and no life-saving serum was available.

Seven and a half of the eight German Panzer Divisions employed in Normandy were engaged by the British Army in the Caen area. This was by design. With the greater part of German forces concentrated in the east, American forces at the western end of the bridgehead were able to overrun the whole of the Cotentin peninsula, in spite of the difficult swampy terrain, and capture the port of Cherbourg. Not until Caen fell, however, after a massive carpet of bombs had been laid down on 7th July, could the invasion be seen to have succeeded and the occupation secured.

Using Caen as a pivot, the whole Allied line swung east, trapping an entire German army in what has become known as the Falaise pocket, because Hitler would not sanction a strategic withdrawal from the area. German POWs overflowed the cages and their wounded were brought in hundreds to the British hospitals. Some were older men, suffering from bad feet and ulcers, the call-up from Hitler's latest recruitment drive. Some were mere schoolboys of fifteen and sixteen years of age, glad to be out of the fighting; some were SS troops, overbearing even in defeat.

The SS troops were splendid specimens of manhood in their black military uniform with silver facings and epaulettes, but Sister Margaret Kneebone of the 39th BGH near Bayeux saw a different side. 'We had to wear boots and gaiters all the time when nursing SS men, for some of them deliberately messed on the floor to insult us.'

The intensity of their hatred came as a shock to British nurses whose profession made no distinction between friend and enemy. One lay on a stretcher, drained by haemorrhage. '*Wasser, Wasser,*' he whispered. When his eyes focused on the khaki battledress of the QA who held the feeding cup to his lips, he spat full in her face. 'English pig!'

They were totally without pity, for themselves or for their comrades. 'Why do you waste your time on him?' a German officer demanded of Sister Kneebone as she tended the eighteen-year-old German youth in the next bed. After a major abdominal operation, he was being given the routine intravenous fluid therapy. She was indeed wasting her time, for the young man had no intention of co-operating in this attempt to save his life. A product of Hitler Youth indoctrination, he was resolved to die for the Führer; he eventually succeeded, after repeatedly pulling out his stomach tube and intravenous needle.

The ordinary German soldier was a different being altogether, an uncomplaining patient who was grateful for anything done for his comfort. In his own hospitals at that time, standards of medical and nursing care were low. Germany was turning out doctors for the armed forces after only two years' training. Equipment was poor. Their bandages were made of paper and, of course, they lacked the great Allied advantage of penicillin. Some captive German doctors even attempted to precipitate the drug by distilling the urine of British soldiers who were being treated with it.

The Falaise battle inevitably caused many Allied casualties. The hospital carrier *Amsterdam* had already made two cross-Channel trips with patients and was mid-way on her third on 7th August when she struck a mine. One half of the vessel was completely wrecked and all in the engine room were lost. As many as possible of her full load of casualties were helped to safety, and the Sister in Charge, Miss Dorothy Anyta Field, QAIMNS, was already in a lifeboat when she realised that many helpless men who were still below decks would have to be abandoned. She insisted on returning to the ship, even as it began to settle in the water, and climbed back on board accompanied by one of her staff, Sister Molly Evershed.

In all, the two Sisters brought seventy-five men from the ward below decks to safety, returning for more after each one was delivered over the ship's rail, even though they knew that at any minute the stricken vessel could plummet to the bottom of the sea. The last to be brought up was a man whose leg had been amputated just before the mine exploded.

No longer able to walk upright because of the angle of the deck, the two Sisters went below for what was to be their last trip. In a final convulsion, the sea closed over the *Amsterdam*, its patients and the two women who gave their lives in their service. There was a fleeting image before the ship disappeared from sight of sturdy Molly Evershed trying in vain to squeeze her hips through a porthole. She was twenty-nine years old and had recently become engaged to marry an Engineer. Miss Field was thirty-two. Seventy-five grateful men wrote to the parents of the two women, who were posthumously Mentioned in Dispatches.

Paris was liberated on 25th August. On 3rd September, five years to the day since Britain and France had declared war, Brussels was freed. QAs exchanged the muddy tents of Normandy for modern accommodation with electric light and flush toilets. A bath was no longer a chilly affair to be taken with one foot in a biscuit tin of hot water wearing nothing at all but a tin-hat.

Conventional indoor uniform and white head-veils could be worn again, for battledress and gum-boots had no place on the bright wards of Brussels' modern hospitals.

Some of the first casualties were Canadians, whose task it had been to clear the pockets of German resistance from the islands in the Scheldt estuary. Until this was done, the port of Antwerp could not be used. Risks had to be taken and the Canadian Major leading his men over a bridge knew well that it might be mined. It was. He now lay, propped up on cushions with his head on one side, as a Sister tried to feed him with rice pudding. He had a hole in his cheek much bigger than his mouth and the trick was to induce the pudding to go the right way. This was a job which could not be hurried and gave the Major the chance to talk between mouthfuls.

'When you've got a minute, Sister, would you mind writing a note to my wife to tell her I'm OK?'

'OK' was scarcely an accurate description of his condition. He could not see the pain on the Sister's face, for he was blind. Even that was not the sum of his afflictions, because he had also lost a leg. There is no other phrase than 'wringing of the heart' to describe the wearisome, twisting sensation that a nurse feels in the upper left quadrant of the thoracic cavity when confronted with such tragedy.

In spite of the disastrous downturn of his fortunes in France, Hitler still believed that the final victory could be his, and that it would be brought about by his two secret weapons, the V1 and the V2. They were his talisman: with them he meant to terrorise and destroy London and southern England to such an extent that Britain would be deflected from her aims in Europe.

The first pilotless flying bomb was launched from Holland on 12th June, to fall on south-east England. 2,000 more landed within the next two weeks, half of them falling on London. Nothing like them had been seen before. Civilians whose ears had become attuned over the years to the drone of an enemy bomber now learned to dive for cover at the odd rattle of an approaching V1, nicknamed the 'doodlebug'. Once the engine cut out, it was usually too late to take cover. The missile with its warhead of a ton of explosive crashed to the ground, inflicting enormous damage.

Dense conurbations such as the Croydon area were favourite targets and St Helier's Hospital at Carshalton was hit twice in five days. On 22nd June a flying bomb landed on the Nurses' Home and injured nurses were wheeled to the operating theatre throughout that day. The Medical Superintendent who was crossing the grounds at the time lost an eye, amongst other injuries, and crawled to his own casualty department on his hands and knees.

On the second occasion, the bomb landed on the roof of the hospital with its engines still running. Second-year student nurse, Inge Fehr (later Samson), a young German-Jewish refugee from Berlin, had just left the ward and was walking downstairs. She had meant to take the lift but when it was slow in coming she decided to walk, which turned out to be a lucky decision for her.

As the flying bomb settled on the roof, the whole building began to shake as if in an earthquake. Ceilings collapsed. Doors flew off their hinges. Screaming patients were flung from their beds. A massive explosion followed and the lift crashed down four flights to the basement. Nurse Fehr hurried to the wards with a rescue team. A twelve-year-old girl lay dead at the entrance to the children's ward, and a VAD with severe facial injuries was carried by on a stretcher.

'I recognised Nurse Grosvenor who had often worked with me. We'd always got on well together and I was sorry when she did not return to the hospital. Not until much later did I learn that she was the Duke of Westminster's daughter.'

Not all flying bombs reached their destinations. Allied planes attacking the launching pads destroyed many on the ground and pilots of the new fast jet planes, the Meteors and the Vampires, found that they could overtake a bomb in flight and, by tipping its wing, upset the internal gyro and send it spinning harmlessly into the sea.

Hitler's second secret weapon was even more deadly, however, because of its silent approach. The V2 rocket which appeared over Britain in September gave no warning rattle. Travelling silently, they homed in on their targets at the rate of 200 a month and laid waste great areas of the densely populated south-east corner of England. As the numbers of homeless grew, ARP and Welfare organisations opened clothing and blanket stores. Mobile Red Cross canteens provided hot soup and sandwiches for thousands of people.

One town, however, had cause for rejoicing. When the big gun at Calais was captured in October 1944 Dover went wild with delight. Sister Betty Le Grys was still at her post at Dover EMS hospital, after four years during which shelling had become an accepted hazard of life.

'One Saturday morning, soon after eight o'clock, we heard the loud-speaker van outside. This often happened, and it was usually to tell us that there would be no bread or milk, owing to enemy action. But this time, the cheerful message was: "Our forces have captured the gun at Calais. No more shells will be fired."

'The town went mad. That day was Dover's special celebration. I gave Jock, the theatre orderly, permission to go down to the town, and later he had some explaining to do to his wife when he appeared on a Newsreel dancing in the High Street with a bevy of nurses. In the evening, I went down to the crowded pub. "Here's one of the nurses from the hospital!" somebody sang out. "Give her a drink, Landlord!"

'We organised a hospital dance as a celebration and the Navy came good with an immensely deceptive "non-alcoholic" punch. We all felt slightly crazy with relief. I doubt if any outsider could realise the sensations we had felt every time we heard that double siren, the signal for another bout of shelling.'

The Allied Front in Europe was now coming up against long-established German defensive positions and progress slowed to a costly, yard-by-yard slog. An imaginative move was planned, therefore, to take the troops in one leap over the Rivers Maas and Rhine to Arnhem in Holland. Had 'Operation Market Garden' succeeded, it would have cut the war short by several months, but it did not succeed. The original air drop of British and American paratroops landed too far from their objective. Bad weather robbed them of air cover and the single road along which supporting troops advanced from Eindehoven became choked with vehicles, while the men were exposed to the enemy's fire on both flanks.

When Number 3 CCS was ordered to Nijmegen to deal with an accumulation of wounded, its ambulances could move at no more than a snail's pace in the convoy of vehicles. Margaret Cromar, TANS, was still with this unit.

'There was one almighty traffic jam all the way from Eindehoven to

Nijmegen. We slept at night in the ambulances and made very little headway amongst all the troops and vehicles, until we were given priority to pass through the Guards' Division. We were exposed on both sides and troops facing outward lined the ditches, their rifles trained on the low-lying fields. Most of the buildings in Nijmegen had been badly bombed but we managed to find a somewhat shaky school which had been used by the Germans as a hospital. Here we set ourselves up and casualties were brought to us immediately.

'We had a lot of seriously injured men and consequently a number of unavoidable deaths, which did nothing to restore the morale of men who were already aware that the original plan had gone horribly wrong.'

After ten days of intense fighting inside Arnhem, the Allies were forced to accept defeat. As many as possible of those men inside the perimeters of the town were pulled back to safety but, of the 10,000 paratroopers engaged, only 2,165 escaped. 6,000, half of whom were wounded, were taken prisoner. Several hundred more wounded remained at large, hidden and cared for by the Dutch at great personal risk.

Number 3 CCS worked on at Nijmegen for eight weeks under constant shelling in a situation that was extremely unpredictable, as the padre discovered when he took himself off for a walk and came back with a handful of German prisoners. When the road back to Eindehoven was cut, which was often, there could be no evacuation of patients. On these occasions, the CCS was overwhelmed with wounded and the staff worked under great strain. The Sisters had reason to be grateful to a Dutch resident in the town who put his home at their disposal so that they might take it in turn to have a twenty-four-hour break while he himself mounted an armed guard over them.

The wounded men extricated from Arnhem were in a state of shock. They were passed quickly down the line, their faces still blackened with camouflage, to the more peaceful hospitals in Belgium. Some were quite unable to speak. Others were pitifully anxious to explain themselves to the Sisters who cared for them. 'I'm not a coward, Sister. I didn't run away ...'

They had been under sustained fire for nine days and, in the end, were without food, without sleep, without ammunition and without support. The failure of 'Operation Market Garden' put an end to all hopes of finishing the war in 1944.

When the winter rains flooded the approaches to the Rhine and snow crippled the jeep-drivers with frostbite, for that darling of all military vehicles gave scant protection to the man at the wheel, the Allied advance came to a halt. At this most unlikely moment, Hitler launched a strong counter-attack in the Ardennes region, which very nearly succeeded in driving a wedge from Liège to Antwerp between the Allied armies. After initial successes which sent Allied troops reeling back in disarray, the attack was contained and repelled – but not before Number 3 CCS had once more been moved to the seat of the action, to the snowbound forests where the plight of the wounded was made more miserable by the bitter weather. Margaret Cromar and another Sister were billeted in a lonely cottage, sharing its discomforts with the poverty-stricken Belgian occupants. Toothbrushes froze solid in the unheated bedroom and their breath formed icicles on the bed-clothes.

The Ardennes attack was Hitler's last fling. Spring brought the Russian armies to Germany's eastern borders and British, American and Free French troops crossed the Rhine into the Fatherland itself.

Margaret Kneebone was now Senior Sister at Number 24 CCS in attendance upon a joint American/British crossing of the Rhine near Wesel.

'The crossing was to take place on the night of Saturday/Sunday, and such was the morale of the troops that a soldier who broke his leg in a traffic accident a few hours earlier was as mad as a hornet to be missing the show. At nine o'clock the next morning, our Commanding Officer, Brigadier Kenneth Thomeroy, came and told us that the operation was under way and what we were to do. As a forward unit, we would hold only chests and abdominals.

'We received the first casualty within three-quarters of an hour of his being wounded and passed him on in good shape after transfusion with blood and plasma. The first day was not so bad, but by the third day we were taking in over 300 patients, Germans as well as our own boys. Inevitably, chests and abdominals built up and they needed a lot of nursing. We sat them up. Now, of course, you get them up and walk them around, but you need more staff for that. There were only four of us Sisters but the orderlies were very well trained. We worked in two duplicated teams of surgeon, anaesthetist, Sisters, orderlies, cooks and stretcher-bearers. The Brigadier held the view that working until you dropped was not efficient. By relieving each other, we could work around the clock. One person in each team was responsible for giving penicillin every three hours, another gave the sulphonamides every four hours. All the patients' medication was marked on coloured cards which showed at once when the next medication was due, for the benefit of the medical units down the line. We had had four years to get the system of documentation polished up and it worked like clockwork.'

It was nevertheless a heavy workload for a small staff of four Sisters. These were the days before the plastic disposable syringe. The glass types then in use had to be sterilised by boiling and they frequently cracked in the steriliser, despite being wrapped in gauze. After each round of penicillin injections, time had to be found for this procedure.

Once across the Rhine, the Allied advance was rapid. Hospitals fanned out in the wake of the troops through towns and villages where pillow slips and sheets hung from every window, signifying surrender, and women with pinched faces watched in silence as the once proud soldiers of the Wehrmacht were marched away to POW cages.

Sisters on busy wards did not welcome interruptions from visiting 'brass hats', and Pat Bradley of the 74th BGH was less than enthusiastic about the pending visit by General Dempsey himself, Commander-in-Chief to the British Second Army. She decided that her first priority lay with the fifty wounded men whose dressings she was responsible for, and appealed to the patients themselves and the orderlies to tidy up the ward.

'When the tent flap lifted and in came the C.-in-C., I hurriedly left my dressing trolley and joined the procession around the ward. The boys had done a·marvellous job. Not a beer-can or cigarette packet in sight. We stopped by one patient who had a bed-cradle in position and, in reply to a question by the General, the medical officer asked me to turn back the bedclothes so that he could show how the man's leg had been treated.

'When I drew back the sheets, not only did I disclose the man's legs but also a rubbish tip of cigarette ends, beer-cans, comics and every conceivable piece of junk which had been whisked out of sight in the ward.

'I believe,' says Pat Bradley soberly, 'that this was my worst moment of the war. My face went scarlet. So did Matron's. There was a deadly hush, for what seemed like an eternity, and then the General threw back his head and let out a huge belly laugh that filled the ward. The relief was enormous and the day was saved.'

Thankfully, during active service a blind eye was frequently turned to the more regimental aspects of army nursing.

As the Allied armies advanced, Allied POWs, some of whom had been captured as long ago as Dunkirk, spilled across the countryside as their camps were liberated. Too impatient to wait for Army transport, they set off for the coast and England on foot, by bicycle or horse-drawn cart – even, in one case, on a steam-roller. Allied wounded being treated in German hospitals were transferred at once to British Military Hospitals, to be spoiled by the nurses and given the best champagne that German Officers' Messes could provide.

In most cases, surgery by German doctors had been adequate but lack of proper after-care had resulted in considerable sepsis. They needed careful nursing and the blessing of penicillin before being sent home to Britain. In the case of sick foreign workers in German slave labour camps, however, medical treatment had been non-existent. One such worker, a Pole who was discovered in a German hospital, had received no treatment whatsoever for a severe jaw injury. He was in a pathetic condition, his jaw a suppurating mass. The staff had not bothered to find out if the man could eat. He had taken no nourishment for several days when the British doctors found him and sank a stomach tube to feed him at once. 'You are the first people to do anything for me,' he told the Sisters.

After the revelation of the inhuman labour camps came the even more shocking discovery of the concentration camps, more accurately termed 'death camps', since their sole object was the extermination of enemies of the Third Reich. One after another, in the secret and remote places of Europe, these heavily guarded encampments with their sinister chimneys came to light. The first was brought to the notice of the British forces by the Germans themselves.

The German Commandant of the Bergen-Belsen concentration camp in Lower Saxony was in a state of mounting panic as the British Front Line drew nearer. He had under his command 60,000 prisoners, of whom 1,500 were suffering from typhus and a further 900 from typhoid. Numerous other diseases raged unchecked through the camp but it was the two killers, typhus and typhoid, which concerned him most, and justifiably. Within the space of a week at most, Belsen would be overrun by the British and the first result, as he saw it, would be the escape into the surrounding countryside of all the inmates. Disease would spread in epidemic proportions across Germany. Astute enough to see that this would be as much of a disaster to the enemy as to the German people themselves, he approached the nearest British HQ under cover of a white flag with a request that they move in at once and take responsibility for the camp. As a result, the area around the camp was declared a neutral zone and a truce of forty-eight hours was arranged to allow for the transfer of administration.

The British inspection party which came to assess the extent of the problem was headed by the Divisional Director of Medical Services, RAMC. He was a man well used to the ugliness of war, but he had to turn aside to vomit when he first set eyes on Belsen concentration camp. The effect on a civilised man was one of total shock.

Ten thousand bodies lay unburied. More were decomposing in open pits. Those prisoners still on their feet were walking skeletons, and the long accommodation huts were full of the dying for whom salvation had come too late. For the last three days before the terrified Commandant decided to approach the British, food and water had been deliberately withheld, in the hope that death would solve his problems.

All who were still alive suffered from the 'Durchfall' (diarrhoea), and, since no attempt had been made to provide sanitation, the situation was beyond belief. There are no words to describe the stench which invaded every intake of breath, which tainted the very clothes of the horrified British party who now moved amongst this corruption.

21

The Collapse of the Third Reich

On 17th April, 1945, British troops moved into Belsen. Under their supervision Nazi guards, both men and women, were ordered to bury the dead, which they did without outward sign of abhorrence or shame. Engineers laid on piped clean water and repaired the electricity supply, which had been put out of action by bombing. Number 11 Field Ambulance and Number 32 CCS, with its team of eight QAs under Senior Sister Miss Higginbotham (MBE), moved in to tackle a medical problem vast enough to put the entire hospital resources of London under strain.

The first priority was to remove all surviving inmates from their foul surroundings, as soon as suitable buildings to which they might be transferred could be found. For this purpose, the Panzer Grenadier Barracks close by the camp were ideal. The 200 German soldiers stationed there were given the option of surrender or of returning to their own lines. Most chose the latter, but Hungarian soldiers who had been undergoing training were left as a labour force, to be repatriated to Hungary when they were no longer needed. One QA was put in charge of the large dining block and kitchen and made responsible for the catering, while the other seven Sisters supervised the cleaning and preparation of wards in the main barrack building.

Within the barracks complex was a German military hospital, staffed by German doctors and nurses, where patients were still being treated, but care for the sick had not extended beyond the hospital walls. The plight of 60,000 prisoners starving to death in the nearby camp had not concerned the German medical staff. Their total lack of feeling so angered the Commanding Officer of Number 32 CCS, who was now Camp Commandant, that he ordered a compulsory tour of the camp for all German personnel.

They went as requested, unquestioning and uncritical. The sights which had made a British Army doctor heave his heart up left no sign of emotion on the faces of these men and women who belonged to what is universally regarded as a caring profession.

Any British officers not engaged in the evacuation and disinfection of the camp scoured the surrounding countryside for food supplies.

The war was still on and food could not be diverted from military requirements, even for this crisis. Farms in the vicinity were ordered to provide meat and dairy produce. Burgomasters were instructed to collect beds and the Nazi camp guards were given bolts of calico and ordered to make sheets without delay. Until proper bedding was available, palliasses of straw had to suffice.

One of Sister Mary Sands' patients was a German who had been one of the courageous few to speak out in the early days against the growing power of the Nazis and their persecution of the Jews. He himself was not a Jew. The Gestapo had come to his house one night and taken him away. Since then, he had spent eight years in various concentration camps and was now little more than a skeleton.

'He was so delighted with his bundle of clean straw,' Mary Sands writes, 'he just wept and wept for joy.'

All the inmates of the camp were lousy. Every woman had a dirty head. One horrified medical officer came upon what he thought was an object covered with a moving white cloth but which was, in fact, a man shrouded in lice. Of necessity, therefore, each inmate was required to pass through a de-lousing centre before being admitted to the prepared wards.

This unpleasant duty was given to the German nurses who utilised the stables of the barracks for the purpose, carrying out their task dispassionately but with the utmost efficiency. Each inmate from the camp was bathed, shaved and totally disinfested before being carried to the new hospital building. Men of the RAMC and Pioneer Corps laboured long with stretchers, transferring patients from their filthy wooden huts in the camp to the bathing station, and from there to the barracks, where there were no lifts to make their task easier.

Enormous problems faced the doctors and the nurses on the wards. Each patient presented a multiple diagnosis. All suffered in varying degrees from dysentery and the effects of malnutrition. In addition, many had heart and kidney disease, tuberculosis, typhus, typhoid, diphtheria or poliomyelitis.

There was no choice of diet. As soon as supplies began to come in from the surrounding farms, the standard meal was a kind of goulash accompanied by bread and potatoes. This was far from suitable for very sick cases, yet control amongst the starving men and women was impossible. Many ate one meal and died. Until further deterioration

in their general health could be arrested, some 300 died every day.
Mass burials were conducted by padres of every denomination.

Among the camp victims were men, women and children of many
nationalities, but the majority were Poles – that race which, like the
Jews, cannot shake off martyrdom. All were uninformed about the
course of the war and totally uninterested. Their preoccupation
with food overrode all other interests. The staff found slices of
bread and meat under their pillows and even sacks of stolen potatoes
under their beds, which the nurses dared not remove for fear of bodily
harm.

As the patients regained strength, they became harder to manage.
They owed nothing to society, least of all gratitude, and some bitterly
resented the restrictions of the hospital. They took to wandering about
at night, stealing food, raiding dustbins and breaking into locked stores.
The Commanding Officer forbade QAs to do night duty, so the wards
went untended except for non-medical guards. The first task of the
Sisters when they came on duty in the morning was to check on who
had died during the night.

Mary Sands writes, 'It was a grisly task and reminded me of dreadful stories of the Black Death in the Middle Ages and the cries of
"Bring out your Dead!" We found bodies in all sorts of grotesque
positions, half out of bed, on the stairs, all with evidence of '*Durchfall.*'

Number 35 CCS arrived to ease the heavy workload which had been
carried so far by Number 32 CCS. A party of German nurses and
their Matron also appeared, begging to be allowed to help. These
women, who worked willingly and for long hours although their own
health was poor after years of inadequate food rationing, gained the
respect of the British Sisters. They were of special value in explaining
the use and dosage of the German drugs which were all that were
available.

Understandably, the German nurses met with resentment from
some of the patients, who never lost an opportunity to humiliate them.
They were all reduced to a state of hysteria one night when Russian
patients invaded their sleeping quarters, shaved the nurses' heads and
stole their uniforms. In the morning, the distraught German women
had no clothes to wear while Russian women patients strutted about
proudly in nurses' uniforms.

The Russian patients were the big trouble-makers throughout the
hospital. As an acknowledgement of the magnificent achievements of

the Red Army against Hitler and of the Russian patients' status as respected allies, they were given arms and some measure of responsibility over fellow patients, a move that was soon to be bitterly regretted. The Russian patients broke out of the hospital at night, marauding the surrounding farms and villages, raping the women, killing sheep and poultry, holding the men to ransom. On one occasion they held the Camp Commandant himself at gunpoint in his own office, demanding more food.

When the last sorry inmates had been removed from the camp, the filthy, vermin-ridden huts were soaked in petrol and burned. The putrid earth was seared with fire. The task ahead was to rehabilitate the survivors so that they could be repatriated at the end of the war. More medical aid arrived. The 163rd Field Ambulance, six British Red Cross teams of doctors and nurses, the 29th British General Hospital and ninety-seven volunteer medical students from the London hospitals moved into the Belsen compound and the barracks hospital.

There were not many laughs in their daily round, but the compulsory nightly disinfesting of themselves provided considerable comic relief for the Sisters. The modern pressure pack had yet to make an appearance on the market and the only available appliance for what was essentially a delicate operation was the old-fashioned and unwieldy Flit gun, which necessitated startling acrobatics in the nude.

Kindness and dedicated medical care eventually broke down the barriers of mistrust between the patients and their nurses and helpful relationships developed. A Jewish woman from Prague, whose lawyer husband had disappeared without trace, was deeply troubled and at last confided in Sister Mary Sands. In 1938, the couple, with a premonition of approaching danger, had sent their two sons to a guardian in Britain. Now the mother was torn with indecision as to whether she should try to contact them again. So much had happened to her in the intervening years since she had seen her sons that she felt she no longer knew them. With some diffidence, she agreed to write to them and was overwhelmed with joy when they replied.

'From that moment on, she had something to live for,' writes Mary, but she adds, 'I feared that she would not survive her freedom for long, since she had a serious heart condition. She had been used as a labourer in the camp, heaving sacks of coal from train to trucks, yet she insisted upon doing her share of work in the hospital although there was no need for her to do so. Every day, she peeled the potatoes in the hospital kitchen.'

One thing in the letter from her sons made her indignant. They had been sent to a Czech school although she had wanted them to be brought up as Englishmen, whom she considered to be the most honourable in the world.

'At the same time,' writes Sister Sands, 'she was concerned that we English might be too soft with the Nazis, not understanding how bestial they could be.'

The facts spoke for themselves. Concentration camps were coming to light at Dachau, Auschwitz, Ravensbrück, Sandbostel and many other sites. The gas ovens used for the extermination of millions of men, women and children were there for all to see. Deaths were meticulously documented in a neatly ordered nightmare created by the Nazis. No attempt was made to hide the fact that, in five years, 35,000 people were put to death at Mauthausen. 203 are recorded as having died of heart failure, in alphabetical order and at two minute intervals. At Büchenwald, five people were sacrificed daily by injecting them with typhus, so that a prophylactic serum might be obtained for German troops.

The German people professed ignorance of these horror camps but some, like an ageing German doctor who had served in the First World War, thought otherwise. 'We Germans,' he said, in utter wretchedness of spirit, 'have been a nation of cowards to let such a situation come about.'

Nurse Inge Fehr, whose Jewish father had once been an eminent professor of ophthalmic surgery in Berlin, went back to her home city after the war and was unable to trace a single living relative. 'There was nobody left in the phone book.'

On 30th April, 1945, with his enemies closing in on all sides, the man responsible for all this accumulated evil took his own life in an underground bunker in Berlin. With his death the infamous Third Reich ground to a halt and its forces collapsed. Not long afterwards, Montgomery's American pilot was taking coffee one morning with the Sisters of Number 35 CCS who had moved from Belsen and were now close to the General's headquarters.

'Waal,' drawled the American, consulting his watch, 'I reckon they'll be signing the surrender just about now.'

All hostilities ceased on 8th May. The liberated countries and poor, battered Britain went wild with joy. Strangers embraced in the streets. Church bells, silent for so long, clamoured from every steeple. Airmen, testing the benign temper of the skies, looped the loop and stood planes on their tails in joyful display. In the mind of every nurse and doctor the incredible truth took root: the killing and the maiming had come to an end at last. The guns in Europe were silent, and there would be no more convoys of bloodied stretchers carrying broken men.

Hospital rules went overboard that day, and there was no keeping a man in bed if he could get up to join in the celebrations. Miss Birch, TANS, last mentioned in the Italian campaign and now stationed at a military hospital at Renaix in Belgium, accompanied the medical officer on a routine ward round. They found all their patients but one had gone, and he too would have taken himself off to the town had he not been tethered to his bed by a blood transfusion.

'Then we might as well join them,' said the MO. Following the sound of hurdy-gurdy music and brass bands, they arrived at the town fair where all the village had congregated to celebrate the victory day. Amongst them were the patients from the hospital. Plastered limbs stuck out from the galloping horses and shiny pigs on the roundabouts and swings. Swathed in bandages, each with a Belgian girl on his arm, the patients swooped down the Big Dipper, blowing kisses to Sister Birch, yelling greetings to their doctor. In the centre of the fairground, sternly guarded by two small boys, was a mountain of crutches.

Kindly, tolerant Miss Birch would never have been cross with 'her boys', no matter what they did. 'Some of them still had their stitches in but luckily they held and no-one was any the worse for the escapade.'

Six days earlier, QA Frankie Newton had been involved in her own private surrender ceremony in Italy. Upon leaving the Indian CCS after the battle of Mount Cassino, she had joined the 12th British CCS as it leap-frogged up the Adriatic coast in the wake of the advancing troops, and was stationed north-west of Rimini on the slopes of the Apennines when the German Army in Italy surrendered. The first indication for the CCS that the war in Italy was over was the appearance of a group of British POWs in ragged uniform. They had walked out of their unguarded camp and now came singing and dancing down the hill to the tents of the CCS. Close behind them came a more orderly company of men in field grey uniform carrying a white flag.

There was great excitement and some confusion when the two groups arrived at the CCS. The German prisoners were led away to a large marquee but their officer, catching sight of Sister Newton, detached himself from the rest of his party and headed in her direction. Saluting her stiffly, he handed her his revolver and asked her in excellent English where he should go.

Frankie was no authority on regulations concerning prisoners of war of commissioned rank and she simply indicated that he should join his men in the marquee. This, however, produced an indignant protest from the officer that he should not be expected to share accommodation with Other Ranks. After three years spent nursing casualties resulting from German aggression, Frankie's tolerance was at a low ebb. Crossly she gave him a hefty push in the direction of the marquee and went back to her ward. After a moment of startled indecision, the German officer took to his heels and was last seen disappearing into the hills. Rumour has it that he turned up in Argentina several months later.

'Oh well,' shrugs Frankie, 'I'm a nurse, not a military policeman. Anyway, he went without his gun.'

Europe was in ruins. Motor transport moved gingerly between tottering piles of masonry, all that was left of Hanover, Dresden, Hamburg, Bremen and Berlin. The task facing the military and civil authorities was immense. Putrid battlefields had to be cleared and disinfested. Thousands of bodies awaited identification and proper burial. Hitler's vast labour force, who had been taken from their homes to work in his factories, were now displaced persons, and were given shelter in special camps run by civil and military medical authorities, assisted by voluntary bodies. The British Red Cross Society, the Salvation Army, the Society of Friends and other charitable concerns supplied food and clothing to the destitute, cared for the elderly, the homeless and pregnant women. They assisted in the disinfesting of prisons and provided delousing stations. Number 3 British Red Cross Mobile Hospital, staffed with doctors and trained nurses, set up a clinic in a ruined château in Belgium to help the citizens of Antwerp who had suffered terribly from rocket attacks during the last months of the war. Numbers 4 and 5 British Red Cross Units opened typhoid clinics in Holland, assisted by Dutch and Swiss Red Cross nurses.

When the Control Commission took over responsibility for refugees in Europe, the military authorities of the British zone in Germany had cared for and repatriated one and a half million people. Some day, someone would need to take a look inside the heads of these men, women and children who had been so ill-treated by their fellow men, to see if the occupying devils bred out of despair could ever be exorcised.

22

The Ultimate Decision

One week after the German surrender, an RAF force of 1,150 men arrived in Norway to take over Oslo airport from the Luftwaffe. They had not expected to find 2,000 Luftwaffe personnel still on the airfield and were even more disturbed to discover a further 12,000 fully armed troops stationed a little further down the road. In this unreal atmosphere, they went warily about their duty. Trouble, when it came, was not from the Germans – who behaved correctly, if sullenly – but from sick and frightened Russians who had escaped from labour camps and were hiding in the woods.

The Duke of Newcastle, who was Second-in-Command of 128 Fighter Wing RAF, was surprised to find a British Military Hospital functioning here in these unstable circumstances.

'Our troubles seemed insignificant when we heard of the chaotic conditions into which the nurses had been flown. Some were even ahead of the 6th Airborne Division.'

As soon as the terrible conditions in the German labour camps in Norway were brought to light, the need for hospitals transcended any consideration of the personal comfort of the nurses. The 79th British General Hospital was established without delay, followed by the 30th and the 75th. To these hospitals were brought the sick and starving inmates of the camps which had provided slave labour for Hitler.

The majority of these were Russians, and the Sisters who nursed them faced deep mistrust as well as a formidable language barrier. Dedicated care, however, eventually won the friendship of these ill-used people. When Russian patients began to offer the Sisters the choice gift of a fish head, they were sensible of the compliment and forebore to hold their noses.

Difficulties arose when the Russian patients learned that they were to be repatriated as soon as they were well enough to travel. This fate so terrified them that they chose to take themselves off into the woods, to live rough and in some cases to hang themselves from the trees rather than return to their home country. Their fears later proved to be justified, as most of those expatriate Russians who returned perished in Stalin's infamous purges. Allied authorities, faced with the Russian leader's insistence on the return of all Russian prisoners, had no option but to arrange their transfer.

In the harshest climate, in the far north of Norway, was the worst camp of all. Anticipating a possible invasion from Russia at this point, Hitler had ordered a line of fortified defences to be built across a bleak and treeless area near Lyngen Fjord. Russians who had been taken prisoner when Hitler invaded their country provided a practically inexhaustible supply of labour, but Lyngen was kept for the sick men. The climate was so severe and the work so arduous that even a fit man could not survive for long. Sick men from all the other Norwegian camps were sent to Lyngen to die, the last ounce of work being extracted from them before they were allowed to quit their miserable lives. Good food was not wasted on them, since they were dying in any case: the rations at Lyngen were smaller than at any other camp.

The work entailed the digging of fortifications through fourteen feet of hard-packed snow and ice with pick and shovel. Thousands of workers died. In the bitter cold of an arctic winter they had no clothing but the remaining rags of what they had been wearing when taken prisoner. Their breakfast was one pint of hot water. Dinner and supper were the same, with the addition of a tablespoon of flour. Twice a week, a small portion of rabbit was provided. Men ate the leather uppers of their boots and fastened the loose soles to their feet with twigs and grasses. According to the evidence of US Colonel Jenney, who carried out several autopsies at the camp, the prisoners had also eaten their dead companions.

When the war ended, these starving wretches were sent to the nearest hospital to await repatriation. The hospital was a German establishment; paradoxically, the very race which had inflicted so much misery on the Russian workers now showed the utmost concern for their welfare and treated them with kindness. Here they waited until well enough to board one of the three British hospital ships running from Lyngen to Murmansk, the *Aba*, the *Ango* and the converted Norwegian luxury vessel, the *Stella Polaris*. It was the *Stella Polaris* which carried out what proved to be the last lift from Lyngen.

Flying the flags of Russia, America and Britain at her mast, she tied up at the port of Kvesmenes in the Lyngen Fjord on 18th July, 1945, and prepared to embark patients. Her Commanding Officer, US Colonel Jenney, three RAMC medical officers, two translators and the nursing staff of five Army Sisters under Senior Sister Miss Barnett,

TANS, all watched from the deck as the gangway went down. Their instructions from Allied Medical HQ were to take on board only those fit enough to travel, but this order was promptly countermanded by a Russian party who unexpectedly boarded the ship and announced that they would accompany the patients. In the opinion of the ship's doctors, many of those who now came on board were too ill to travel but, regardless of circumstances, the Russians insisted that no-one must be left behind.

They came on board, each carrying a bundle of possessions, and were sorted into categories as far as possible. Those suffering from tuberculosis were given cabins with port-holes; 'open' tubercular lesions went to the top deck. The very sick were carried on board by German stretcher-bearers.

The nursing required during the voyage was intensive but the Sisters could be proud of the fact that, of all these very ill men, only one died during the voyage. Most of them slept for long periods, some would occasionally break out into a sad folk song. Their troubles were not over, however. On reaching the port of Murmansk, the doctors on board submitted to the receiving party on the wharf a list of those patients who should be carried ashore by stretcher-bearers.

This caused instant commotion amongst the Russian officials. A female Red Army Captain who appeared to be in charge barked out commands on the dock. Red-faced with anger, she issued counter-orders to the effect that no stretchers or stretcher-bearers would be supplied. The seriously ill men who had been nursed with such care during the voyage from Lyngen now had to get off the ship as well as they could without help. Russian bystanders on the quay looked on with indifference while their own sick countrymen struggled on crutches down the gangway. One man suffering from advanced tuberculosis died before he reached the wharf. Only those who had not long to live were carried by stretcher, and they were unceremoniously dumped on the quay, exposed to the weather and totally untended. There was nothing to be done. This was Russian territory and the American and British hospital staff could only stand and watch, sick at heart.

With the war in Europe brought to an end, the Allies switched all their military weight to the Far East and South-East Asia. A steady stream of troopships began to leave Britain for India carrying men and hospitals which were no longer needed in Europe. Japan was now on the defensive. Burma had been won back and the Japanese forced to retreat into Siam, leaving thousands of their dead behind. Pioneers of the Sanitation Squads and Royal Engineers faced a massive cleaning-up task before the battlefields were made wholesome once more. Miss Esther Somerville, newly appointed Matron of the 38th British General Hospital in Rangoon, was a Regular QA whose sang-froid was legendary, but even she was shaken by the carnage.

'To my dying day, I will remember the smell of death as we sailed up the Irrawaddy into Rangoon.'

After Rangoon, Malaya waited to be reclaimed. Singapore had to be redeemed, as well as all the islands of Indonesia. There was still a long way to go.

Borneo was the next target of the Australian 9th Division. In the spring of 1945, they made a successful landing at Tarakan. With the assault troops went the all-male advance party of the 110th Australian Casualty Clearing Station, consisting of doctors and orderlies. Ten days later, Theatre Sister Marie Dickie and Senior Sister Barbara Millard (ARRC, later Kilgour), both of the Australian Army Nursing Service (AANS), were flown in by flying boat from the nearby island of Moratai. Their arrival on the congested beachhead caused a certain amount of confusion amongst the troops, who had not considered screens necessary for showers and latrines until that moment. A great welcome awaited them from the hard-pressed medical officers of the unit. One of the doctors had been put out of action by a sniper, leaving a depleted staff to cope with the considerable casualties which accom-pany any landing. Until the two Sisters arrived to relieve him of the nursing, the Commanding Officer, Major Dorsch, slept on the floor of the tent which housed the most seriously ill men.

A captured Japanese hospital in good repair with several small wards and a good theatre made an excellent base for the CCS. Additional ward space was provided by six long tents erected in the grounds. The Japanese had plainly vacated the building in some haste, leaving be-hind medical books and reports and knitting patterns for their peculiar one-toed socks. They also passed on the patronage of an obliging hen who paid a daily visit to lay an egg in a box placed in one of the wards. As usual after Japanese occupation, all the drains were blocked and water supplies had been interfered with, but Army Services quickly restored these.

The Front Line was the jungle which surrounded the hospital. A

Field Ambulance Unit gave on-the-spot medical aid, and casualties reached the hospital wards shortly after being wounded. One of those who did not recover from his wounds was the Australian Victoria Cross holder, Derrick. His bed was taken soon afterwards by a Japanese officer in a similarly moribund condition.

As soon as they could be moved, patients were evacuated on the hospital ship *Manunda* to the island of Moratai, where the 2nd/5th Australian General Hospital was working under uncomfortable conditions. The solid rock formation of the island made the digging of latrines impossible and the only method of disposing of sewage was to erect seats over deep clefts in the boulders and to burn the excreta every day. Wooden seats could not be used as they would be destroyed in the flames but the metal substitutes became white hot, and many a poor sufferer was taken to hospital with a burnt bottom.

Sister Faith McCullough can be forgiven for cheating one night when she had to get up to go to the latrines.

'It was during a terrific storm so I pulled on my gum-boots and picked up my umbrella. Since I only wanted to pass water, I decided to squat down in the open. In all that rain, I reckoned my contribution wouldn't make much difference. The obligatory guard was hovering a little distance away but the night was pitch dark. At just the wrong moment, a great sheet of lightning lit up the whole camp and I was spotlighted, sitting under my umbrella, as plainly as if it had been daylight.'

British and American nurses were also working in the Far East. A number of Royal Naval vessels, including hospital ships, moved to the Pacific at the end of 1944 and were now playing their full part alongside the American Navy. When the American 7th Fleet moved in for the attack on the island of Okinawa, the hospital ship *Tjitjalengka*, a Dutch ship with Dutch administration but staffed with Royal Naval medical personnel, was lent as replacement for the American hospital ship which had been put out of action by Japanese Kamikaze suicide planes.

'It was tremendously exciting to be in the midst of all the great ships of the American Fleet,' writes 'Bobby' Robinson (later Velanoff), one of the Royal Navy Sisters on board. 'As the assault troops went in, we sailed in a square at four knots an hour a few miles off-shore and waited for casualties.'

The patients were brought by a destroyer which sailed alongside the hospital ship, matching its speed, while one by one the casualties were transferred by breeches buoy, a delicate operation made more difficult by rough weather.

'Other ships in the area who were trying to cling to the cover of darkness were glad to see the back of us when we eventually sailed, several days later, with a full load of casualties and ablaze with lights from stem to stern.'

Casualties in this theatre of war were taken to any one of a number of hospitals set up on Pacific islands by American and Australian medical services and flown or ferried from there to Australia. A team of Australian Sisters and also six Royal Naval Sisters accompanied casualties on Dakotas adapted to carry stretchers. This was a considerable ordeal for the Sisters until their cotton dresses were replaced by flying jackets and boots to combat the cold in unpressurised cabins at high altitude. The Royal Naval hospital ship *Oxfordshire* was moored in Sydney harbour to act as a base hospital until the new Royal Naval Auxiliary Hospital ashore at Herne Bay was ready to receive patients. When that opened, the *Oxfordshire* put to sea once more to help with the increasing number of burned seamen resulting from crashing Kamikaze pilots.

The greater the threat to Japan, the more desperately courageous her troops became. Okinawa, the most important of a string of islands tailing off the southernmost point of Japan, was won only after three months of hard fighting. The Americans took few prisoners. Rather than surrender, Japanese commanders committed traditional Harakiri by sword. Their soldiers, being lesser men, destroyed themselves with hand grenades.

News of these reverses could not be kept from the Japanese people, who were already learning how it felt to be on the receiving end of a bombing attack. The American Air Force was teaching hard lessons to a nation which had done all the destroying up till now. There was a rush to construct air raid shelters in the big cities of Japan, using POWs as labour. Amongst the half-starved wretches shovelling dirt and breaking rocks were five women dressed in rags. They were scarcely recognisable as those Australian Army Sisters who had been captured three years earlier in Rabaul.

Allied Intelligence was well aware that thousands of men, women and children had been held as prisoners ever since the fall of Singapore, but of their whereabouts they knew little. They rightly suspected that large internment camps lay hidden in the dense jungles of Sumatra, Java and Malaya, but every effort to locate them had failed. No survivor had ever returned from airborne parties of guerrillas sent by the Allies to investigate. When British POWs were freed from Japanese camps in Burma in a near starving condition, fears for this unknown multitude held in secret places increased. When it became known that Japan was experiencing a food crisis and that her own troops were reduced to a small ration of rice, Allied leaders realised that release would have to come quickly if the lives of these internees were to be saved.

The means to a speedy release was put into their hands by the Western scientists who had just perfected the atom bomb, a weapon of such lethal potential that it would undoubtedly bring the war to an end. In so doing, the destruction of people and property would be on a scale never before experienced. Those within a mile of the explosion would die instantly; thousands more would face a slow death by radiation.

The alternative was to carry on with a grinding war, fighting yard by yard until the last soldier in Japan was killed. Okinawa had proved that. In this case, conceivably another million Allied troops would lose their lives on Japanese soil, and thousands of helpless internees would perish.

The two courses of action were debated; the decision to employ the bomb was taken.

Looking ahead to probable action by the Japanese forces abroad when the bomb was dropped on their homeland, the Allies guessed that one of their first actions would be to exterminate all prisoners. In the light of documents captured later, this proved to be an accurate assessment of the way in which the Japanese mind works (see Appendix D). Consequently, in the few days left for action between the decision to use the bomb and the dropping of it, Allied representatives were secretly dropped by parachute into the jungle in areas where camps were thought to exist. Upon receiving the signal that the bomb had been dropped, they were to present themselves immediately at the nearest Japanese HQ and demand to be shown all internment and POW camps. By acting with speed, they hoped to forestall any attempted massacre.

Five men, highly trained in survival techniques, were dropped over the jungle in northern Sumatra. Major G. F. Jacobs, a South African in the Royal Marines, was leader of the party, the rest of which was made up of two Australian wireless operators, a Dutch Sergeant who had fought with the Dutch Underground movement, and a Chinese interpreter. They went to ground to await the signal from South-East Asia Command in Colombo.

The Japanese Government was given one last chance. An ultimatum of unconditional surrender was offered and rejected. Although their homeland was now in a state of disintegration and economic chaos and the Japanese Navy had ceased to exist, the Japanese military leaders preferred to fight to the death.

There remained no other course open to the Allies, in their opinion, but to drop the bomb. On 6th and 9th August, atom bombs were dropped on Nagasaki and Hiroshima with terrible effect. It brought about immediate capitulation; World War Two was now truly over. It was time for Major Jacobs to show himself.

23

Internment: Bankinang and Palembang

It is necessary at this point to back-track to Sumatra as it was in 1942 when Japanese troops were overrunning the country. Of those refugees who made the last, ill-fated dash for freedom from Singapore and who survived shipwreck, hundreds were already imprisoned. Muntok jail on Banka Island overflowed with castaways. On the mainland, Dutch colonists were driven from their homes and put behind wire, together with any survivors from Singapore who were still trying to escape.

Many refugees had used the cross-country escape route successfully, including the wounded who had been passed along from the islands by doctors and nurses, but the chance was past for all the hundreds of troops and civilians who now assembled around the empty harbour of Padang, mesmerised into inaction by the wide, indifferent sea. After all the striving to reach this point, they were too late. There was nothing further to be done but await the arrival of the Japanese and capture.

The doctors and nurses amongst them were perhaps luckier than the rest in that they had their work to occupy hands and minds. The two women doctors, Marjorie Lyon and Elsie Crowe, with six QAs - Kit Woodman, Canadian Mary Charman, Naomi Davies, K. M. Jenkins, Lydia McLean and Louie Harley - three Colonial Service Sisters, Sarah Service, Mrs Macduff and Mrs Malmanche, and five members of the Indian Military Nursing Service worked on at the Salvation Army Hospital while awaiting their own inevitable capture.

From the hospital windows, they watched British troops being led into captivity under Japanese guard.

'They turned and waved to us as they went,' writes Kit Woodman. 'It was awful to see them go. They had done so much to cheer us up over the last difficult days, with a sing-song every night.'

The military status of Army Sisters had never been recognised by the Japanese and QAs were not awarded any of the privileges supposedly due to POWs. Since these were rarely observed by the Japanese in any case, this lack of distinction was of little consequence. The QAs were interned, a few days later, in Padang Convent with the civilian nurses and doctors and 2,500 other women and children of all nationalities. The majority were Dutch colonists who had been living in the area, but there were also French, Belgian, American, Australian, Indian, Eurasian, British as well as Sumatran native women, drawn from all walks of life by chance, shipwreck and the fortunes of war.

At first, rations were adequate. Boredom and learning to live together without friction were the chief worries. Tensions built up amongst so many different cultures existing side by side with no privacy at all, and in this respect, the nurses, accustomed to self-discipline by their training, were noticeably more able to adapt to communal living than many of the civilian women who had led a sheltered existence until now.

The children, ranging in age from three months to eleven years, created a welcome diversion. While mothers of different races were still at a loss to understand each other, their children quickly worked out a common language. Their inventiveness in a total absence of toys entertained everyone, but this was before hunger turned charming children into selfish thieves.

Their Japanese masters lost no time in establishing rules of conduct expected from the women. 'Tenko' (roll-call), during which they were made to stand for hours in the sun until a satisfactory tally was reached, could happen at any time of the day. The women quickly learned that failure to bow before even the lowliest Japanese soldier brought instant punishment – a vicious slap to the face or a blow from the butt of a rifle. The Japanese had no respect for their own womenfolk and could scarcely be expected to entertain anything but indifference towards the women of their enemies. As time went on, it became obvious that the survival of interned women was immaterial to them.

A building which had housed the Brothers of a religious order (Fraters) was handed over to Dutch nuns for use as a hospital for POWs and internees, but the British nurses were not allowed to work here for fear of collusion with the troops. Instead, they organised daily clinics in the Convent grounds to deal with cases not needing hospital attention, although their scope was limited as there were no drugs or dressings other than those brought from the Salvation Army Hospital. The complaints they dealt with at this stage were minor, as the women and children were still in good health and reasonably well-fed.

Providing food for their thousands of prisoners was a responsibility which the Japanese were not prepared to shoulder for very long, however, and the women were told to feed themselves. The sole Japanese contribution was a cup of rice per day for each person. A local trader was allowed into the camp compound to sell vegetables, meal and coffee to those who had money. Most of the Dutch women had been allowed to bring money and jewellery with them into internment, and one Belgian woman, a millionairess who had managed to hang on to her jewel box when she was shipwrecked, had enough potential capital to keep the circulation of money flowing throughout captivity by paying others to work for her.

Shipwreck, with its chance paupers, created a new working class who had to earn money in order to live by any means available. The nurses, all penniless, stuck together and pooled resources. Kit Woodman trimmed eyebrows and sold paintings made from a collage of anything available. Mary Charman ran a laundry, which was not an easy task when the soap ration was minuscule, and Naomi Davies, with little Jean Duncan already in her care, became 'minder' for several other children who followed her about the camp like the Pied Piper of Hamelin. Coconut shells could be scraped and polished with a sliver of glass to make cups. Shady hats were made from plaited grass. All these could be sold to buy a banana or a handful of spinach.

As the first Christmas in captivity drew near, the women were determined to make it a day of happiness for the children. Christmas dinner, in the shape of eight inquisitive chickens, was enticed through holes in the bottom of the perimeter fence with trails of rice, straight into the pot. But despite the effort to make it otherwise, the day brought nostalgia and heartache for all. Mothers with young children pined for news of their husbands and older children who were imprisoned in other camps. No communication between them was possible, no meeting permitted. The British Sisters had received no mail from home, nor were they allowed to write letters. Their parents knew only that their daughters were missing. When one of the women, who had a fine singing voice, sang 'Silent Night', even the most resolute of them wept. They wept for their children, their families and for themselves. Fortunately, perhaps, they did not know that ahead of them stretched three years of trials which would take them far beyond the solace of tears.

A year passed, during which the effects of malnutrition began to show. Insect bites turned septic and developed into non-healing ulcers.

No measures could be taken to combat malaria, despite Dr Lyon's continual demands for quinine. She had many confrontations with the Japanese, and nurses would watch, heart in mouth, while Japanese officers grew apoplectic with rage. She never showed the slightest fear of them and, angry though they were, they never harmed her, although her requests were consistently ignored. Her staunch supporter in all her protests was a woman barrister who had made a special study of the terms of the Geneva Convention. Mrs Holle's frail appearance was deceptive. These two completely fearless women made a formidable team.

After Christmas 1943, the women were moved to Padang jail. Always adept at extracting the maximum discomfort from any situation, the Japanese ordered that the move would take place during the hottest time of the day and that all women would walk, carrying their possessions, even those who were sick. Dr Lyon promptly sought out the Camp Commandant and blazed away at his callousness. This was one battle which she won. To the astonishment of the rest of the internees, two ambulances arrived to transport the sick.

The jail had been left in an indescribably dirty condition. The civilian men who had been imprisoned here may have believed that their place was being taken by Japanese soldiers. Whatever the reason, it was so filthy that no-one could think of moving in until it was cleaned up. The first priority of the nurses was to scrub out a room suitable for a sick bay, while Dr Lyon waited outside with her patients under the shade of a tree.

A little Dutch girl of six years old, gravely ill with diphtheria, was causing the doctor great anxiety. Having no serum or any drugs with which to treat the child, Marjorie Lyon could only watch helplessly as her condition deteriorated. The moment came when it was obvious that, without an immediate tracheotomy, the child would die. The swollen membranes of her throat were rapidly closing the airway. While Sister Naomi Davies fanned away the flies, Dr Lyon, without anaesthetic, made an opening into the trachea with a small knife and inserted an airway tube. The child, who was too deep in coma to know what was happening, began to breathe more easily and by the time she was carried into the still damp sick room, the crisis was over.

Conditions at the jail were vile. Built to accommodate 500 people, it now housed 2,500 women and children for whom there were only thirty lavatories. These were in the form of a continuous row of seats with halfway partitions between each but open in front, the whole suspended over a row of pits. Because of the huge population of the jail, these rapidly filled up, but it was several weeks before Japanese soldiers, suitably protected with face masks, brought oxen carts to clear away the excreta.

'The stench and filth were unbearable,' says Kit Woodman, 'but bear it we did. To add to our miseries, the men had left a legacy of bugs, thousands of them. As fast as we killed them, more would appear. Some people were becoming quite dotty through lack of sleep.'

A fresh crisis now arrived, worse than the bugs, worse than the unemptied lavatories. The Japanese sent one of the Brothers from the Frater House with instructions to collect all the young girls. Frantic mothers sought to hide their daughters.

'The whole camp supported the mothers of these young girls,' says Kit. 'We hid them on the top of cupboards and underneath the beds and then we stood guard over them. When the Brother returned to the Japanese empty-handed, they came themselves to see why their orders had been disobeyed. With drawn revolvers, they demanded that we hand over the girls, but the whole camp of 2,000 women made a stand, and stuck to it. The atmosphere was tense but the revolvers were not used, and the soldiers were compelled to go away without the girls. We felt we had won a great victory.'

When some weeks later the women were moved to a camp in the jungle, they went gladly, feeling that nothing could be worse than Padang jail. They were moved in batches of 500, taking everything they could carry. Women with small children struggled to carry suit-cases filled with clothing while their precious pots and pans were slung around their necks. If a child could walk, no matter how young he was, he had to look after himself and carry something.

Their new home was in the heart of dense jungle at Bankinang, directly on the equator. The heat was overwhelming. 'Our first thought was,' says Kit, 'how we were going to live in that heat, perhaps for years.'

The camp was new and had been efficiently laid out to take advan-tage of a jungle stream. The water flowed first to a row of troughs in a large coolie-type shed which served as a bath-house, then via the latrines back to the jungle, disposing of excreta in a sanitary fashion. Four large sheds with 'basha' (straw) roofs each held 500 people, allowing a space of six feet by two feet for each person on two-tiered bamboo platforms. There was a hospital hut which could accommodate seventy-five patients, but apart from a few wash-bowls there was neither equipment nor medical supplies. A few blankets and pillows had been donated by Dutch women and this was the extent of the comfort which could be offered to the sick. Beri-beri and other deficiency diseases were now making an appearance and the hospital was always full. All the nurses worked there in shifts but could do little for the sick apart from washing them and attempting to make them more comfortable on their platforms of bamboo.

The first funeral at the new camp brought the heartening discovery that the civilian men's camp was not far away. Certain of the men were detailed to act as grave-diggers, thus presenting an opportunity for messages to be passed, despite severe punishment if caught by the guard. In this way, women learned of the whereabouts of their husbands and were able to exchange news.

One day the word was passed that a truckload of men would be passing close to the women's camp and all who had relatives in the men's camp were alerted. As the truck came in sight there was wild pandemonium in the women's camp: wives climbed up the fences and even poked their heads through the basha roofs of the huts in an attempt to catch a glimpse of their men. Infuriated guards dashed about, belaying the women with their rifle butts, all to no effect. By a piece of clever organisation, the truck was temporarily halted exactly outside the women's compound for a few frantic moments while the men searched for a familiar face amongst the excited, ragged women. Orders barked by near-hysterical guards were drowned in an uproar of greetings before the truck moved on once more and the women climbed down from their perches. They were punished by being made to stand hatless in the sun until their guards thought that scores had been settled.

The basic ration was reduced and those without money had to make even greater efforts to earn some. Hunger was constant and food the sole topic of conversation. Tree-felling parties to provide wood for cooking were welcomed by the women for the opportunity they gave to go outside the compound into the jungle where, acting on advice from native women amongst them, they were able to find edible leaves.

1944 slid into 1945 with little to mark the passing time in the camps but continued loss of weight and an expanding cemetery. This time, no-one bothered to greet the New Year. There were no old people or babies left in the camp. Every child's death sent Dr Lyon storming in rage to the Japanese, demanding food and medicine, all to no avail.

In this, their third year of imprisonment, a new and more virulent form of dysentery struck the camp. The victim would collapse in the morning and be dead by nightfall. The doctors suspected cholera, but they had no means of clinically confirming this diagnosis. The nurses, with no disinfectant of any kind, struggled to contain the outbreak, but deaths continued unabated. Now, too, beri-beri was to be seen in its advanced stages where sufferers, plagued by a diabolical craving for salt, swelled to grotesque proportions with oedema. When the basic rice ration was again cut, this time to less than half a cup per person, the internees could only accept the fact that the Japanese meant to starve them slowly to death. Many lost the will to live and died.

The nurses never lost hope. They continued to help Dr Lyon and Dr Crowe with the sick and the dying although they themselves were so weak that every movement, even talking, was an effort. The apathy of malnutrition affected them all. One of the Dutch girls, Judith Sybers, remarked one day with some truth, 'If we stay here much longer, we won't want to leave.'

Fuel for cooking was as important as the food itself. Fire was needed to cook the rice and boil the water, which was otherwise undrinkable. Under these circumstances, the next move of the Japanese Camp Commandant was one of pure sadism. No more wood-foraging parties were allowed outside the camp perimeter, with the result that the compound was very soon stripped of every twig, leaf, piece of bark or handful of grass. The women were reduced to digging up tree roots and drying them for fuel.

For Kit, the breaking point came when she went to light her fire one morning and discovered that the roots she had been drying overnight in the embers of the hospital fire had been stolen. Kit had a working partnership with Mary Charman whereby Mary made herself responsible for their washing and Kit for the cooking. The theft of the roots was a disaster which temporarily swamped Kit.

'I burst into tears and cried and cried, for there would be no food that day for Mary and me. I was quite desperate and didn't know what to do, when Emmy Hanedoes came along to see what was upsetting me. She went away and came back with three pieces of dry wood. It was the most wonderful gift.'

Emmy was a Dutch girl who drove the guards wild because she was so tall that they had to stand on tip-toe to slap her face.

Kit later found her culprit, one of the dear children who had grown into lawless, unlovable rogues. They would cause much heartache after the war when parents tried to steer them back into the ways of civilisation, but that was a problem for the future. The end of the war was nowhere in sight for the internees in Sumatra. There was no news from outside. Any questions put to the Japanese produced the stock answer, 'The news is good.'

Another large internment camp for women was established at Palembang in Sumatra, in a swampy area on the River Moesi. Amongst the hundreds of prisoners brought here were the Australian Army Nursing Sisters and the Colonial Service Sisters who had survived the sinking of the *Vyner-Brooke* and two Sisters of the QAIMNS, all of whom had originally been imprisoned in Muntok jail on Banka Island.

In spite of dire consequences had they been caught, at least two nurses managed to keep a diary. One was Sister Phyllis Briggs of the Colonial Nursing Service, and the other Australian Sister Betty Jeffrey, whose book *White Coolies* is based on her diary.

Of the time in Muntok jail, Phyllis Briggs wrote, 'We became acquainted with hunger from the start. Japanese guards threw pieces of bread through the railings at us and had great enjoyment in watching some of the male prisoners scrambling for scraps. I just could not bear to watch such a degrading scene.'

Almost the last prisoners to be brought to the jail were a Russian Jewess and her little boy, Mischa. The father had been drowned when their ship sank and, a few days after her arrival, the mother herself died of pneumonia. Fortunately, the boy was too young to understand his tragic circumstances and one of the women, Mrs Mary Jenkin, whose own son was far away in England, took charge of him. She made for him a little mattress stuffed with grass and let him sleep by her side on the concrete platform which she shared with thirty-eight other women.

Mary Jenkin had chosen to remain in Singapore with her husband to the last. She had worked as a member of Mrs Cherry's Malayan Auxiliary Nursing Service and finally attempted to escape with her husband and twelve other men in a launch. They had all been captured and brought to Muntok jail. After the prisoners were segregated and moved to the mainland, Mary Jenkin, like many other women, never saw her husband again.

The move was done in stages, the wounded being left until the last in the care of the Colonial Nursing Sisters and, on arrival in Palembang, they were taken to a hospital there run by Dutch nuns. Once again, British and Australian Sisters were not allowed to nurse their own troops. Women prisoners were accommodated in several houses which had belonged to Dutch colonists until recently and the men were taken to a camp not far away, but with which there was no possibility of communicating.

The discovery that a certain empty house in the women's camp was to be taken over as a Japanese Officers' Club was bad news for everyone, but especially for thirty-two Australian Sisters who lived next door. They were filled with misgivings when ordered to scrub out that house and two others across the street which were to serve as an annexe. Their fears proved to be justified when, on the night of the Club's opening, the summons came for six girls to present themselves next door.

There was no possibility of dodging the issue, so fourteen Sisters turned up instead of the required six, feeling that there might be safety in numbers. All had gone to great lengths to make themselves look as unattractive as possible, with unkempt hair and wearing men's shirts, outsize shorts and boots. The two Japanese officers awaiting entertainment were stunned. Why, they asked, did the girls not make the best of themselves, and would they like money for lipstick?

The answer to this and all other advances was an unequivocal 'No'. The evening dragged on while the girls were plied with soft drinks and the men struggled to make small talk but the frigid atmosphere eventually proved too much for the exasperated hosts and the girls were sent back over the fence unharmed.

Four of their colleagues in another room at the Club were not so lucky. Their suitors were not to be put off and, after the softening-up process at the Club, they led the protesting girls across the road in the direction of the annexes, about whose function there was now no doubt. But the girls would go no further. They refused to enter the annexe and stubbornly walked up and down the road while angry officers barked orders at them. At each delay, the men grew more violent, more determined to have their way. At the point of desperation, one of the Sisters had a blinding flash of inspiration. Remembering that the Japanese have a pathological dread of tuberculosis, she suddenly collapsed in a paroxysm of coughing which lacked only a rush of blood from the lungs for complete realism. Horrified, the Japanese officers melted away, leaving four very shaky Sisters to return to their anxious friends.

The affair was not yet over. An order was issued that rations would be withheld from the whole camp until the girls complied with the wishes of the Japanese officers. No food was delivered the next day, or the day after that. Clearly, the situation could not be allowed to deteriorate to the point of starving all the internees. In utter misery, the Australian Sisters sought for some way out of the impasse. When it seemed that, in the end, some women must be sacrificed for the sake of the others, last minute relief was obtained from a Dutch resident of Palembang who was still at liberty and who managed to smuggle into the women's camp a small quantity of flour. On the fourth day, before further developments could take place, a Dutch doctor was able to get a message to the Japanese Resident concerning the goings-on at the women's camp. The Officers' Club was promptly closed down, to the intense relief of all the internees.

When, a little later, volunteers to nurse at a native hospital were asked for, there was a certain amount of hesitation and mistrust. Upon learning, however, that the person seeking help was a Dutch Dr Hollweg, who had been the Red Cross representative in Palembang before the war, four Sisters consented to go; two QAs, Mary Cooper and Margot Turner, the latter now fully recovered from her ordeal at sea, and two Colonial Sisters, Jenny McAllister (later Taylor) and Mrs Olga Neubrunner.

Dr Hollweg ran a very busy native hospital with the help of his wife and one other doctor. When the team was enlarged by the addition of the four Sisters, it was able to accomplish a great deal of satisfactory work amongst the sick people of the district. It continued for several months, until one day the Kempei Tai, the dreaded Japanese Military Police, paid a visit.

Dr Hollweg and his wife, who were accused of communicating with the enemy, were beaten up and taken to the jail along with the other doctor. They were not seen again. Without explanation, the four British Sisters were also imprisoned in the same jail. Their home for the next six months was a cell four paces wide, without sanitation or washing facilities. Their bed was a rush mat on the stone floor, their only visitor a sparrow. 'The longest six months of my life,' says Dame Margot today.

They were allowed out of their cell for toilet purposes for five minutes only every morning. When the muslin dresses they had made for work in the hospital wore out, the guards gave them native sarongs to wear. Murderers and thieves in the same block would stand and stare as the Sisters passed by to exercise, astonished to see white women in native dress and in such deplorable condition. Even these hardened criminals were moved to pity and would pass little offerings through the cell bars, sometimes a cigarette tin of hot coffee, sometimes a banana. Their daily ration of food was two small portions of cooked rice accompanied by cold tea or water.

The health of the four women began to suffer. Jenny McAllister, who was showing symptoms of typhoid, caused her friends much anxiety, but their request for a doctor was refused. The guard made one concession, however. He gave them back the haversack of provisions which had been confiscated when the women first arrived. With the oats, dried milk and sugar it contained, they were able to make a kind of porridge which undoubtedly saved Jenny's life. At the end of six months, still without being offered any explanation, the women were sent back to the Palembang camp, four emaciated scarecrows scarcely recognisable by their colleagues.

After eighteen months in the Dutch houses, the women were now moved into the camp which had just been vacated by the men, into basha huts in an area of mosquito infested swamps well below sea-level. It was a camp which had little to commend it but for Mary Jenkin, at least, there was a small measure of comfort. A little hand-made stool bearing her husband's initials had been left behind, perhaps intentionally.

By this time, all the women were suffering from malnutrition. Rations, which had been meagre enough in the Dutch houses, were reduced again. In their debilitated state, the women had little resistance to the infections of this fever-ridden environment and the malaria and dysentery which stronger women might have withstood killed them off like flies.

The hospital hut was always full and the Sisters were glad of extra help when Dr Margaret Thomson and Colonial Sister Netta Smith were amongst a fresh batch of internees. Netta and the doctor had been imprisoned in a camp further north at Jambi ever since their capture on the island of Sinkep.

Every appeal to the Japanese for drugs was turned down. 'We think nothing of your Red Cross,' they told Sister Mavis Hannah, as they tore the brassard from her arm on one of the many occasions when she badgered them for medical supplies. 'There is plenty of room in the cemetery,' was their stock reply.

But the cemetery was filling up. Phyllis Briggs' diary for 1944 makes grim reading:

March 4th Mary Anderson died. She made a will leaving her belongings to her friends and to me she left a linen frock and a piece of mosquito netting which I share with Mary Jenkin.

Valda Godley died and Mrs Colley is ill.

May 14th Mrs Curran Sharp died.
We are made to cut the grass with parangs which are blunt in the hot sun while a Jap officer watches us from the shade. Poor Maudie Hilton cut her finger. She stood on a pile of dried mud and announced quite solemnly ... 'This picture will go down in history. It will not be forgotten in a hundred years.' [Maudie died a few months later.]

But it's no use going into the ethics of things. We just have to get on with it.

Getting very short of water and the well is very dry. Hardly any vegetables sent in for us. A few people allowed outside the camp to search for edible plants. Weed soup.

June 19th Missionary Sally Oldham (Lancashire) died. Working parties sent out with chunkals to cultivate new areas for sweet potatoes. Everyone is getting weaker and thinner. I try to fill up on water.

Mary and I made to stand in the hot sun for an hour because we did not see Fatty (Jap officer) go by when we were cutting the grass and so we didn't bow to him. He was wearing yellow silk pyjamas. The Japs complain that the children laugh at them and pull faces. I felt ill and fainted again. McKenzie is ill with dysentery.

July 27 Grace Guer died. She was so young and pretty. All the missionaries are ill, Miss Cullen and Miss McIntosh the worst.

Ena Murray and three others had to stand in the sun as a punishment for putting water in the wrong places when they watered the Jap gardens. The next day, they had to work all morning from 6 am until 11 am emptying the contents of the septic tank on their gardens.

Mary woke up one night feeling something heavy on her chest. It was a large rat. One of the Chinese nurses had her toe-nails nibbled.

A surprise visit from a Japanese dentist brought hopeful patients queueing for attention to their long-neglected teeth, but their enthusiasm melted away when it was discovered that he used no anaesthetic. One poor women was left in a state of collapse, half demented with pain, after he had removed the broken stump of a tooth with a chisel.

Despite the horrific hardships which had to be endured, there was nothing craven about the women. They despised their Japanese captors and never lost an opportunity of showing it. In this respect, the Australian girls could be counted on to give the lead. As Mavis Hannah recalls, they were expected to carry water for the Japanese officers' baths 'and we never failed to pee in it before it was delivered.'

The next entry in Phyllis Briggs' diary is for August 4th. 'Only a tea-cup of water to wash in now. The wells have all dried up and we long for rain. The clouds come and go again. Every morning when I awake, my legs feel numb and I have a pain like permanent toothache in my feet.'

A few days later, there was an event to put all their miseries to flight, at least for a little while. Allied planes appeared over Palembang and bombed the oil refineries at nearby Pladjou. To the wild delight of the women, the Japanese at the camp were thrown into an immediate panic and, in a sudden rush to make amends, produced a sack of mail. The internees had their first news from home in two and a half years. In addition, Red Cross boxes were distributed for the first time. Through cracks in the fence, the guards could be seen stuffing their pockets with packets of cigarettes – but even so, for each women there was a ration of twenty-two cigarettes, four lumps of sugar and a tiny portion of mouldy chocolate. It was a tremendous boost to the morale to know that the Allies were fighting back. They had no idea that the invasion of Europe had taken place and that Normandy was almost won.

The Japanese were now determined to conceal all traces of the camp from the air. Washing could not be hung in the compound. A strict black-out was enforced and cooking fires were forbidden during the hours of darkness. These measures were not enough to allay their fears, apparently, for they decided that the women must be hidden away before another Allied plane returned to investigate.

Phyllis wrote of their departure: 'We left the camp at 2 pm, carrying our bundles and with tin cans and other precious possessions tied around our necks and were driven down to the river to board one of the old ferry boats which used to run between Penang and Butter-worth. A lot more women joined us at the first stop who had come from a camp in Bencoolen, a number unable to walk including several Dutch nuns suffering from beri-beri and malaria.

'Next morning at dawn, we sailed down the river. The air was fresh as we neared the sea and we hoped that we had said goodbye for ever to Sumatra with its mosquito swamps, and that freedom was getting nearer. We had each brought a bottle of boiled water and a little cooked rice. I took a spoonful of my precious sugar. This always did me good whenever I felt particularly weak, and I used to keep a little store in a face cream jar for emergencies.

'We were at sea all the next day and it was night once more when we approached Banka Island. To get ashore, we had to go by coal lighter and, with great difficulty, we had to scramble down a narrow iron ladder into the depths of this filthy, pitch-dark boat. The sea was rough and we were tossed about like corks. Some of the women became hysterical. By the time we reached Muntok jetty, I scarcely had the strength to climb up the ladder and would have fallen backwards into the sea had not two Japs at the top caught me and dragged me onto the jetty.

'They wanted us to march in threes but, in our condition, this was quite impossible. We staggered the length of that wretched jetty. It seemed as if we trudged for miles but I suppose it was only about a quarter of a mile long. The Japs kept shouting at us to hurry and I was almost in tears. My legs felt like jelly. Finally, we reached the lorry that was waiting for us. Mary Jenkin and I were the last to climb on board.

'We drove to our new camp and found it was a huge place, although we could not see much in the dark. The huts had not been lived in so they were free of bugs. We were grateful for the cooked food that awaited us, prepared for us by the men whose camp was a short distance away. We were filthy with coal dust but there was no water, so we lay down on our bamboo bali-bali (sleeping platform) too weary to unpack or bother with anything.'

At first the new camp seemed wonderful compared with Palembang. Situated high above sea-level, it was swept by fresh breezes, and the women hoped that they would be able to build up their strength here and halt the rising toll of deaths. Fifty-five had died since their captivity began. In this they were to be cruelly disappointed.

The first disillusionment came when rations were cut once again. The customary ten sacks of rice for 500 women were cut to six, which gave a ration of two ounces of rice per person per day. This was followed by a piece of unfathomable Japanese logic. A weighing machine was produced and an announcement made that all women would be weighed monthly. There was never any indication as to whether their masters were disturbed, delighted, amazed or appalled at the results, which showed that few of the women were now over six stone and that all of them were on a downward trend.

Even in their emaciated condition, hard work was expected of them. They were ordered to sink the heavy posts for a perimeter fence into rock-hard ground with no other tool but a chunkal. Every blow jarred bodies which had no cushioning fat left.

Not long after their arrival at the new camp, an unknown and virulent fever made its appearance. In the absence of a better diagnosis it was dubbed 'Banka fever'. Victims were suddenly struck down with a raging temperature accompanied by acute irritation of the skin. Unconsciousness quickly intervened and few recovered. The doctors believed it to be a form of cerebral malaria but, with no quinine at their disposal, they were powerless to treat it.

The first Australian Sister to contract the disease was Wilhelmina Raymont of the 2nd/4th Australian CCS, a close friend of Mavis Hannah of the same unit. Mavis went to the Japanese officers and asked for quinine.

'We knew there was some in the Red Cross boxes, and the cinchona trees whose bark is the source of quinine were not far away. I begged them. I said I would do anything they wanted if only they would give me quinine for Ray. They laughed at me. They gave me nothing. And she died. I will never forgive the Japs for that.'

At this moment in the conversation, this very strong woman seemed to deflate. Her voice, usually vibrant and firm, fell to a flat murmur. 'It was all pretty awful,' she said, and that is the nearest thing to weakness you will find in Mavis Allgrove today.

The men in their camp seemed to be faring no better. Whenever a relative of one of the women died his belongings were sent to her via the ration truck. The small, labelled bundles were becoming an everyday occurrence. One day, Mary Jenkin found a pair of boots with her name on; in this way she learned that her husband had died.

Phyllis Briggs was filled with concern for her friend. 'She became very quiet. She was unable to cry, but she was determined to hang on herself for the sake of their twenty-one-year-old son, Robert, in England.'

The sickness spread. The water with its foul taste was highly suspect, as were the primitive sanitary arrangements, but both were outside the control of the internees.

'There was no drainage of sewage,' writes Phyllis Briggs. 'One had to squat on bamboo slats with a foot on either side of a foul, open tank which rapidly filled up. Years later, I still had nightmares of that seething mass of huge maggots. Some of the women volunteered to clean out the tank in order to earn money for food. Ena Murray and her sister, Norah Chambers, Audrey Owen, Margot Turner and Netta Smith were among the splendid women who did this filthy job for a few cents each.'

Deaths became a daily occurrence and the Japanese ordered the women to dig the graves themselves, a task which was beyond the strength of most.

No Allied planes flew over Banka. There were no letters and no news from the outside world, just sickness and starvation. Many women ceased to care. They turned away from the little food which was available, gave up the fight and died.

'A sort of mask came over their faces at the sight of food,' says Mavis Hannah. 'I know how it felt because it happened to me after I burned my foot. I had been heating some food for a patient to make it more palatable and a Jap passing by kicked the tin I was using as a pan off the fire, so that the boiling oil went over my foot. The burn went septic and I had a bad time, completely losing my appetite. It took me one and a half hours to eat half a coconut-shell of rice. I took it in tiny amounts to keep it down and took my mind off the food by counting the leaves on the tree above me. Only by doing this could I prevent myself from being sick.'

'Even when our friends died, we were apathetic,' writes Phyllis Briggs. 'Miss Penny, Miss Prouse, Olga Neubrunner, all dead. Mrs Brown and Dorothy McLeod. Dorothy had been such a cheerful little person, a great one for sweeping the drains, and in the early days of our captivity her singing was a joy to hear.'

Three more Australian Sisters died: Rene Singleton and Blanche Hempstead of beri-beri, Shirley Gardham of dysentery. At this camp, seventy-seven women and children died in three months. When the order came to leave, everyone was glad to quit this pestilential place. The miraculous dawn skies and the fresh sea breezes were a cover-up for killer diseases.

The women were packed close together on the open deck of a small ship and remained like that all night. They sailed at dawn, and then sat in the sun all day without shade as they crossed once more the strip of water to Sumatra. Most were suffering from dysentery and although the nuns had been able to get hold of a few bedpans, the only way to empty them was in the sea at the end of a long rope. Iole Harper, AANS, was one who volunteered for this dangerous job, balancing on a ledge which ran around the hull while two colleagues held her tight against the strong pull of the sea.

Once more they sailed up the steamy River Moesi and tied up at Palembang wharf, watched by a group of Japanese officers. Amongst them was Yamasaki, who had at one time acted as Commandant of the women's camp. He had never previously shown any concern for their welfare, but now he took a look at the decks crowded with sick and dying women, where the more able tried to protect the others from the relentless sun with their own bodies. The smile faded from his face. He barked an order. A Japanese soldier was sent running away and returned with an officer who jumped down amongst the women and began giving injections to the most seriously ill.

Betty Jeffrey, AANS, comments in her book *White Coolies*: 'This is the first time we have ever seen a Jap actually do something to help the sick.'

From the ship, the women were herded into a train, Phyllis Briggs supporting her friend.

'By this time, Mary was so ill, she could hardly stagger along. I managed to get her in with the hospital patients who were lying on the floor of a goods waggon, while I spent the night in a crowded compartment where a poor mad girl called Gladys moaned and clutched at us all night long. We were in pitch darkness and all the windows were closed. In the morning we were each given a little loaf made of tapioca flour and allowed off the train to visit the water tank.

'I was asked to go and help in the hospital waggon where Mary was. This was a closed truck which had previously been used for coal. There was a large pot of water which had slopped over and mixed with the coal dust where the patients were lying. Dr Margaret Thomson, Miss McKinnon (Colonial Nursing Service) and Mrs Rover, a

German trained nurse who was married to a Dutchman, were helping to look after the sick. There was scarcely room to move without treading on someone. The patients were mostly Dutch nuns suffering from dysentery who kept asking for bedpans the whole time. We emptied them through a small opening in the door which had to be completely shut every time we neared a village. The heat and the smell were almost beyond endurance.

'We spent a day and two nights in this atmosphere. The Japanese guard did his best to give us some air, but the steel door was too heavy for us to move. Once he handed us a bunch of bananas, and at one stop we were given a little rice. When we left the train we were ordered into lorries which took us on a long journey to an abandoned rubber estate. We had been three days and two nights without sleep. Seven women died on that journey. Others collapsed on arrival and did not recover.'

'Belaloo' rubber estate at Loeboek Linggau in northern Sumatra had been given the 'scorched earth' treatment before its owners left, and it was now desolated. Leaky huts awaited women who were no longer strong enough to repair the holes in the roofs.

Phyllis Briggs looked at it all with sinking heart. 'Everything was dripping wet. Mary and the other patients were put into the hut which was to be used as a hospital and laid on the damp bali-bali. I went to collect our possessions from the luggage which had just arrived and discovered that many of my precious things had been stolen en route, including my sewing needles. I wept. I had only a few cents left with which to buy food and without my sewing needles, I could not earn money. I did not know how I was going to manage, so I sold my last bit of jewellery, Mother's gold bracelet. I got a hundred francs for it on the Black Market.'

The nurses still undertook the care of the sick, although they themselves were ill with beri-beri, their limbs swollen and covered with inflamed red patches. They could only work for an hour at any one time, but they continued to do whatever they could to help the dying. Almost everyone now suffered from terrible ulcers and jungle sores which were treated with rags soaked in palm oil, but even rags were precious and had to be used again and again. One dedicated nun, whose self-appointed task it was to do all the hospital washing, boiled up these filthy rags every day in an old oil drum and put them in the sunshine to be cleansed.

The absurd weighing ritual continued and the graph of recorded findings continued downwards. Mavis Hannah was now four stone six pounds. The women ate anything they could lay their hands on. Miss McKinnon experimented with snails and nearly died of typhoid. Some Indian families began to eat rats until several died as a result.

On 8th May, 1945, the unbelievable happened. A sack of letters was delivered, stained with rain and all two and three years old. The women had no means of knowing the reason for this move, or what attack of self-doubt had prompted the Japanese into this gesture of generosity. The date meant nothing to them but to the Japanese it meant that the Western Allies had now only one enemy to concentrate upon: a good mark now might not come amiss in the future.

For the nurses, all young women with anxious parents grieving for them in various parts of the world, the letters sharpened the wretchedness of their condition. To see the familiar handwriting of the person who dwelt in the comfortable image of 'Mother', the presider over teapots, maker of cakes and recipient of childhood troubles, here in the squalor of a Japanese internment camp, was almost too much to bear.

They saw no hope of ever rejoining the world they had once known and, as each day of wretchedness followed another, many let slip their precarious hold on life. Irish Mary Cooper, QAIMNS, died now, as well as Colonial Sisters Ena Castle and Mrs McFie, Australian Sister Gladys Hughes and missionary Miss Dryburgh, who had brightened the life of the camp in the early days with music, training a choir to perform great choral works which she produced from memory. There were no longer any women strong enough to dig the graves; the task was taken over by the older children, who were now stronger than their mothers.

Phyllis Briggs could not fail to note the deterioration of her friend's condition. 'Little Mischa was taken care of by Mrs Colley and Miss Cullen, and Mary was taken back into hospital where I hoped the extra rations would help her. I tried to coax her to take a little soup but her mouth was very sore and, in the end, she could not digest anything. From 10th August, I realised that she could not live much longer. Indeed, her poor emaciated body was in such a state that we hoped it would not be long. Helen McKenzie (a Colonial Sister) was very good and helped me to bathe her every morning and make her as comfortable as possible. Every night, I spread the piece of mosquito netting over her. At this stage, we were all so weak that we could not do as much for one another as we would have liked.

'On 16th August, Mary was much worse. She dozed all day and then, at seven o'clock in the evening, she said, "I can't do any more. I'm going to join Charlie."

'I told her I would see Robert, her son, when I got home and I would tell him how brave his mother had been. She gave a little smile, and died within the hour.'

With little expectation of being able to fulfil that promise, Phyllis Briggs applied herself once more to the daily quest for food. Another batch of letters arrived, causing bewilderment in the camp: there were references to brothers being 'demobbed' and folk in England going on holiday. Was the war over? Had they been forgotten? Would anyone ever find them, deep in a Sumatran jungle?

24

Freedom

Major Jacobs' party did not have to wait long for the signal from Colombo that the atom bomb had been dropped and that the war was over. They immediately left their hiding place in the jungle and presented themselves at the Japanese Military HQ in the town of Medan in northern Sumatra.

At that time, there were 80,000 armed Japanese in Sumatra and a strong Air Force. Major Jacobs' party of five had no way of knowing whether this considerable force of warriors, as yet unbeaten in any battle and far away from their devastated homeland, would accept the fact of surrender, or whether they were even aware that capitulation had taken place. Boldness was the only card Major Jacob had to play, and it worked.

Confused by the speed with which events had turned so dramatically against them, the Japanese were unprepared for the sudden appearance of an Allied officer in their midst. Before they had time to grasp fully the situation, Major Jacobs, with a convincing air of authority, extracted from them grudging acquiescence to his request to be shown all the internment and POW camps in Sumatra.

He was adamant about the need for haste, for he had no intention of allowing the Japanese time to dispose of the evidence by exterminating the captives. At his insistence, his team were taken on a whirlwind tour of all the camps, most of which were deep in the jungle and unlikely to be discovered by any chance exploration. They went by truck and plane, knowing that at any time their Japanese drivers and pilots could cause them to disappear without trace if they chose.

Major Jacobs' immediate reaction upon seeing the camps was to signal HQ Colombo that the task was greater and more urgent than anyone had foreseen. If the lives of thousands of sick and starving people were to be saved, doctors, welfare officers, food and medical supplies must be dropped without delay by parachute, the only method of delivery until air-strips could be enlarged to take the big, long-distance planes.

The women at Bankinang internment camp did not believe the rumour that the war was over. Such stories had been in circulation since the first year of captivity, and little attention was paid to the Eurasian girl-friends of the Japanese guards who spoke of a huge bomb dropped on Japan which had finished off the war.

One day in August, QA Kit Woodman, now down to five and a half stone in weight, and her equally frail friend, Mary Charman, carried their food bowls to a place at the far end of the compound to enjoy a meal of boiled scraps of flour dough. By dint of scrimping and saving they achieved this treat of *barmi* (Chinese noodles) once a week, and they chose to enjoy it in what little privacy the camp offered, away from the crowds of aimlessly wandering women in the compound.

There was a strange tension about the camp that day. The guards were behaving in an uncharacteristic fashion and the women, who had grown sensitive to the slightest change in atmosphere, since their lives might depend upon it, grew more cautious.

Kit and Mary ate their food warily, with one eye on the compound. They had learned that if trouble was brewing, the sensible course was to keep out of it.

There was a sudden stir at the main gate, and men who looked like giants alongside the squat Japanese soldiers appeared there. The realisation dawned on the women that these were European men, but such was the apathy induced by malnutrition that Kit and Mary finished their meal before making any move to investigate.

'Do you know,' said Kit calmly, as if they had not all prayed for this day for three and a half long years, 'I believe we're free.'

Caution was by now built into their natures and, in fact, would never leave them. They marvelled at these tall men whose legs were so wonderfully straight and hairy after the smooth-skinned, bandy Japanese, and they were grateful for the willing hands which took over the chopping of wood. But the greater significance of their freedom was not fully comprehended until a Dutch woman of awesome faith produced a Union Jack, which she had kept hidden for this day. As the flag of the Rising Sun was hauled down and the Union Jack was run up the mast to flutter bravely over the camp, excitement and pent-up feelings effervesced.

'It was as if the sight of the British flag released in every one of us a sudden burst of energy,' says Kit.

The confirmation came when the Japanese Commandant sent for the camp committee and a formal announcement was made that the war was over.

Reunions between wives and husbands in the nearby camp were almost too overlaid with emotion to be endured. With the help of those women who were not involved, the wives made frantic attempts to improve their appearance. They went to the meeting adorned in bits of borrowed finery, albeit patched and darned, but face powder made from ground-up rice could not disguise skin blotched by mal-nutrition and pocked with the septic bites of insects, and there was no concealing the folds of flesh hanging from the skeletal frames of women who had once been large.

Even so, Major Jacobs, in his book *Prelude to the Monsoon*, could write: 'the spirits of the women internees (at Bankinang) were higher than at some of the other camps. At the men's camp, about a mile away, the morale was very low. This confirmed a trend we had pre-viously noted. Perhaps the women were more adaptable or had greater inner resources than the men, but they seemed to withstand the rigours of internment more stoically.'

And of the women, the nurses survived in better shape than most, because they had a job to do. One whose morale had never flickered, at least not publicly, was Miss Spedding, Matron QAIMNS. Weigh-ing, at the end, less than five stone, never really well during the years spent in captivity as a result of the severe shrapnel wound she received during the attack on the *Kuala*, she survived with spirit undaunted and dignity unimpaired. When, shortly after liberation, prophylactic injec-tions were arranged for the internees, Miss Spedding looked coldly along the line of Japanese orderlies armed with syringes and declined.

'Thank you,' she said, 'I will wait for a British orderly.' Never for a moment, throughout all the difficult years, had she behaved other than as a Matron of the QAIMNS, a woman of authority. She was later awarded the OBE.

Release of prisoners did not follow automatically. It would be some time before British troops could land and take over the running of the country from the Japanese. Air-strips had to be enlarged and the minefields surrounding the whole island had to be cleared before Allied planes and ships could approach. The unpleasant truth had to be accepted that, for the present, the internees had to stay where they were, and the Japanese had to continue to administer the camps, albeit under a very different set of rules.

This was hard news, especially for the men, filled with hatred for the Japanese as they were and thirsting for revenge. However, thousands of starving men and women roaming at will through the jungle would have had a poor chance of survival, especially since a revolutionary movement was afoot amongst the native population. Encouraged by the newly formed Republic of Java, Sumatrans were demanding liberation from their former masters, the Dutch, whose only place of safety for the present lay within the camps.

Under the terms of the surrender, Japan was responsible for the safety of prisoners until relieved by the Allies, and the onus of this pledge was now placed firmly on their shoulders by Major Jacobs. Conditions for internees rapidly improved. Sacks of rice arrived, carried for a change by the guards. Food began to pour into the camps.

'I sometimes think,' says Kit Woodman, 'that this sudden abundance of food was the most awful thing the Japs did to us.'

Despite Major Jacobs' plea to eat sparingly, the long-starved internees found that control was impossible. They could not stop eating.

There had been one important omission on the list of camps given to Major Jacobs. No mention had been made of the Loeboek-Linggau women's camp on the Belaloo rubber estate, a site so remote that it might easily be overlooked, which is perhaps what the Japanese intended. 1,000 women might have remained there, shut off from the rest of the world until aid, when it came, would have been too late, had it not been for the unrelaxing vigilance of Major Jacobs.

British legal authorities were seeking accounts from anyone involved in Japanese atrocities, so that the criminals could later be brought to justice. The facts of the massacre on Banka Island now came to light when Stoker Ernest Lloyd RN, recently released from Palembang camp, sent his story to Major Jacobs.

He had been amongst those men about to be killed by the Japanese on the beach. When instructed to blindfold themselves before being bayoneted, Stoker Lloyd and two companions had sought to escape by jumping into the sea. A hail of bullets followed them, killing the other two men and seriously wounding Stoker Lloyd so that he floated in a semi-comatose condition into the shelter of some rocks. When he struggled ashore some time later, he found piled up on the beach the bodies of twenty-two women, riddled with machine-gun bullets. Twenty-one were identifiable as Australian Army Sisters.

Realising that these nurses must have been part of the large group who left Singapore on the *Vyner-Brooke*, Major Jacobs concluded that the considerable number as yet unaccounted for were probably in some camp which had not yet been brought to his notice.

Determined insistence on his part eventually extracted the reluctant admission from the Japanese that there existed one more camp which he had not been shown. Every possible obstacle was put in his way when he demanded to be flown there without delay, which was not surprising since the Japanese could feel nothing but shame at the scene which would confront this envoy of Admiral Lord Louis Mountbatten.

People in the free world were celebrating with church bells and fireworks, but no hint that the war was ended reached the women internees at Loeboek-Linggau. Their lives became increasingly at risk as their captors grew more jittery and quick to anger with every day that passed. Medicines which might have eased the last hours of dying women and saved others remained locked in the guard hut. Three more Australian Sisters were buried in the cemetery at the top of the hill. 'Mitzi' Mittelheuser, Winnie May Davis and Dorothy Freeman died in wretched circumstances with only an old rice sack to cover them, never knowing that peace had come at last.

Everything changed after the visit of a high-ranking Japanese officer, who had felt it expedient to get to the camp before Major Jacobs. On 24th August, ten days after the end of hostilities, all women who were still able to walk were ordered to assemble on the hill near the guard hut. The Commandant addressed them from the top of a table. He was in a genial mood, which at once spread alarm and distrust among his hearers.

'Now we are all friends,' he informed them. 'The war is over. Soon British and Americans will come.'

In silence, the women wandered away, confused and withdrawn. Not until the guards brought heaps of fresh vegetables for them did the truth sink in. Cabbage and spinach were usually left in the rain to spoil for forty-eight hours before the women were given permission to pick them up. Down from the guardroom came quinine, serum, powdered milk, vitamin tablets and butter, the contents of the Red Cross parcels which could have saved so many lives, and a sack of three-year-old, water-spoiled letters.

Despite these last minute attempts on the part of the Japanese to improve the women's condition, Major Jacobs was appalled by what he saw.

'They were so short of food that a banana skin had become a delicacy. They had no clothes any more. The majority wore crude shorts with sun-tops made from old rags. To protect their feet, they had *trompers*, rough, native slippers made of wood with pieces of rubber or cloth nailed across the foot to keep them in place. Some built up mental defences by withdrawing into themselves and time and events ceased to have meaning for them.'

Japanese clothing stores were hastily put at the disposal of the women. Men from the nearby camp, who were mostly Dutch as few of the British had survived, came to cut firewood for them and to mend the leaking roofs of their atap huts. Some took rifles and went into the jungle to shoot deer and wild pig, and soon more food than the women could eat was being brought into the camp. In an amazingly short time, their physical condition improved and they were able to take the first steps towards normality. Their ordeal was over: no more 'tenko', no more face-slapping or being made to stand for hours in the sun for punishment, no more unrelenting hunger.

'All I want now,' wrote Betty Jeffrey in the diary she need no longer conceal, which later provided the material for her book *White Coolies*, 'is Mother, home, and some bread and jam. It is almost too much to believe that this may happen any day.'

On 16th September, the Australian Government sent two planes for the sixty-five Australian Sisters they expected to evacuate: one plane would have been sufficient for the twenty-four survivors. Twelve had drowned, twenty-one had been shot and eight had died in camp. Three Colonial Sisters had also died in this camp, and one QA. The survivors were taken at once to Singapore, which was rapidly becoming the centre for released prisoners.

Phyllis Briggs was in the first batch of women to leave the camp. 'We left at dawn. I wore a Japanese private's uniform complete with yellow boots and carried a small pack containing the linen dress left to me by Mary Anderson when she died. We went by train to the airport and at one station I saw a native selling sweet, sticky cakes. Without a second thought, I pulled off my boots and handed them out of the window. He gave me the whole tray.'

During this immediate post-war period, it must have seemed to Allied Administration that the flood gates of the Far East had been opened as the prisoners of the Japanese were released: 122,000 men, women and children, sick in mind as well as body, had to be helped back to civilisation and, in many cases, transported to the other side of the world. From Japan itself, from Borneo, Java, Sumatra and the

Dutch East Indies, from Shanghai and Hong Kong, they were brought along a chain of hospitals which led home.

The Japanese had been loath to give up Singapore, the scene of their great triumph over Britain, and pockets of resistance fought on for a while after the capitulation. Snipers had to be cleared from the dock cranes before the first hospital ship, the *Karoa*, could tie up.

Sister Maureen Ferris, last mentioned in connection with the Chindits, was now one of the *Karoa*'s nursing staff waiting to embark POWs as soon as they had been given a thorough medical check-up. Until the ship was ready to sail, 'Open House' was held on board for anyone who cared to join the Sisters in the dining saloon for tea.

Maureen had never starved. 'We had been so spoiled. We used to turn up our noses at tinned milk but these people loved it, drank it neat. They would sit ogling a plate of bread and butter and then, not being able to wait any longer, would fall upon it, getting right down to it. Then they would realise what they were doing and would try very hard to be polite.'

The released nurses were taken at once to the Alexandra, once more a military hospital. It had been left in a chaotic state by the departing Japanese and a formidable task faced the incoming British unit. All the lifts were broken, the X-ray machines destroyed and ward furniture smashed or non-existent. There were no beds, sheets, pillows or blankets, no instruments, not even a jar in which to stand a thermometer; the whole place was indescribably filthy. The unit had exactly two days in which to clean and equip the building as a working hospital. Japanese soldiers were commandeered for fatigues and made to clean up the mess they had created. A tireless worker for the hospital was Lady Louis Mountbatten, who consistently cut through the trammels of red tape in order to get the work done and equipment replaced in time.

One of the first women patients to arrive was Sister Margot Turner, QAIMNS. The Assistant-Matron of the Alexandra, Miss Mary Frith (later Taylor), was shocked to recognise in this gaunt woman with a yellow complexion and two missing teeth, a contemporary from her own training school at Bart's Hospital. Sister Turner had lost her teeth during an unfortunate encounter with a Japanese soldier, when she had been slow to bow.

Proper beds with mattresses awaited women whose bony frames had grown accustomed to sleeping on concrete or bamboo. Smooth sheets cossetted them and every care was lavished on them. To the released women, however, their nursing colleagues looked distinctly odd – 'such big bosoms and behinds!' They in turn looked odd to the hospital staff. Phyllis Briggs, although rapidly putting on weight, was still under six stone and covered in scabies. To her great mortification, a bug hopped out of her pack on to the pristine hospital sheets. She had come a long way from being the immaculate Colonial Sister Briggs of the Alor Star Hospital.

One overriding thought had occupied her mind ever since her release: the whereabouts of her fiancé. She began her search for Tony Cochrane. Singapore teemed with released POWs and almost all were searching for relatives and friends. The British Red Cross Society had lost no time in opening a Missing Persons Office, but there was no happy ending for Phyllis. The man she had promised to marry, that night in the resuscitation department of the Kandang Kerbau Hospital when all Singapore was going up in flames, was posted 'Missing, believed killed'.

After an exhaustive search, QA Naomi Davies found the father of young Jean Duncan. Jean was now twelve and a half years old. Her father was in poor shape after imprisonment in Changi jail, but a reunion with his only surviving daughter became possible after his health improved, and Naomi was able to relinquish the charge she had taken upon herself when the *Kuala* was wrecked. No doubt influenced by the woman who steered her through a nightmare period of her life, Jean eventually trained as a nurse. Naomi became godmother to her first child.

A less satisfactory conclusion was reached for that other orphaned child, the little Russian boy, Mischa. After the death in camp of Mary Jenkin, his self-appointed guardian, the little boy passed to the care of two of the other women, Mrs Colley and Miss Cullen. Now about to marry, Miss Cullen applied to adopt the boy, but the Jewish Society would not allow this. Instead, they undertook to trace the child's family. He was sent to Shanghai to live with relatives he had never seen.

The streets of Singapore were crowded with disorientated men and women who were trying to pick up the threads of a life they had left three and a half years ago. Voluntary bodies moved in to reassure and help in every way. The Hon. Mrs Begg of the Women's Voluntary Service occupied a chair in the foyer of the Adelphi Hotel every day from 8 am until midnight, answering questions, arranging contracts, sending off cables. Another WVS member toured the streets in a van loaded with hot cottage loaves and handed out hunks of bread smothered in butter, each with a dollop of jam.

'That girl can never know the thrill she gave us,' says Kit Woodman. 'The bread tasted so good.'

Those nurses whose medical tests had proved satisfactory were allowed to leave hospital and were living in some style at the Raffles Hotel. Some, like Kit, were putting on weight too quickly, but control of eating was impossible at this stage, as Maureen Ferris was to find when the HMHS *Karoa* set sail for Britain with her first batch of released POWs.

She had a ward of seventy-five men, '. . . and three Japanese "ladies" whom I put in the side ward. I was too busy to look after them and put them in the charge of an orderly. "They bints in the sideward," he used to call them.

'The most dreadful fights broke out in the ward. I would go steaming down there and it would be – "Sister, he's got half a potato more than me!" – and when I did a ward round, I would find under their pillows perhaps a chop bone or bit of bread.

' "Look," I'd say, "we'll get cockroaches and rats all over the ship!" but it was no use. They would cry when I took the food away from them.

'Since we could not restrict their diet, we let them have what they wanted. They would all sit up and burp afterwards and my RAMC corporal, who was a solicitor's clerk in civvy street, would go round with a large Winchester bottle full of indigestion mixture. Everyone had a dose. We just could not restrain their eating because they got so upset. Serving dinners was a nightmare, as no man could have more than the other.'

Fortunately, Maureen Ferris was endowed with great reserves of patience and understanding. She needed both on that voyage.

'When we first embarked the patients they had to go straight away on the nominal roll, Army fashion. That was the thing that counted in the Army – the nominal roll. But when I went amongst them asking the usual – Name, Rank, Unit – they would burst into tears. "Don't worry," I told them. "We'll do it later."

'Some poor lads, their minds had gone. They were like children. We used to take them by the hand and say, "Come with Sister." I used to think of their mothers, overjoyed to be getting their sons safely home and then seeing them as they really were.

'The "cages" were two small wards, each containing six bunks, which were reserved for patients who needed restraining. On every trip the *Karoa* made, they were always full. At one time I had five RAMC medical officers in the cages. Their minds had gone. All these men came from Changi and other camps on the island of Singapore.'

Fresh camps came to light with every week that passed. Thirty Indians, comatose and close to death from starvation, were found on one of the smaller islands of the Pacific and were nursed by Australian Sisters of the 2nd/9th AGH on the island of Moratai. There was no co-operation from the Japanese, who pleaded ignorance of the camps even when disclosure was imminent and inevitable. Allied officers had to remain one jump ahead of their wily, defeated enemy if they were not to be hoodwinked.

An American officer being driven across country in Japan remarked upon a party of white women working in the fields; he was told by his Japanese driver that these women were the wives of Japanese farmers. He drove on without further enquiry. Had he stopped to investigate, he would have discovered that these were prisoners captured in New Guinea and the islands who were still being made to work as slaves for the Japanese. Amongst them were the six Australian Nursing Sisters captured at Rabaul.

Confined within a former hospital building under strict guard, the women had no means of knowing that the war had ended, although their suspicions were aroused by the dejected attitude of their guards. When one day it was reported that an American jeep had been sighted on a distant highway, two of the women decided to investigate.

Successfully evading the guard one night, Kathleen Parker of the Australian Nursing Service and a civilian nurse cut across the fields to the nearest road, hoping that an American vehicle might pass that way. They had not long to wait. Running out from the bushes which concealed them, they stood with arms outstretched in the path of an approaching jeep, bringing it to an abrupt halt. Two American officers in the back leaned forward to investigate but the Japanese driver, quickly recovering himself, shouted to the women to get out of the way and made to drive on, attempting with his bluster to conceal the fact that the two ragged women were speaking English. This time, the Japanese deceit was uncovered. The Americans intervened and heard the full story of the still captive women. Recrimination against the Japanese followed swiftly and the women were released at last. Freedom however, was short-lived for one of the Australian Nursing Sisters. Miss Callaghan died a year later from tuberculosis contracted whilst in the hands of the Japanese.

Some of the repatriating ships went in the opposite direction. To the hospital ship *Amavapoora* fell the task of transporting sick Japanese personnel from Sumatra back to Japan. Also on board were four Japanese medical officers, who were openly astonished to learn that the Japanese patients would be treated by British Army Sisters. Obviously, if the roles had been reversed, such a situation would have been unthinkable. The patients themselves had expected no treatment whatsoever and presented a testimony of thanks to the Sisters at the end of the voyage. Word had reached even higher places, and when the *Amavapoora* docked at her port of disembarkation in Japan, bouquets of flowers expressing the gratitude of the Imperial Government of Japan awaited the Sisters. At that point, the fact that Britain followed a different book of rules in war may have taken root.

Sister Maureen Ferris's final voyage on the *Karoa* was concerned with repatriating Australians who had been taken prisoner in New Guinea and the surrounding islands. The fact that many of them were very sick men made their conduct no less predictable. At every port of call around the Australian coast, men not due for embarkation slipped ashore.

'Some of them on the Dangerously Ill List! They would be waiting for us at the next port, standing on the jetty, waving "Hallo, Sister!"

' "Where have you been?" I would demand.

' "Been to see me auntie," they would explain as they climbed back into bed. All sort of fictitious "aunties" surfaced, who, it seemed, had to be visited.'

Maureen, who lives today in a charming Suffolk cottage, is good-humoured and easy-going, but as she speaks there is a touch of iron beneath the banter.

'I won't buy a Japanese car. The Norfolk and Suffolk Regiments from round here were the ones taken to Singapore and thrown in to defend the island. The poor devils had been all those months at sea with no training. They had never even seen a jungle. They were either massacred or captured straight away. You can still see some of them around here, hobbling up and down the roads, limbless or blind.

'I really don't often think about it now. It's only when I'm chatting to someone like this that it all comes back.'

The last word is from Kit Woodman.

'Most of us feel quite indifferent towards the Japs. They are cast in a different mould. Forgiveness is a different thing entirely and I cannot go along with that, noble as it may seem. The Jap does not want to be forgiven. He is what he is and certainly does not seek forgiveness. Nothing will make any difference to him, and all the forgiveness in the world is a waste of time and energy.'

Epilogue

It was a shabby Britain which welcomed back the released POWs. Almost every commodity was in short supply but Kit Woodman and her fellow QAs were suitably honoured with the award of Associate of the Royal Red Cross (ARRC), a priority certificate entitling them to a rubber hot-water bottle and an invitation to take tea with Queen Mary. Her Majesty opined that Margot Turner's four-day ordeal on the raft must have been very uncomfortable.

Many of the nurses mentioned in this account retired from the profession at the end of the war and buried their war-time memories in a new life of domesticity and motherhood. Some of the VADs who had not nursed before the war found so much satisfaction in their chosen war effort that they went on to undertake full training. A number of Service Reservists joined the Regular forces and carved out a distinguished career for themselves.

Miss Olga Franklin, CBE, RRC, survived imprisonment in Stanley Internment Camp, Hong Kong, to become Matron-in-Chief of Queen Alexandra's Royal Naval Nursing Service.

Matron Monica Johnson, later Dame Monica Golding, DBE, RRC, and Sister Margot Turner, later Dame Margot Turner, DBE, RRC, each in turn became Matron-in-Chief of Queen Alexandra's Royal Army Nursing Corps. (Queen Alexandra's Imperial Military Nursing Service became a Corps in 1949, known after that as QARANC.) Both matrons held the rank of Brigadier after Regular Commissions were granted in 1949.

When the ingredients of victory in the Second World War are analysed, the part played by the nurses should not go unremarked. Soldiers, sailors, airmen and civilians in bombed Britain would have been in a sorry state without them.

3,076 British nurses, civilian and Services, lost their lives. The names of some of those who died during incidents reported in this book can be found in Appendix C. All their names are to be found on the Roll of Honour in the Nurses' Chapel in Westminster Abbey.

Australia, New Zealand, Canada, India and South Africa all sent their volunteer nurses, and each country has its memorial to those who did not come back.

The events recounted here took place forty years ago and the numbers who attend the annual reunions grow smaller each year. But as far as the nurses of the Second World War are concerned, the term 'old lady' applies to somebody else. They share a comradeship forged in difficult times and memories of splendid human endeavour which have obliterated the tragedies. They remember the loyalty of men transformed by war into nursing orderlies with no qualification other than a kind heart. They remember the unsung selflessness of the doctors, and they remember the lighthearted courage of the men they nursed.

A tailpiece can now be added to the story of 'Mischa', the little orphaned boy who was cared for by the women in the Japanese internment camp.

At the end of the war, he was taken to England by the missionary, Miss Gladys Cullen and later identified by a Displaced Persons organisation as Isadore Warman, whose parents had been living in Malaya at the time of the Japanese invasion. He was reunited with an aunt and uncle living in Shanghai and when, some years later, all foreigners were expelled from China, he went with them to live in California. His life from then onwards followed the pattern of any American boy growing into adulthood. In due course, Isadore married and raised a family. There the story seemed to end except for the mystery surrounding his early years which had not been revealed to him.

In 1982, his wife's cousin, living in England, happened by chance upon a book dealing with the internment of women by the Japanese; "Women Beyond the Wire." by L. Warner and J. Sandilands. (Michael Joseph 1982). There the missing years of Isadore's life, the shipwreck and internment, were laid bare. As a result, he was able to visit England, to thank in person the women who had cared for him and nursed his mother before she died.

For this extra information I am indebted to Marilyn Branston, cousin of Mrs Isadore Warman and to Phyllis Thom.

Appendix A

Fever Song

An original poem contributed by ex-QAIMNS Kitty Jones
(now Hutchinson).

And did you serve in India, lad,
Or Burma's wild green land?
And did you have the fever there
Till you could scarcely stand?
And does the fever catch you still
When England's winds blow bitter chill?

And does your head throb once again
As it did then, my lad?
And do you feel the dulling pain
The same as you once had?
And do you, soldier, curse the day
When under those hot skies you lay?

And do you shake and shiver, lad,
And ache to lay you down,
As you did then, short years ago,
Under the jungle's crown?
And do you sigh for water now,
And drink the salt sweat from your brow?

And do your limbs feel far away
In ague's sudden grip?
And do you like the price you pay,
The fever-cup you sip,
For being young in England's isle
When Hitler saw his war-god smile?

Or do you think of well-known friends,
Men of your Company,
Who, uncomplaining, met their ends,
Nor looked for sympathy;
But under Asia's brassy skies
Died with this England in their eyes?

Their rotted bones in jungles lie
Six thousand miles away –
Lad, what's a fever? You won't die.
You'll live another day –
But God forgive, if you forget
They paid, in agony, our debt.

Kitty Hutchinson, East Grinstead, 1

Appendix B
George Medals

George Medals awarded to civilian nurses between 1940 and 1942:

1940
Junior Nurse Violet E. Reid, working in a mental institution

1941
Nurse Vera Anderson, on ARP duty at Nottingham
Matron Miss J. E. Burton, Coventry and Warwickshire Hospital
Sister Emma Horne, Coventry and Warwickshire Hospital
Staff Nurse Mary Fleming, Grove Park Hospital
Senior Assistant Nurse Aileen R. Turner, Grove Park Hospital
Matron Mrs Boulton, Sir Robert Geffery's Home, Mottingham
Assistant Nurse Mary S. J. Newman, Southampton
Matron Miss E. G. Thomas, West Bromwich and District General Hospital
Works Nurse Marjorie E. Perkins, Coventry
VAD Dorothy M. White, BRCS Horsham and Worthing
Nurse Mary F. Thomas, ARP Casualty Service, Woolwich
Assistant Matron Miss Catherine McGovern, RRC, Royal Chest Hospital
Staff Nurse Patricia Marmion, Royal Chest Hospital
Staff Nurse Ruby Rosser, Grove Park Hospital

1942
Assistant Nurse Mrs Knee, City Hospital, Exeter

Appendix C
Mortality Lists

The mortality lists below have been obtained by referring to the following sources:
Queen Alexandra's Royal Army Nursing Corps Museum at Aldershot
Nurses' Roll of Honour, Nurses' Chapel, Westminster
Commonwealth War Graves Commission
Surviving Nursing Sisters

Army Sisters who lost their lives in disasters at sea:

At the sinking of the:
SS *Stentor*
'Taffy' Davis, Eileen English, C. D. Manfield, Joy Walters.

SS *Ceramic*
E. E. Bevis, N. M. Clement, J. Coulter, C. M. Cribb, R. N. Essex, M. E. Evans, A. M. Gardner, M. A. Hood, E. K. Hollis, G. L. Knight, K. D. McBryde, M. D. McGregor, M. Maxwell, D. M. Morris, C. M. Nicholson, M. Nolan, M. M. O'Sullivan, J. Pitt, B. M. Sutherland, K. Toohey, H. A. Tudor, G. Waters, L. M. E. Wheelock, K. F. M. White, A. R. Wingate, W. M. F. Wood.

MV *Strathallam*
J. H. Davidson, T. Doran, E. Hadridge, E. M. Mawston, H. Porterfield.

HMHS *Newfoundland*
Matron A. McInnes Cheyne, U. Cameron, D. M. Cole, P. Gibson, A. M. Laughlin, M. Lea.

HMHC *St David*
S. E. Dixon, W. A. E. Harrison.

HMHS *Talamba*
M. L. Johnson.

HMHC *Amsterdam*
D. A. Field, M. Evershed.

HS *Centaur*
Australian Army Sisters M. L. Adams, H. S. J. C. Haultain, Matron A. Jewell, E. V. Kind, M. A. McFarlane, M. Moston, A. M. O'Donnell, E. M. Rutherford, E. A. Shaw, J. W. Walker, J. Wylie.

SS *Khedive Ismail*
R. F. Airey, J. K. Atkin, E. M. Bateman, A. Brown, I. Burrows, E. A. Dalgarno, E. D. Dann, M. E. Davies, G. Dervan, A. W. Dewar, B. O. Dowling, M. Farrelly, C. M. Fitzgerald, G. W. Harvey, V. F. Hastings, N. Q. Humphrey, Matron E. M. E. Ievers, M. Jarman, M. F. Johnston, W. E. Kells, M. J. Kells, M. E. Leckey, B. E. Leech, M. J. Littleton, J. N. McLaren, M. L. McMillan, I. Moore, S. Morgan, P. Nuttal, B. Pirie, S. G. Richardson, H. M. Robertson, D. E. Senior, M. Smith, I. Spence, K. M. M. Taylor, J. M. G. Thomas, M. A. R. Urquhart, K. H. Walker, R. A. Warwaick, M. S. Whitaker, G. M. White, A. A. Willis, E. J. Young.

The Malayan Campaign: Service, Civilian and Colonial Service nurses who were killed in action; drowned; murdered by the Japanese or died in internment camps in Malaya:

Colonial Service and Civilian nurses
Matron Brebner, Sisters V. Boston, Brooks, J. Cameron, E. Castle, Mrs Cherry nee Sister Law, I. E. Darlington, J. E. H. De Ambrosia, M. J. Forgie, M. A. Gentles, A. F. Gibson, M. E. Green, D. Hirst, F. Holgate, W. M. Jones, M. Keddie, A. C. Keir, V. M. Leefe, M. J. Livingstone, G. Logan, R. E. Low, E. C. Lowry, C. M. MacPherson, E. F. McConachy, O. L. Mac-Farlane, N. S. McMillan, J. Milne, J. C. Morrison, L. Murray, M. B. N. Mustill, I. M. Nelson, M. Nicol, M. Perry, M. Robinson, J. D. Scott, A. M. Sim, M. Skehan, E. M. Smith, G. Somerville, D. G. Strange, J. Y. Thomson, E. M. Try, M. M. Waugh, M. Wilde, M. A. Woodyear-Smith, V. J. Wright, A. M. G. Young, Olga Neubrunner, R. Mcfie.

QAIMNS and TANS
Principal Matron V. M. S. Jones, Matron W. Russell, Matron C. L. M. West, Sisters E. N. Ayres, C. F. Black, C. H. Clewett, E. K. Carroll, L. Coward, D. V. Dunlop, M. R. Finley, M. H. T. Fowler, A. J. Hervey-Murray, M. A. Hodgson, M. J. Jones, R. H. Dickson, M. Cooper, B. LeBlanc-Smith, A. M. C. McClelland, H. Montgomerie, A. W. Muir, E. D. Pedlow, L. S. Symonds, J. B. Wright, N. Sullivan, D. H. Tombs, B. L. Wells, M. E. Gale, A. A. Ingham, A. MacGregor, Strachan, E. M. Wilson. B. Morgan
Indian Military Nursing Service
Matron N. Sweeney, G. M. De Souza, E. Eastwood, B. H. Hollands, L. E. James, B. M. Joyce, S. Kantha, J. Lim, N. T. Lord, P. M. Sebastian, A. Sutharisanam, A. Arivannandam, R. A. Taylor, I. G. Woolger, L. M. V. Anderson, N. C. St. J. Hussey.

Australian Army Nursing Service
Matron Drummond, Matron Paschke, Sisters Bates, Balfour-Ogilvie, Beard, Bridge, Calnan, Casson, Clarke, Cuthbertson, Davis, Dorsch, Elmes, Ennis,

Freeman, Farmaner, Fairweather, Gardham, Halligan, Harris, Hodgson, Hempstead, Hughes, Kinsella, Keats, Kerr, McDonald, McGlade, Mittelheuser, Neuss, Raymont, Russell, Salmon, Schuman, Singleton, Stewart, Tait, Trennery, Wilton, Wilmott, Wight.

Appendix D
Official Diary of the Taiwan POW Camp

The official diary of the Taiwan POW camp was captured intact. The following is a copy of the official translations of part of the entry dated 1 August, 1944.

The following answer about *the extreme measures for POWs was sent to the Chief of Staff of the 11th Unit (Formosa POW Security No. 10).*

Under the present situation, if there were a mere explosion or fire, a shelter for the time being could be held in nearby buildings such as the school, a warehouse, or the like. However, at such time as the situation became urgent and it be extremely important, the *POWs will be concentrated and confined in their present location and, under heavy guard, the preparation for the final disposition will be made.*

The time and method of this disposition is as follows:

(1) *The Time*

Although the basic aim is to act under superior orders, *individual disposition* may be made in the following circumstances:

(a) When an uprising of large numbers cannot be suppressed without the use of firearms.

(b) When escapes from the camp may turn into a hostile fighting force.

(2) *The Methods*

(a) *Whether they are destroyed individually or in groups, or however it is done, with mass bombing, poisonous smoke, poison, drowning, decapitation or whatever, dispose of them as the situation dictates.*

(b) *In any case, it is the aim not to allow the escape of a single one, to annihilate them all, and not to leave any traces.*

(3) To: The Commanding General.
The Commanding General Military Police.

Reported matters conferred on with the 11th Unit, the Kiirun Fortified Area HQ and each prefecture concerning the *extreme security in Taiwan POW Camps.*

I hereby certify that this is a true translation from the Journal of the Taiwan POW HQ in Taiwan, entry 1 August, 1944.   (*signed*) Stephen H. Green
This is Exhibit marked 'O', referred to in the affidavit of James Thomas Neheniah Cross. Sworn before me this 19th day of September 1946.   (*signed*) P. A. L. Vine
Major, RM

Certified as exhibit 'O' in Doc no. 2687

Acknowledgements

My sincere thanks are due to the following men and women who have assisted me with their recollections:

From the Australian Army Nursing Service:
Mavis E. Allgrove (née Hannah), Moira Atkins, ARRC (née Crittenden), Joan Crouch, ARRC, Dorothy Gellie (née McCrum), Betty Jeffrey, Barbara Kilgour, ARRC (neé Millard), Faith McCulloch, Joan Paige, ARRC, Gwen Pegg (née Cocks), Ellen Savage, GM, Vivian Statham, MBE, ARRC (née Bullwinkle), Dorothy Tinsley (née Bush), Nell Williamson, RRC (née Marshall), Dora Wood (née Church).

From the Civil Nursing Reserve:
Betty Cowieson (née Le Grys), Eileen Edelston, Dorothy Larson, OBE (formerly Mrs Brown), Joyce Robertson (née Atkins).

From the Colonial Nursing Service: Netta Smith, Phyllis Thom (née Briggs).

From the Queen Alexandra's Imperial Military Nursing Service and Reserve:
Miss Birch, Freda Brown (née Davis), Miss Chesterfield, ARRC, Marjorie Cocksedge, Robina Dagley (née Campbell), Mary Davies, RRC (née Currie), Zena Deakin (née Potter), Ursula Dowling, RRC, Eveline Duff (née Rowston), A. M. Elliott (formerly SSAFA), Dame Monica Golding, DBE, RRC, Matron-in-Chief (née Johnson), Sheila Fox, GM (née Greaves), Joan Grottick, Teddy Head, Naomi Hedley, ARRC (née Davies), Kitty Hutchinson (née Jones), Mary Irish (née Howard), Yvonne Jeffrey, Wyn Jenkins (née Wallace), Gwendoline Jones, RRC, Margaret Kneebone, RRC, Yvonne Lander (née Hunter), Marjorie Lloyd, Judy Martin (née Price), Joan Moore (née Hunter-Bates), Sheila Mullins (née McDowell), Frankie Nicholls (née Newton), Kitty O'Connor, May Parry, MBE, Grace Peasley, RRC, Principal Matron (née Clark), Kit Philbrick, ARRC (née Woodman), Miss Robins, Mary Sands, ARRC, Anne Sharwood (née Collings), Maureen Shaw (née Ferris), Marjorie Smith, Esther Somerville, RRC, Helen Stanger, RRC (née Wright), Pat Stephens (née Bradley), Olive Sweeney (née Holmes), Mary Taylor (née Frith), Enid Thomas, Hilda Thomas (née Edwards), Kathleen Thomson, RRC, Dame Margot Turner, DBE, RRC, Matron-in-Chief, Sheila White.

From the Queen Alexandra's Royal Naval Nursing Service:
G. A. Cooper, RRC (née Ramsden), M. A. F. Edwards, Olga Franklin, CBE,
RRC, Matron-in-Chief, Phyllis James, Barbara Lambert, Minnie Lindsell (née
Murphy), Lucy Reynolds (née Dixon), T. Velanoff (née Robinson).

From the Territorial Army Nursing Service:
Elsie Burrows, Margaret Cromar, Mentioned in Dispatches, Jean Mitchell,
RRC, L. K. Perry, Kathleen Smith.

From the Voluntary Aid Detachments:
M. C. Cox (née Mew), Phyllis Harris, Dorothy Lewes (née Jacobs), Sadie
Wilson (née Apperley) VAD 1914-1918.

Louise Carter (née Lansley), Civilian Nursing Sister; Joan Cavell, First Aid
Nursing Yeomanry; Dorothy 'Jane' Dye (née Harper), Civilian Nursing Sister;
Jess Frost (née Edwards), Civilian District Midwife; M. E. Jackson, RRC,
New Zealand Army Nursing Service; T. McLachlan, ex-civilian Resident of
Singapore; E. H. Monteith, laboratory assistant, RAMC; His Grace the Duke
of Newcastle, ex-RAF; Marison Orfeur, wartime student nurse; E. Rolph, army
casualty; Inge Samson (née Fehr), German refugee student nurse; Nancy
Stowell, Princess Mary's Royal Air Force Nursing Service; Rachel Taylor (née
Cashmore), student nurse; Mrs Wardle, for the diaries of Nursing Sister
Luker, QAIMNS, RRC.

I should also like to thank all those publishers who have given me permission
to quote copyright material, in particular Cassell (London), Houghton Mifflin
Company (Boston) and McClelland and Stewart Ltd (Toronto) for the quote
from Winston Churchill's *The Finest Hour*, Volume II of *The Second World
War*, and Doubleday and Company Inc (New York) and Heinemann (London) for the extract from *Crusade in Europe* by Dwight D. Eisenhower.

Bibliography

Attiwill, Kenneth, *The Singapore Story* (London: Muller, 1959)

Bowden, Jean, *Grey Touched With Scarlet* (London: Robert Hale, 1959)

Bowie, Col. David, RAMC, *Captive Surgeon in Hong Kong* (published by the author)

Boys, Doreen, *Once Upon A Ward* (Published by the author, 1980)

Cambray, P. G. and Briggs, G. G. B. (compiled), *War Organisation: The Official History of the Voluntary Aid Detachments* (London: 1949)

Carew, Tim, *The Fall of Hong Kong* (London: Anthony Blond, 1960)

Churchill, Winston, *The Second World War* (London: Cassell, 1954)

Cottrell, Anthony, *RAMC* (London: Hutchinson, 1943)

Crew, F. A. E., *The Medical History of the Second World War* (London: HMSO, 1972)

Donnison, F.S.V., *History of the Second World War: Civil Affairs and Military Government* (London: HMSO, 1972)

du Cros, Rosemary, *ATA Girl* (London: Muller, 1983)

Edge, Geraldine and Johnston, Mary, *Ships of Youth* (London: Hodder & Stoughton, 1945)

Eisenhower, Dwight, *Crusade in Europe* (London: Heinemann, 1948)

Fergusson, Bernard, *The Wild Green Earth* (London: Collins, 1952)

Ford, James Allen, *The Brave White Flag* (London: Hodder & Stoughton, 1961)

Gilmour, Oswald, *Singapore to Freedom* (London: E.J. Burro, 1943)

Jacobs, G. F., *Prelude to the Monsoon* (Cape Town: Purnell, 1965)

Jeffrey, Betty, *White Coolies* (London: Angus & Robertson, 1954)

Jones, Katharine (ed. Harrison, Ada), *Grey and Scarlet* (London: Hodder & Stoughton, 1943)

Lampe, David, *The Last Ditch* (London: Cassell, 1968).

Macfarlane, Professor Gwyn. Alexander Fleming. *The Myth and the Man.* pub. Chatto & Windus.

Montgomery, Bernard, *The Memoirs of Field-Marshal Montgomery* (London: Collins, 1958)

Oliver, Dame Beryl, *The British Red Cross in Action* (London: Faber & Faber, 1966)

Plumridge, J. H., *Hospital Ships and Ambulance Trains* (London: Seeley, 1975)

Smythe, Sir John, *The Will To Live* (London: Cassell, 1970)

Wilmot, Chester, *Struggle for Europe* (London: Collins, 1952)

'Grey and Scarlet': Magazine of the Royal Australian Nursing Corps.

Cabinet Papers, Public Records Office, Kew, London

Central Chancery of the Orders of Knighthood

Naval Nursing Service Records
Official History of the Shaw-Savill Shipping Line
QARANC Gazette
QARANC Museum Records, Aldershot
RAF Archives, Ministry of Defence, London

Index